33

W9-ANP-473

Change in an African Village
Kefa Speaks

No man is right all the time.
   —A Chewa saying

KEFA VILLAGE

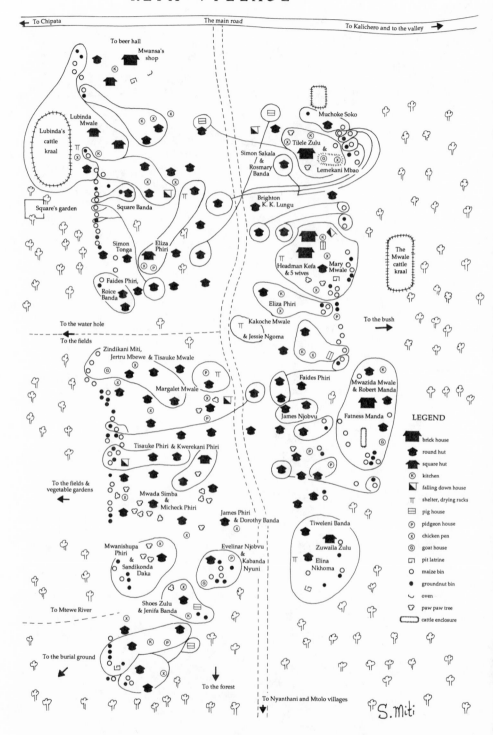

To Chipata · The main road · To Kalichero and to the valley

To beer hall
Mwansa's shop

Lubinda Mwale

Lubinda's cattle kraal

Square's garden

Square Banda

Simon Tonga

Eliza Phiri

Faides Phiri, Roice Banda

Muchoke Soko

Tilele Zulu

Simon Sakala & Rosmary Banda

Lemekani Mbao

Brighton K. K. Lungu

Headman Kefa & 5 wives

Mary Mwale

The Mwale cattle kraal

Eliza Phiri

To the water hole

To the fields

Kakoche Mwale & Jessie Ngoma

To the bush

Zindikani Miti, Jertru Mbewe & Tisauke Mwale

Margalet Mwale

Faides Phiri

Mwazida Mwale & Robert Manda

James Njobvu

Fatness Manda

To the fields & vegetable gardens

Tisauke Phiri & Kwerekani Phiri

LEGEND

◼	brick house
⬟	round hut
⬢	square hut
Ⓚ	kitchen
◣	falling down house
⊤⊤	shelter, drying racks
⊟	pig house
Ⓟ	pidgeon house
Ⓧ	chicken pen
Ⓖ	goat house
⌑	pit latrine
○	maize bin
●	groundnut bin
⌣	oven
▽	paw paw tree
⬭	cattle enclosure

Mwada Simba & Micheck Phiri

James Phiri & Dorothy Banda

Tiweleni Banda

Mwanishupa Phiri & Sandikonda Daka

Evelinar Njobvu & Kabanda Nyuni

Zuwaila Zulu

Elina Nkhoma

Shoes Zulu & Jenifa Banda

To Mtewe River

To the burial ground

To the forest

To Nyanthani and Mtolo villages

S. Miti

Change in an African Village

Kefa Speaks

Else Skjønsberg

KUMARIAN PRESS

With thanks to

The Honourable Chief Chikuwe, Headman Kefa Mwale, Community Development Assistant John Phiri, Sylvester Miti, Brighton K.K. Lungu, Agnes Banda, Rachel Ngwenie, Dorothy Wilson, Tyford Nyirenda, Square Banda, Tilele Zulu, John Mbao, Mwada Simba, Micheck Phiri, Timeke Daka, Faides Phiri, Dorothy Banda, Simon Sakala, Mwanishupa Phiri, James Phiri, Tisalire Banda, Kwerekani Phiri, Kabanda Nyuni, Evelinar Njobvu, Shoes Zulu, Jenifa Banda, Kathontho Mwale, Mwanishinga S. Mbewe, Katherine Daka, Lelia Adona Mbewe, Janet Lungu, Zenaida Mwale, Mary Mwale, Jones Mwale, Gilbert Zulu, Peter Nyirenda, Erik Aaberg, Elisabet Helsing, Marit Kromberg, Beatrice Mutala Skagestad, Vigdis Varn, IDZ, PRIO, NORAD . . .

. . . and many others who made this study possible.

Copyright © 1989 Kumarian Press, Inc.
630 Oakwood Avenue, Suite 119, West Hartford, Connecticut, 06110-1529 USA
All rights reserved under International and Pan-American Copyright Conventions. No part of this book may be reproduced or transmitted in any form or by any means, electronic or mechanical, including photocopy, recording or information storage and retrieval system, without prior written permission of the publisher.

Printed in the United States of America
Second Printing 1990
93 92 91 90   5 4 3 2

Edited by Barbara A. Conover
Cover design & illustrations by Maxine Marcy
Book design by Marilyn Penrod
Typeset by Apex Typesetting, Inc.
Printed by McNaughton-Gunn
Skjønsberg, Else.
   Change in an African village: Kefa speaks / by Else Skjønsberg.
     p.   cm. — (Kumarian Press library of management for development)
   Includes bibliographies.
   ISBN 0-931816-57-2
   1. Ethnology—Zambia—Kefa. 2. Kefa (Zambia)—Social conditions.
3. Social change.   I. Title   II. Series.
GN657.R4S59 1988
306′.096894—dc19   88-26685
                                             CIP

CONTENTS

VILLAGERS

Headman Kefa Mwale	Chewa village leader; about 75 years old
Keterina Daka	Kefa's first wife; about 60
Janet Lungu	Kefa's second wife; about 70
Regina Shawa	Kefa's third wife; about 60; of the Ngoni tribe
Lelia Mbewe	Kefa's fourth wife, and his favorite; about 50
Nyamanda	Kefa's last wife; about 50
Kakoche Mwale	Kefa's father; blind; about 90
Jessie Ngoma	Kakoche's wife, and mother of Wickson Mwale
Mwazida Mwale	Kefa's sister; about 60
Robert Manda	Mwazida's husband, a rich Kefa village cattle owner; about 60
Vast Manda	Robert's son, also called Tisatenji; divorced and childless; about 35
Fatnes Manda	Vast's sister; divorced; mother of Lucy, 6, and Joseph, 11
Lemekani Mbao	Kefa and Mwazida's Ngoni half-brother; about 60
Tilele Zulu	Lemekani's wife, and mother of 8; a hard-working cotton grower; about 50
Joseph Mbao	Lemekani's crippled son; 20
Alines Mbao	left school and lives in Kefa to help her mother; 15
Esinaya Mbao	goes to school and helps her father weed; 12
Nelli	stays with her grandparents, and her parents live in Lusaka; 8
Malisawo	Tilele and Lemekani's last-born; 6
Square Banda	crippled and lives alone; considered the first in African medicine; about 50
Mwanishupa Phiri	mother of Nyawa, 10, and two other children who live outside Kefa village; about 40
Sandikonda Daka	Mwanishupa's husband; used to be a tobacco grower, but now is troubled permanently by a bad leg; owner of a few pigs and some chicks; 60
Lubinda Mwale	deputy headman with a bad temper; happened to kill a man and had to go to jail; about 65
Mwanijinga Mbewe	Lubinda's wife, and the mother of Bernhard, who cultivates in other people's fields with Kathontho's oxen
Mr. Tembo and Mr. Mwanza	government bricklayers who came to Kefa village to construct model houses
Chaputa Mbewe	father of Asters Mbewe; 45
Tiku Banda	Chaputa's wife, who was made a widow when Chaputa died from the blow inflicted upon him by Lubinda
Shuzi Zulu	ardent vegetable grower who refused to be observed by us; 25
Jenifa Banda	Shuzi's wife, and mother of two children; currently pregnant; 20
Mwada Simba	the mother of children in Lundazi; about 45
Micheck Phiri	Mwada's husband, who loves his wife (and fights with her); about 30
Henly	Mwada's grandson; 10

Kwerekani Phiri	permanently employed by the Public Works Department; comes to Kefa village during weekends to drink beer and to see his wives; 60
Jessie Tonga	Kwerekani's first wife, and mother of Alick, Samu and Kambula
Tisauke Phiri	Kwerekani's second wife, and mother of several school children
Aida Mbewe	Chaputa's mother and Asters' grandmother
Zindikani Miti	Kefa's nephew and heir, the son of Margaret Mwale; owner of the banana plantation; about 35
Gertru Mbewe	first wife of Zindi, and mother of Maggi, 13
Tisauke Mware	second wife of Zindi, and mother of Nisosi, 5
Dorothy Banda	mother of Gidson, 4; Unice, 2; and Mavuto, 1, who died; 20
James Phiri	Dorothy's hard-working husband; 25
Kabanda Nyuni	brother of James and father of two small children
Evelinar Ngona	Kabanda's wife; occasionally possessed by spirits
Sonile Ngona	mother of James and Kabanda, who shares her resources with them and their families
Andrick Banda	used to fall sick during weeding season; 65
Rahaby Sakala	married James Njobu without contracting proper marriage
Mtole Mbao	Kefa's Ngoni half-sister, and Rahaby's extended mother
Emeria	Rahaby's daughter; 2
Brighton K.K. Lungu	sociological assistant who used to work in Lundazi, but whose leg was destroyed in an accident
Romance Tembo	Brighton's mother; about 55
Ajesi Kamanga	Brighton's aunt, who died just after the survey had started
Tilolele Banda	Brighton's sister, and mother of two (9, 3); widowed
Rachel Lungu	Brighton's sister, and mother of two (7, 5); earns income by serving as waitress in a beer hall
Misho Sakala	shared a sleeping hut with Brighton; son of Tilolele
Faides Phiri	female head of household, and mother of 5 sons, 4 of whom stay with her in Kefa village and help her to cultivate; about 40
Yanzulani Nkoma	said to own several houses in Chipata; works as a builder and only comes occasionally to Kefa village
Mwaniyana Zulu	Yanzulani's wife; sells fish which she buys in Malawi and Luangwa Valley; mother of 2 sons (12, 9) in Kefa village; two grandchildren also stay in the village
Kamaswanda Njobvu	basket maker who came from Petauke and asked to stay in Kefa village to make and sell baskets; married to Grace Zulu in Petauke; contracted informal marriage with Rahaby
Brackson Njobvu	Kamaswanda's brother, who helps him in his trade
Simon Sakala	bike owner and hard-working vegetable grower; extended son of Mtole Mbao
Tisalire Banda	Simon's wife, and mother of Emmelia, 3, and Rothia, 1–1½, who died; 20
	and other incumbents from an additional 28 households...

INTRODUCTION

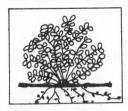

Chakudza siciyimba ng'oma
What Comes Does Not Beat a Drum

It was the ambition to make the past known to the future that led the residents of Kefa village to participate in the study that comprises this book. They seemed to take it for granted that their own hand-to-mouth agriculture would soon disappear, and that a future of clean shirts and tractors lay ahead, even if it would not be their future. They wanted their grandchildren, some of them already in school or working in town, to know how they, their elders, had worked and lived; how they sweated in the maize fields to prepare the parched soil in September and October, broke their backs to harvest groundnuts in April, savored the conviviality of the beer pots in August, and took part in the numerous ceremonies that unfolded throughout the year. They wanted to share with others the village joy of seeing children multiply and grow, herds increase, and granaries be replenished.

Kefa is a very ordinary Zambian village. Virtually every adult village resident grows his or her own food and also some for sale. A total of 250 people live in the village, which is situated in Eastern Zambia close to Chipata town, and most of them belong to the matrilineal Chewa people.

Like most ordinary African villages, Kefa is undergoing rapid changes. The fact is that traditional rural ways of life have little resistance to the transformations wrought by the global political economy. And as economic links between town and villages are tightened, forces that had cemented village living erode. Lost in the modernization process are not only mud huts and grass roofs, but also a way of life dominated by sharing and reflection. Unfortunately such entities leave no visible remains behind; yet their disappearance leaves us poorer than before. It is to make the invisible losses visible that I have written this book.

I myself am a Norwegian rural sociologist. At the time of the study I was working for a Rural Development Programme in the area. It was my third fieldwork in a third world rural setting and my previous field experiences had helped me to clarify the method we would use—a time study—and the overall goals. I had three basic aims: first, to account objectively how villagers live and work; second, to disclose why people do what they do; and third, to describe village life within a frame of reference that is endemic to the villagers rather than to the expatriate sociologist. Of course, this latter endeavor can only meet with partial success. However sensitive an author is, to tell a story is a very personal affair. I do however hope that villagers, in Kefa and elsewhere, will recognize at least some of the flavor of village living when reading this book. The Chewa words of wisdom—*no man is right all the time*—can also be the motto for this village diary.

The first objective—the recording of village life—was achieved through a time allocation study. To gather the time data, the Rural Development Programme for which I worked employed five local people, each one hand-picked because he or she spoke at least some English. After sixteen months in the village, the team had observed eight men and eight women heads of households for 6,400 hours, or more than 500 (wo)man days. It was quite some achievement, by the people thus closely followed for such a long time, and more so for the team of observers. One day Agnes Banda made this entry in her notebook:

> "I could not record all Tisalire's activities. She was too busy doing so many things. Her main activity was pounding maize, but she also breast-fed her lastborn, chatted with her neighbour Timeke, smoked a cigarette that she had got as a free gift from Square Banda, and ate the groundnuts that Timeke shared with her."

And there were other problems: Brighton K.K. Lungu, the only member of the team who was a Kefa village resident himself, wrote this in his notebook:

> "Some of the activities recorded here are not accurate. For example, by the time Lubinda went to see Mr. Manda I was not there as I had to go to the bush. The time was between 5:09 and 5:25, but as I do not know exactly I can only guess. I do not want to cheat the government* so please do not blame me. I do not know what to do about this and I am so very sorry if you find that my way of assisting you is no good."

Half-done or inaccurate observation days were excluded in the final analysis of the time study. They were not many and their exclusion is not likely to have influenced the validity of our data, which are presented in Appendix A.

The second objective to reach behind what we saw to comprehend—why the villagers did what they did—made close local collaboration an absolute necessity. As the time allocation study progressed, the team members were encouraged to jot down events, discussions, or just

---

*The Provincial Community Development Department, the Chief of the area, and the head-man all warmly supported our study, as did the Integrated Zone Development Programme under which I worked as rural sociologist. For this reason we were looked upon as "the government."

anything they would reflect on while on duty recording daily activities or while they lived alongside their fellow villagers sharing in their work and leisure. The large amount of qualitative data that resulted is very much the essence of this book. Most of it was collected and written down by Sylvester Miti, who was the team supervisor. Being a Ngoni, he had been brought to the village from Chief Mpezeni's area. Brighton K.K. Lungu and Tyford P. Nyirenda also did a wonderful job reporting on daily Kefa village affairs.

It is the men's perspective that dominates the book even if it has been written with the clear ambition of giving the women villagers the central place in the community which is truly theirs. However, because male villagers are less busy than the womenfolk, the men in the sociology team had more time at their disposal to write down small talk, discussions, and major events in which their observed persons—that is, the men in the sample—participated. It is also a fact that a man's perspective carries more weight than a woman's in a village like Kefa. Yet, as we shall see later on, a women's perspective is by no means absent. The problem, however, was this: As village women are so busy catering to most village needs, so also were the female recorders Agnes Banda, Rachel Ngweme, and Dorothy Wilson (all from the immediate vicinity of Kefa village) who kept busy recording daily activities and had little time for stories. And once their daily work was done, they then drew water and cooked for the men in the sociology team. The male perspective is the public perspective, the one loudly spoken. The following story serves as an example:

Sandikonda Daka, a much respected village elder, felt himself fenced in by the time observation study in which he had been asked, and to which he had agreed, to participate. One morning soon thereafter we heard him complain to John Scout Phiri and a few others who had no ardent business just then. Mr. Daka said: "When I woke up this morning I found the recorder seated at my porch waiting for me to come out so that he could start recording all my doings. Now there are plenty of things that a person does inside his house early in the morning, like chatting privately with the wife, and even doing his business with her, that should not be recorded. I do not think it is right, even for people in the government, to watch everything that goes on in a marriage. I am determined to take this matter to the headman because if this is going to continue it is bound to cause some grave problem around here."

John Scout tried to calm Sandikonda by commenting "But to record our businesses is their job. They want to tell others about how we live and work and about the problems we face when the rain is not enough and our young people stay on in the towns." Simon Sakala, who had joined the small group, said: "Unless they come very early, they may not catch us at home. I, at least, am off very early and I never tell the mother of my last born [the wife] where I am going. So it is better that the recorder comes early, if he wants to spend the day with me."

Hundred Banda, however, supported Mr. Daka wholeheartedly: "This is very bad, indeed. I for my part fully accept Mr. Daka's complaint. If I were to find a girl outside my house waiting to observe the mother of my children while we were doing our thing, I would know how to deal with that girl right away. And if she reported me for assault or anything I shall gladly stand judgment, if indeed I have done anything wrong. Truly, at dawn people do many things inside their house that should not be recorded and I would refuse to have any observers near my house at that hour."

Having received such support, Sandikonda continued: "What has this village become? Now we cannot even play with our own wives for fear that somebody is listening at the door. We all paid money for our wives. They are entirely ours to do what we please with. They cannot be disturbed against our wishes."

It was a fair complaint. We took care to solve the problem to Sandikonda Daka's full satisfaction. From then on the morning shift of recorders waited at a safe distance from the house of the person to be observed until it was quite clear that the house had shed its cloak of nightly privacy and a new day had begun.

Active involvement of the villagers in selecting the information that would become this book was the third ambition of the study. Thanks to the honorable Chief Chikuwe and the Headman Kefa Mwale, such close cooperation was secured right from the start when a village meeting introduced the idea of making Kefa village the focus for our study. The Chief himself recommended Kefa village to us, knowing that headman Kefa was a man of wisdom and authority. Kefa was also selected because the community had been appointed as a model village of the Chipata District and would soon be transformed according to the government's plans of appointing model villages to become spearheads for rural development. Brick houses and tap water would be the benefits soon to be bestowed upon Kefa.

It was the headman and the village meeting that gave us the approval we needed to participate in village affairs. It was also the headman who persuaded the few village residents who at times got tired of the time observations that this was a job needing the participation of the whole village. Of the people selected for observations only one man—Shoes Zulu—decided not to participate. Of this occasion Sylvester Miti reported:

"Shoes Zulu has been away from the village for some days, but now he is back. When he returned he told us: 'Let me rest, I am tired of being followed around. I do not want to have people watching me any more.' Jackson Phiri, his friend, supported him and said: 'Why don't you just say no. They cannot put you in jail for refusing. I would never have participated in such a study. I tell you, Mr. Zulu, this study is useless to me.' Sylvester Miti, the team leader, reported this small problem to the headman, and Mr. Kefa Mwale said: 'I shall talk to Shoes and to Jackson, and if they go on arguing I shall tell them to leave my village. Here we want everybody to cooperate. I am not at all happy about this because when we had our meeting everybody was asked to give their opinion. At that time neither Jackson nor Shoes protested and we all agreed that this study was something we would do together. And now these problems arise! ' "

It was not a big problem. We did not want to force anyone to participate: quite the contrary. Shoes was replaced by somebody else. No wonder he got tired of being followed around! We asked a lot from many people. Yet virtually everybody contributed, and many did so in a manner we would never have expected. James Phiri was one of them. One day James came to talk to us, and this is what he reported:

"This morning when I woke up the recorder was outside my house as usual. But, when I went to the vegetable garden to water tomatoes, the recorder remained behind in the village. And when I returned home he asked me where I had been and what I had been doing and for how long! Surely this is not right, at least before I was never observed in this way. How can this man observe me when he is not even there to see what I am doing. I tell you this because if our survey shall be worthwhile it must be done well."

In Chapter 1 Kefa village is described in general terms through its villagers. Kefa village is primarily the Mwale family, that is, headman Kefa Mwale and his kin. But there are also many other village *residents*, as the villagers with some knowledge of English prefer to call themselves. The headman's position is central not only because of Kefa's personality but also because of the rights and duties that the headmanship confers upon him. His position is further cemented by the past. Kefa Mwale comes from a family of headmen and he secured his headmanship by establishing his own village in the 1940s. The formation of Kefa village was partly the result of the colonial administration resettlement policy. Hence central political and administrative decisions have from time to time had obvious repercussions in Kefa village.

In Chapters 2 and 3 the mainstay of Kefa village living is rendered in some detail. Land, soil, and labor are the most basic productive factors in the village. Most villagers base their existence on subsistence cultivation, even if cash crops and economic considerations increasingly influence what people cultivate and how. Still, agricultural production is precarious in Kefa and cultivation is pivotal to the social fabric. Production results determine family size and division of labor, status, and outside contacts.

The farmer's calendar is a strict and utterly demanding one. There is a time for everything, for hoeing and planting, for weeding and scaring off predators, for harvesting, repairing tools and houses, and for socializing around a pot of beer.

The production side is only one part of the Kefa picture; enjoying the fruits of one's labor is another. Chapter 4 focuses on consumption, that is, food preparation and meals. In subsistence society food must be made anew every day by every household. There is no work on which Kefa women spend more time than food preparation. The technology they use is simple. It is women, with their many duties at home, who are ultimately responsible for their family's well being. Once made, the daily meals allow for relaxation and togetherness, and beer drinking provides these to an even greater extent. Of the many joys of village living, beer has a special place, at least for the beer drinkers and the many women who make brewing their business. But alcohol is also a source of strife and wastage, particularly now that beer has become a commodity rather than a free gift.

Agriculture and food preparation are the most basic of all village activities, but most villagers perform other tasks to live well. Chapter 5 shows how animal husbandry, petty trade, crafts, and beer brewing are means through which industrious village residents earn at least some money. To earn at least something is everybody's concern, but this is not an easy goal in a society where there is so little. And yearning for money has also caused trouble among friends and family members.

It is against the background of cultivation, food preparation, and various economic undertakings that Chapter 6 introduces Kefa family structure and family life. As the economic base for Kefa village is slowly changing, so is family life. In a society where school has taken over much of the educational role of the elders, and where young men earn money to pay their own brideprice rather than depending on their elders, growing up in Kefa village is no longer what it used to be. Yet many things remain, if not the same, at least basically unaltered. Women elders still advise the girls during puberty ceremonies. Marriage counselors still help quarreling spouses come to terms. And village meetings are still called to solve problems that arise when people who are not married get together or spouses do not heed advice and continue to work against rather than in support of each other. Divorce and death remain facts of village life and have to be handled properly to reduce distress or destitution.

In Chapter 7 the disruptive forces of illness, witchcraft, and death are described. In these respects, too, Kefa village has its specialists, the healers and the witch doctors. There are also coping mechanisms such as special foods, village dances, and expulsions of unwanted village members. Because life is hard, villagers are used to meet uncertainty. Healing herbs and roots, amulets, and rituals are part of a common village stock of knowledge. If there is no cure, people join together from near and far to give a common voice of consolation to the suffering. Whatever happens, there is a village order, which when threatened with disruption, is promptly reinforced by headman Kefa's traditional superior, the honorable Chief Chikuwe.

Village life is changing in rural Zambia, and Kefa village has become a forerunner of this change. Chapter 8 relates how Kefa village came to be appointed model village for the district. Within a couple of years, the physiognomy of the village changed as every mud hut was replaced by a brick house. It was all part of President Kaunda's effort to develop the rural areas, but the price paid by the Kefa residents to transform their village was high. During no year were there more funerals in the village than during the time when the model house constructions were at their peak, nor were there more village meetings. Yet, the villagers pursued their endeavor of turning Kefa village into a model village. That they succeeded is a witness to the organizational skills of headman Kefa and the hard work and patience of his villagers.

Appendix A renders the findings from the time study, which focused on the everyday activities of eight men and eight women during more that 6,000 hours. The Appendix describes in detail how the villagers worked in agriculture, prepared food, and performed other economic activities. It includes data on eating and drinking, leisure, and minor activities. Data from a recall study yield additional light on the Kefa cash economy and on traveling. Family decision-making patterns as perceived by spouses are also described. The Appendix explains methodological issues concerning the time allocation study and the basic concepts that were assumed. Finally, simple statistics show that Kefa compares well with other villages in the district and in Zambia in regard to demography and basic socioeconomic characteristics. Kefa is unique, yet representative.

One word about the footnotes at the end of each chapter and the appendixes. Their purpose is to give more detail to selected aspects of rural living without unduly interrupting the reader. The dominant approach throughout the book has been to visualize village life rather than to explain it. Zambian twentieth century history has been left out, as have the Chewa kinship system and the linkage between Kefa and the global political economy. The style is very much determined by the way the young local sociologist assistants to the study expressed themselves, and academic terminology has been avoided as much as possible. The story about Kefa village aims to break with a tradition that describes and analyzes non-Western societies at a level of abstraction that makes them unintelligible or uninteresting to the untrained eye. Yet it needs to retain a linkage to that same tradition. This objective is reached by means of the time study and the footnotes.

Many social scientists take care to disguise the people and places they write about. This is not the approach of this book. One reason is that the Kefa village residents wanted their grandchildren and others to know how they as individuals worked and lived, not in the abstract, but in a very real sense. As do possessions, names too seem to hold a different meaning to Chewa people than to Westerners. While we cherish our names as talismen that can protect us against the transcience of life, the Chewa seem to have a deeper interpretation of identity and change. To them a name is like a garment, suitable at certain periods in life, slightly out of place or outmoded at others, and able to be exchanged for something more appropriate.

Nyanja is the language of the Chewa. The old Dictionary of the Nyanja Language, compiled and written by missionaries and edited in 1929, puts it this way:

> Anyone may give a child its name, though of course it is the father or the mother that receives or confirms it . . . A relation, brother or sister, or even an outsider, may make 'friendship' with the babe and give it their own name, or the name of their brother or sister. The father very often gives the child a name. . . Names are closely associated with friendship, which is almost a covenant, so that the one who gives a child his name creates a covenant or lifelong friendship between them. . .
>
> Names are changed at puberty, the idea most likely being that a change of life involves a change of name. Similarly, when two make a covenant of friendship or love, they change their names, which is at once a declaration to each other that such friendship has renewed their lives, and a declaration to others of the fact and its constancy. There is a great deal of philosophy in all this, and when there is no need for a register of names in the fixed formulas of the registers of formal civilization but, on the contrary, a need for free growth of form under the changing sky of a normal heathenism, the African philosophy of naming is certainly more natural and perhaps as useful as our own. Changes of names may, however, take place from a variety of motives. A journey to a great distance may so impress a person's life that he comes back with a name taken from the limits of his travel. Political relations may change his name. (p. 117)

For this and other reasons, many people have many names. One may reflect courtesy to foreigners who seem unable to remember names they are not familiar with. To accommodate, a person picks any name that comes into his mind; hence, the villagers Prison, Government, Iron, Whisky and Shoes. There is also influence of the Church. When villagers join it, they may change their names or add Christian names to their other names. Thus Mulumbenji became Emelia, Lemekani John, and Chada Simon.

Second names, or clan names, present a limited choice. Though the Chewa traditionally inherited property and positions through their mother, the clan name is that of the father. Most clan names, like most first names, have a meaning. Phiri is "hill," Njobvu "elephant," Mvula "rain," Manda "grave." Clan names indicate blood relationships, but with time clans have become so extended that Phiri, Banda, and Mwale are found all over Chewa land, in Malawi as well as Zambia and most clan members are unable to trace their origin to a common ancestor.

I have called many of the people in the book by the names that I learned when I was first introduced to them, but this is not always the case. In addition, though I have used real names and real situations, and have linked conversations and events to those names, anybody writing about the "real" world is unlikely to be able to prevent her imagination from subtracting and adding facts and feelings to bring forth not the "real" thing, but its reflection as it appears to her. I hope that Kefa village residents, neighbors, and visiting friends and relatives will understand.

This book, the final outcome of the study, is only my responsibility. I have written it in Norway, thousands of miles away from Kefa village. However, headman Kefa and his village residents have been following its progress, hoping, with me, that it will fulfill the aspiration that we all have invested in the study, that of making ordinary village life known and cherished by villagers and urban residents of Zambia, and elsewhere.

CHAPTER 1   THE VILLAGE AND ITS PEOPLE

Ciswe cimodzi siciumba culu
One White Ant Does Not Build an Ant Hill

In the village almost everything is free, and there are plenty of possibilities for people to practice together-ness, and also traditional talents like dancing nyau and cimtali dances and to dig for mice. Labor is inex-pensive and can be paid with other goods than money. What is not good is the belief in witchcraft, the dislike of hard work, and the lack of transport.

A villager's view

The Village

A village is the people who live in it, and through its residents the village both acquires and develops its individuality. When we made our census of Kefa village in 1977 we counted fifty-six households,[1] or nuclei, people staying together and sharing most of their food, money, and labor. One hundred and twenty men and women and almost the same number of children, each one with his or her definite place in the community, with a roof over the head and somebody to share in joys and sorrows, with groundnut and maize fields and tools to work the ground. While about half the households had a male and a female head and children, in many homes there were no adult men and a few consisted of only one person. In others a grandmother lived with a grandson and daughter, or a husband lived with two or more wives. Togetherness was still a key element to Kefa village living.

Sylvester Miti, who was from the Ngoni people, described the Chewa[2] village in this way:

"Kefa village has been created by a combination of people who have come together from different places and for different reasons. In my home area in Chief Mpezeni new villages are also being formed because of hunger, but in such villages the only new members are wives and children. In this way our Ngoni villages consist of large families. As each family grows, the elders are respected accordingly. Each elder leads his own segment and solves its problems before matters are brought to the headman's attention. But here in Kefa village there are no such segments. Instead the village is divided geographically. The village residents differentiate between *Kumidindo*, which is the northern part, *Pakati*, the middle, and *Benemwale*, the southern part of the village, where most of Kefa Mwale's family live. And it is my observa-tion that those living in the various sections cooperate accordingly."

The Mwale, the Phiri, the Sakala, and the Zulu were the four main families in Kefa village when we started our study. There were also a few other people not connected by birth (but often through marriage) with the four. Needless to say, we cannot include all in our story, yet each one contributes to making Kefa village the unique place it is. We shall, however, introduce at least a few, to underline the purpose of this book, which is to go beyond statistics, generalizations, and abstractions to bring the focus to the individual and his and her interplay with the surroundings.

We asked headman Kefa about his village residents and he said:

> "I have Zindikani Miti here, my nephew who has come from Jumbe in the valley with his Bisa family. They are Bisa[3] through the father, but belong to the Chewa people through the mother Margaret, my sister. Then there is Konala Sakala and his family members, who came here from Kumbwi village. I also used to have the Phiris from Chiduka village, but now all of them have left [they were expelled from Kefa village because one of them killed headman Kefa's son]. In the southern end of my village, from Lubinda's house up to that of Robert Manda, is my own *Cigawa* section, the Mwales. Some of them like Lekemani and his relatives [sisters] claim to be Ngoni through their father. And there is Zuwaila Zulu, who came from Malambo to live here with us, but he is only one person and not a family like the others." (Headman Kefa does not count his wives and their children.)

The headman's own family, the Mwale, and the Phiri family, were the first to settle in Kefa village, back in 1942 when the village was founded by headman Kefa himself. In the 1950s the Sakala family, moving from their own village of origin somewhere near the Malawian border, came to live in Kefa village. It so happened that Konala Sakala and Kefa Mwale used to be workmates some time past, and when Konala was in trouble in his own village, he came to headman Kefa and asked if he could become a Kefa village resident. He brought his sister and her children along with him, and later on he married Kefa's sister Mulumbenji, or Emelia, as she came to be called when she joined the Reform Church.

In 1966 the Zulu family came, two brothers and their wives. The elder brother had killed a relative and spent several years in prison. With Zambian independence he and many others were pardoned, but back in his village he did not feel wanted. Thus he arrived one day at Kefa's house to ask for residenceship. Kefa took him to Chief Chikuwe, who permitted him to stay in his chiefdom if he promised never to kill again. And so he promised.

Being headman, Kefa Mwale has more wives than any one else, and having more wives he has more land under cultivation, and with more land he can afford to marry more wives. Keterina Daka, seventy years old, is the first wife. Though Kefa had had at least three wives before her, they are no longer with him and do not count. Being Kefa's first wife, Keterina enjoys much respect in the village. She is old but she still cultivates her own field and even helps Kefa in his hybrid maize field.

Keterina and Kefa have many children, but only Zenaida Tikambenji, Mwale, who is forty-five, lives in Kefa village. Zenaida's first husband died. She is now the second wife of a husband who lives and works in Petauke, 100 kilometers away. The husband sometimes comes to see her, but not very often. Zenaida has five children. Three live in Lusaka and the Copper Belt where they work or go to school. Only Ruthi, who is twelve, and Nabien, who is ten, are with the mother, and at night they sleep with Keterina, the grandmother. Zenaida's three-year-old grandson, Moriss, also stays with her. He is the pet of the Mwale family, usually found on someone's lap or back. Everybody, including the headman, his greatgrandfather, spoils him.

Gilbert Zulu is Zenaida's son from her first marriage. He lives in Ndola, where he has been working for the railways for many years. Although he is married with four children, he is contemplating a divorce. It is said that he wants to marry a new wife who is younger and better educated than the old. Gilbert has great plans for the future. He wants to buy a tractor and become a farmer here in Kefa village.

Janet Lungu, seventy years old, is Kefa's second wife. She lives with her granddaughter Agnes. Kefa sometimes helps Janet with money, but she mostly manages by herself and by whatever her children and grandchildren give her. Kefa and Janet are not on particularly good terms, nor are they on bad terms. In fact they do not meet often, though Janet lives next door to the other Kefa wives. Like them, she too has a room in one of the two brickhouses that Kefa has built.

Regina Shawa, forty years old, is the third wife of the headman. She is Ngoni and Kefa paid bridewealth—*lobola*—of one cow and 1 kwacha (about U.S. $1.20) for her. "A girl must marry so that the parents can earn," Regina told us. When families are joined in marriage *lobola* plays a much more important part among the patrilineal Ngoni than among the Chewa. Regina married Kefa about ten years ago. They have no children. Regina too has her own field and garden, and she is known as a hard-working cultivator.

Adona Lelia Mbewe, who is forty-five, is the wife Kefa used to love the most. She and Regina fought because of a disagreement concerning a hen. When Kefa involved himself and beat Regina with a stick, Regina became very upset, not because Kefa beat her but because he took sides in a quarrel between his wives. But Adona Lelia was also upset. Kefa loved her very much and promised that he would not marry additional wives. But now he has married a fifth wife.

The fifth wife, Nyamanda, comes from Kamanga village, just across the road. A widow, she is well known for her skills in brewing beer. Since Nyamanda married headman Kefa, Lelia does not weed her maize. She says she wants to go to Lusaka to stay with her sister's daughter. Kefa is afraid that if she goes, she may not come back. Lelia too was a widow when she married Kefa eight years ago. She has no children. Lelia's brother is a messenger at the Chief's court. Because he receives a cash income, Lelia does not worry so much about the future. If she divorces the headman, her brother can help her financially.

Kefa Mwale has two sons in the village, David, who is seventeen, and Paskale, who is fifteen. The boys' real mother divorced Kefa some time ago and returned to her own village. As a consequence the boys are supposed to be fed by their two other mothers, Ketrina and Lelia. But this does not always happen. Their mothers consider the boys lazy and sometimes refuse them food, thinking that this tactic will persuade the boys to help them weeding their maize fields. Even the headman cannot seem to make the young boys work, and he often herds his cows himself without the help of his sons.

Mary and Jones Mwale are also under headman Kefa's care. After both their father, the headman's brother, and their mother died, they decided to settle in Kefa village. Mary, who is divorced, used to live in Lusaka. When her husband decided to marry a new wife, she went to stay with Kefa Mwale in his village, leaving her daughter behind in Lusaka. Now Mary is a successful grower of cotton and manages well by herself. Of course she is young and strong. Jones, her brother, is occasionally employed by the tobacco board to buy up other farmers' tobacco at harvest time.

Elida Mbewe was another Mwale relative, a much respected elder, a mother, grandmother, and greatgrandmother of many. Not only the headman but also many others called her *amai*—mother. When she died, Kefa slaughtered a cow to feed the many mourners who came to grieve her.

So far we have introduced less than 10 percent of the village residents. Throughout the rest of the book, many more will appear on the scene, some frequently—as indeed they are more visible in the village—and some only briefly. However always at the center, by virtue of his position as village leader and his skills and political wisdom, is the headman himself, Kefa Mwale. Like every other headman, Kefa is the owner of the village and thus, as we shall see, he conducts his own and the village's affairs.

The Headman

"I was born in Mpindila village in Chief Chikuwe's area in 1903, or about that time. I was named after my father's father, Mr. Kefalimani Mwale from Kasungu in Malawi. As my mother's brother was a headman and my mother's mother's brother was the owner of his village, it was clear from the beginning that I would be headman."

In his youth, like most other young men, Kefa Mwale travelled widely in Zambia, driven by the need for cash to pay taxes and also by the desire to see the world. And so he did.

"I have seen so many places in Zambia and also in Malawi and Rhodesia. In my young days, I went all the way to Salisbury (Harare) before the Great East Road was built in 1928, [connecting Chipata, the Eastern Province capital, with Lusaka]. For five years I worked as a laborer for the Public Works Department, mostly in the Northern Province. I married a Bemba woman who produced three children. Later I went to Kitwe on the Copper Belt, so I also know town life. But, as I am a Chewa and my home is here in the Chewa homeland around Chipata, after some time I longed for my own people and I came here. In Chipata I got the job as a houseservant to an English family, and later on I was the messenger in the Agricultural Station at Kalichero in Chief Chikuwe's area. At that time I had a wife and several children, who stayed not so far away, at Mtolo village.

"The land at Mtolo village was not good, and my family did not eat well, and that is why I decided to move. I was lucky. My boss, the agricultural officer at Kalichero, told me that I could have new land if I could bring enough people with me to form a new village. Land was being reallocated and the government helped to settle people on land that until then was reserved for whites.[4] My boss said that he could not give land to individuals, but if we were many we would have sufficient land to make our own village.

"I discussed the matter with headman Mtolo, saying to him, 'Let us go and make a new village where land is fertile and abundant for all of us.' Mtolo did not want to go, but he accepted that I and my family left him. It was good for all of us, because those who stayed behind took over our fields."

It was not only luck, or the fact that Kefa Mwale came from a family of headmen, that made Kefa into the "owner of the village." In 1941 a program of resettlement was started to relieve pressure on reserves that until that time were the only areas allowed for African settlement. Large areas of fertile land had been reserved for white settlers in the 1920s, a policy that had led to a mass movement of Africans and congested conditions on the African reserves. As time passed, the white settlers never reached the numbers the British colonialists had hoped, and living conditions among the Africans were deteriorating rapidly. The resettlement program of the early 1940s was established to relieve pressure on the reserves and to introduce modern agriculture in the form of soil conservation measures. It was as part of this program that the energetic Kefa Mwale took his family and formed a new village—Kefa village.

Headman Kefa described how it happened:

"When I left Mtolo to build my own village, I did so because of *njala*— hunger. I welcomed those who wanted to improve their standard of living, making it clear that they who wished to share my land must cooperate and abide by my decisions. I went with my family in order to live well, not with the intention of becoming *mfumu ya mudzi*—village headman. Those who joined me did so of their own free will.[5] This is why those who want to live in my village now must cooperate. If not, I tell them that they may go back to where they came from. If there are problems I discuss them with my village residents. If we cannot come to terms, I take the problems to the Chief.

"When we first came to the area that was to become Kefa village, we walked about and carefully studied the vegetation and the water sources. In this way we decided that here was where we wanted to be. The same was the case when we chose our gardens. We watched the way trees, bushes, plants, and even the grass grew, in order to pick the most fertile soil for our new fields. During the rainy season we planted a special grass that tells us where the water remains under the surface when the soil dries up. Thus we determined where to dig our waterhole, and it is from there that the women draw water for us.

"The people who came with me were my father, Gabson Kakoche Mwale, two of my uncles, two brothers, my sisters and their families,[6] and people from the Phiri family from the neighboring village of Chiduka. During harvest we cleared our new fields, leaving it to our wives to harvest alone, while we worked hard cutting trees and clearing new ground in Kefa village. We also built temporary houses here in Kefa village. We worked hard, very hard. To build a new village is a tough job.

"The Department of Agriculture helped us by sending laborers to clear my fields according to the new method of cultivation. Through them we learned how to make contour ridges to keep the soil from disappearing with the rain. The Game Department also helped us to protect our fields against the elephants which were at that time a great trouble.

"Today my village land is still plentiful and fertile. We rarely shift our fields. Only when a cultivator is absent for some time is the field allowed to rest. Since we came to Kefa village there is no starvation. We are now 250 people in my village. And all is well. Our only problem is that young people go away. So they did in the past, but now they never return, and we miss them. They seem to think that happiness dwells in town, while some of us see only misery there."

"A village is not only a social entity, it is also an administrative unit. The headman functions as the head also in this respect. He is the link between the various families within the village, to other villages and to the traditional and modern administrative structures. The allegiance of the headman to the Chief is part of the former. A number of villages within a defined area form a chiefdom ruled by a chief owing allegiance to the paramount. In local matters the subchiefs with their councillors comprising headmen in major villages within their area, act independently and settle disputes with the exception of those of certain categories which have to be referred to the paramount or administration." This Bruwer wrote about rural structures at the beginning of the 1950s.[7] It aptly describes the duties and linkages of the headmanship today.

When asked about his duties, this is what Kefa Mwale said:

"A good *mfumu*—headman—must cooperate with people. If his own residents disobey him how can he expect people from other villages to respect him? In some villages the residents do not come together to solve problems and decide things. But, if people solve their problems without the aid of the headman, they will think that he is useless to them. A headman should be concerned with problems facing every family in his village. In order to do so he has his *induna*, the deputy headman. The *induna* is picked from among the most worthy village residents. It is only by respecting others that the *mfumu*, the headman, can make people respect him.

"A headman must not be greedy. In the past a headman received gifts of free beer from whoever brewed, but this custom is changing. Today people make beer not because of plenty, but because they have run out of food and need money. They want to sell and not to give beer away. I do not mind if I do not get any beer. Some still give, but not as they did before.

"Earlier the *mfumu* dissolved marriages when there were problems in a household and a marriage needed to be broken. Now this decision is made by the court. The change is good because one can easily be hated for dissolving somebody's marriage. Otherwise it is difficult to be *mfumu* now. In the past, villagers paid more respect. Only mad people did not obey the headman's words. Today anybody with money does as he pleases, disregarding the headman's decisions. Yet, when in trouble, he comes to me. And I help, as I do not want to pay him back with his own behavior.

"It is my job to make people aware of the needs of the Chief and the government. The government depends on all of us. Without the cooperation of the *mfumu* it is difficult for anyone to gather villagers together and secure their attention and cooperation."

A headman is like a father to his village. He represents it in the outside world and coordinates and leads its internal affairs. Kefa Mwale is a strong and active leader. Frequently he calls his people together for discussions, and he listens. But he also emphasizes that everyone who wants to live in his village (and only the headman is entitled to call the village "his") must cooperate with him and abide by his decisions. And people do, at least most of the time. There is a saying: *Mfumu ya ndeu simanga mudzi*—"a bellicose chief does not keep a village."[8] Not only has Kefa "kept" his, he has made it grow to become one of the larger villages in the chiefdom. "Kefa has in so many ways tried to better his village. All the time he is teaching people knowledge, cooperation, and understanding. That is why it is easy to stay with him and abide by his rule," Brighton Lungu explains.

The Chewas are matrilineal,[9] or more specifically, they used to be.

Nowadays, increasingly more Chewa men who can afford to pay brideprice,[10] just like the patrilineal Ngoni, so that their children will belong to their own family and not that of the mother. The headmanship also used to follow the mother's family; a man would inherit his position as headman from his mother's brother. A Chewa family, as we shall see in Chapter 6, is very large. A man has several mothers and even more maternal uncles; thus a headman is likely to have a number of sisters' sons all eligible for the position as headman. It is the village elders who chose the new headman from the nephews of the former headman, often according to the former headman's advice. And a woman may also be appointed.

This was the tradition, but today tradition is set aside, even by those who used to be their bearers. Said headman Kefa:

> "I am a Chewa, but it is my intention that my daughter Zenaida becomes headwoman after me, and not my sister's son Zindikani Miti. I know it is the Ngoni,[11] and not we Chewas, who have the custom of taking son or a daughter to succeed them as headman, but the world is changing. Nowadays Chewa pay brideprice just like the Ngoni, so that the children will belong to the father's family. In this way we believe that we have compensated the wife's family adequately with money or cattle for the children she produces. People no longer want to depend on their mother's family, or their sisters' children. They want to depend on their own children. When it comes to my succession I shall not hesitate to say that I will not accept that my sister Margaret's son becomes headman after me. My grandson Gilbert Zulu (Zenaida's son) is an educated man, and when he grows older he will be the best leader of this village. Then he can rule the village for his mother."

It is not that Kefa favors his daughter Zenaida rather than the nephew Zindikani to head the village. Instead, he wants his grandson Gilbert to become headman. At the moment Gilbert lives in Ndola working for the Zambian Railway. Gilbert plans to earn enough money to buy a tractor and return home to farm.

Kefa knows that some people will oppose his plan to make Zenaida and Gilbert leaders of Kefa village. In order to secure the headmanship for Gilbert, Kefa is seeking the support of the young men in the village. He seems to think that the young men will support a young headman and that together they will be able to overrule the traditional elders. Some people say that to reach this goal, Kefa plans to give new land only to people who are related to him (and consequently are likely to support him), or who plan to cultivate only for a short period of time. In that way he will make plenty of cleared land available for Gilbert when he comes back home. (Chapter 2 discusses in greater detail this allocation of land.)

A headman does not decide village affairs entirely alone. Without the support either of village elders or his deputy headmen—his *induna* (and the former group usually includes the latter)—it may be difficult even for a strong headman like Kefa Mwale to rule the village. At the onset of the study the headman had two deputies: Eliah Phiri, who was head of the Phiri family, and Lubinda Mwale, the richest man in the village, the owner of a herd of about fifty cattle. Both of them were elders with their own definite views on the succession of the headmanship. And as *induna* they were influential members of their community.

Fate seemed to play into Kefa Mwale's hands in his endeavor to make Gilbert and not Zindikani his successor. Within only a few months Kefa village lost both its deputy headmen. After each of them was involved in a killing, one was expelled and the other had to go to prison.

One day headman Kefa's son proper, Dandaulani Mwale, a man of about forty, was found dead hanging from a tree in the bush, not far from the village. As the tree was very small, it was obvious that somebody had placed him there. The village residents immediately suspected Laimen Phiri. Laimen had threatened Danda, saying that he had stolen 26 kwacha from him, money that Laimen had given Danda for safekeeping at a time when the two were the best of friends. A village meeting was called and Laimen was accused of murder. At the meeting Laimen admitted to the deed. As a consequence he and his entire family, including his father Eliah, the deputy headman, were expelled from the village, and later on from the chiefdom, according to the Chief's wish. The case finally ended up in the court in Chipata, as we shall see in Chapter 5.

It was only a few weeks later when the second tragedy fell upon the village. Lubinda Mwale, a long time deputy headman and Kefa village resident known for his short temper and sharp tongue, was approached by his neighbor, Kwezekani Mbewe. Mbewe shouted at him because the dog of a relative of Lubinda had eaten four of Kwezi's hens. Annoyed at this futile complaint, as the dog was not even his, Lubinda chased Kwezekani from his door with an axe-handle. In the process the handle fell upon Kwezi's head and cracked his skull. The following day Kwezekani, who by then could not talk, and could hardly walk, was taken to the hospital, where he died. Lubinda's own son-in-law, who worked with the Chipata police, took the old man to prison, where he remained for a year, when a mild sentence and his own poor health allowed him to return to Kefa village.[12]

It was a shattering time for the villagers. Some weeks later, when they had returned to their everyday routines, Kefa summoned them to a meeting to elect new *induna*. Pointing out that both his deputies, though village elders, had contributed to poisoning village peace with their hatred, the headman announced that time had come to think differently. This is a time, said Kefa, when changes take place, and when it is no longer obvious that the elders are much wiser than the youth. Many sons and daughters from Kefa village had been to school until adulthood and knew things that their parents had not even heard about. These were youngsters who drove cars and even tractors, and who were acquainted with new ways of cultivating. When the villagers elect new deputy village leaders, they should not ignore these people, for they need young blood.

The headman invited his village residents to propose candidates, but nobody said anything. Kefa Mwale then submitted his own, and they were Jackson Phiri and Jenelani Khosa. He introduced both to the village in terms of their family connections and their relationship with most of the people present at the meeting. Jenelani was away drinking beer when he was suggested as new deputy, and had to be brought from a nearby house of beer. When he arrived, he and Jackson were placed high on chairs brought out for this purpose so that they would be seen and respected by the rest, who were squatting on the ground as usual.[13] When the meeting was invited to respond to Kefa's choices, some pointed out that they were too young to handle village affairs, and especially the personal problems that so often are referred to the headman and his deputies. But Kefa answered by mentioning once more how the two were related to the major families in the village.

It was the industrious farmer Nason Phiri who reminded the new *induna* that they must behave well and not be short-tempered. And Lemekani Mbao, himself a nondrinking man, suggested that it would also be better if the deputy headmen reduced their beer habits. Hearing this, Jenelani, having just arrived from the beer hall, cried out that the villagers no longer wanted him to enjoy himself if they wanted to stop him from drinking beer. If that were the condition, he would flatly refuse to become a deputy headman!

"We do not want you to stop drinking, but only to reduce your beer habit," someone reassured him. Thus the discussions went on and on, until it was quite clear that everybody had had a say and was happy. And, once more, headman Kefa had got his way. Then Jackson Phiri, the new deputy headman, spoke: "As everybody knows, one has not one, but two homes, the village of the father and the village of the mother. For this reason, I request that you, Mr. Kefa, inform our parents of what has happened here. Only then can we be assured that we are really the new deputy-leaders in Kefa village."

So it happened that the deputies in Kefa village are youngmen and not elders.[14] Because Jackson Phiri and Jenelani Khosa are friends of Gilbert, Kefa thinks they will support Gilbert as his successor. But deputy headmen depend for their office on how village residents judge their character and performance. Whatever headman Kefa does, the village residents ultimately decide. And as yet they are undecided. Sylvester has filed this report:

"Jackson was appointed deputy by Kefa, but because he is young [around thirty] he is not certain whether he will keep the job. In fact, Jackson thinks that this is a job more suitable for an older person. He is afraid that he may be bewitched, and as he is still young he does not have sufficient knowledge about charms and medicines to protect himself. Lemekani, Kefa's brother, also thinks Jackson is too young. He has been complaining to the brother and asking him why he appointed a youngman like Jackson to solve village affairs problems when there are elders more acquainted with village ways and better able to settle disputes and make people cooperate. Even Jackson's mother is not happy that her son was appointed deputy headman. She too thinks that he is much too young and that it was wrong of Kefa to select him."

The village meeting is the official center of events. Here most communal decisions are made, or at least the problems in need of a decision are presented to the village residents. The village meeting also serves as a forum for debate and problem solving as we shall see later on, particularly in Chapter 7. The headman calls his villagers together often and he usually presides over the meeting. When he is away, his deputies do so.

Headman Kefa is old and wise. He never dominates a meeting. He knows that the final decisions rest with him, and he can well afford to listen to his residents. Anyone can talk at the meeting—men speak more frequently than women, but young people rarely do so. They know that the elders have had more experience than they and that it is by listening that they will learn.

Village events are also shaped elsewhere, some openly at ceremonies or at neighborhood gatherings, and some clandestinely at night, when the villagers claim that only witches move about without fear. The role of witchcraft—and, even more, the fear of witchcraft—plays an important role in shaping village affairs. (We shall learn about this in Chapter 7.)

The Past

To understand fully underlying currents that shape the events of the village and give them significance, it is also necessary for us to see today in the light of yesterday. For this reason we went to the village elders and asked them about the past, and how village living used to be.

Zindikani Miti answered for many when he said, "I do not have a proper history of where my grandparents came from and how they lived. But my parents were never caught as slaves by the Ngoni.[15] When they ran away it was from hunger. It drove them to Mtolo village and drove me to Kefa village. But I cannot say anything about the past better than Kakoche Mwale and his son Kefa."

We then talked to headman Kefa, the sturdy and vivacious man in his early seventies, the most lovable leader of his village, the honored husband of five wives, a man who had traveled widely and seen so much. But Kefa said, "If you want to know about the past you must talk to my father. He knows better than I or anybody else in the village what happened before."

I had passed the mud-and-wattle house of Kakoche Mwale many times, but it was only now that I noticed him. He was usually sitting quietly in the shade of his house on an old and worn deck-chair, a gift of long ago from an English employer. He was small, withered, and very old. He had, in fact, lived through ninety rainy seasons, and ninety harvests.

His eyesight had failed him years ago, but not his insight, even if he used it mostly to look back. When he started to talk about olden times, young people joined us to learn about their past. Kakoche had seen a lot of things happen. What had happened of late he did not seem to think much of. It was no longer the world he knew and loved.

"In Africa there is much confusion now. People no longer abide by the rules, they no longer pay respects to their fellows. There is too much selfishness. If there is food, those who have it no longer share. They forget their friends, and when they do somebody may die from hunger. If there is beer, do not forget that every villager is your friend and a friend must be invited to drink. To drink beer means to drink in the company of others. If somebody does not take beer, he should still join the company. Togetherness is what is important. Nobody can be so busy that there is no room for others in their lives.

"Now we have independence. What does it mean? If a man has money he no longer wants to accept his relatives. He will not shake hands with people like me because he thinks I am dirty. Money makes people proud. Before, it was different. It was better. During those days we would share good things with each other. When brewed, beer was brought to the middle of the village and there were special houses where we would all eat together. Not only beer and food but knowledge too was shared. Indeed Europeans are haughty but not as proud as some of these Zambians. You see a visitor and greet him 'Zikomo'[16] and he answers 'old man, why do you greet me? I don't know you.'

"What is independence? We are asked to grow maize to earn money, but when you want to sell you already have to have money to buy the sack to put the maize in. How can I earn money when I have to have it to earn it? Before, the Chief informed us what the government wanted from us. During those days the cooperation between the government and villagers was good. Not so today. Now, people come to the village, people we do not know and whom we have never seen before, and they tell us what to do and what not to do. This is not good."

Kakoche belonged to the Chewa people. He was born in Kasungu in Nyasaland (Malawi) when the Ngoni chief Mpezeni was occupying the

Chewa country of Mkanda. He was a child during the 1880s when the British, Portuguese, and even a few German colonialists fought to gain power over the lands west of Lake Nyasa. He was a young boy in 1898 when the British defeated the warrior tribe Ngoni in battle. Around that time Kakoche's father died and his mother decided to take her children and her few belongings and go home to her paternal village in Luangwa Valley. They walked for three weeks, sleeping on beds made of leaves and grass.

About 1910 Kakoche and a group of other young men went on foot to Bulewayo, Southern Rhodesia (Zimbabwe), to work in the mines.[17] The distance from what was then Fort Jameson (Chipata) is 1200 kilometers as the crow flies. The journey took six weeks, during which the men slept in the bush and enjoyed hospitality wherever they could find it: *Illi tere nkulinga utayeda naye*—"only when you have walked with a man can you know him."

Many men went south to return with stories of strange sights and events, and with new clothes, tools, and money for the tax imposed by the English administration. The railway between Lusaka and the south had been opened in 1906, but to travel by train cost money, and it was to earn money that Kakoche and friends went away from home. They might have sold themselves to one of the many contractors who moved around in the rural areas in search of labor for the mining companies in Southern Rhodesia and later on the Copper Belt. But to do so meant to have no choice as to employer and employment. It was in order to be free to choose their employment that Kakoche and his group preferred to walk rather than to ride on the train with a prepaid ticket.

> "I worked underground for one year knocking stones with a hammer," related Kakoche. "Working in the mine was okay because we earned money. Not much money, but things were not as expensive as they are today. Besides, we had no choice. Because we all had to pay the head tax, the mine work was good. We miners were paid ten times the wage of an ordinary laborer, but the underground job was very tough. We saw people die as did one man in our group. Stones fell upon him and crushed his life away."

Kakoche's first wife was Ntambo Sakala from Mpindila village, Msekera. As was the Chewa custom, Kakoche went to live and work in Ntambo's village when they married. (Maybe it's a good thing that the wife and not the husband is the family's main breadwinner!) Only a few years after he returned from Southern Rhodesia, Kakoche was forced to leave home once again. By then he was the father of five small children.

> "In the last year of the European War [1918] I and many other relatives were recruited to serve the army. We worked as porters and spent most of

the time in Nyasalan [Malawi] far away from home. We carried headloads
and made food. It was hard work and there was little to eat. Many died.
God chose those who would return home to be with their families once more.
    "We never saw the enemy."[18]

In Mpindila village people, cattle, and crops thrived as a result of
natural fertility of the soil and the hard work and care of the village
residents. But soon their prosperity was to end. In the beginning of the
1920s the area around Fort Jameson (and other places in Zambia) was
declared "Crown Land" by the British. The traditional owners of the land
were forcefully evicted to make room for potential European settlers![19]

It was a period of despair. Thousand of people were displaced, family
roots were cut, homes were torn down. And new land had to be cleared,
new homesteads built, new villages formed. During this time of confusion Kakoche and Ntambo separated. Kakoche went to his mother's village
in Luangwa Valley. Ntambo with her youngest children took a new husband and settled in his village.

Kefa Mwale was the oldest son of Kakoche and Ntambo. He remained
with the Mpindila village residents when they settled in Chiparamba some
15 kilometers farther northwest. Here they soon discovered that the maize
did not grow and the cattle did not thrive as they did in the old village.
It was for these reasons that, twenty years later, Kefa broke away to make
his own Kefa village.

Fortunately, the Europeans' relationship with Kakoche was not only
that of economic exploitation and geographic displacement. Dutch missionaries taught him how to read and write Nyanja. An English employer
taught him carpentry and gave him saw, hammer, and plane. Still, these
skills remained peripheral to his life. "The most important things I learned
from my father was how to get along with people and to share my food
and beer," headman Kefa told us.

It was only when Kefa set up his own village that father and son came
to live together once more. By then Kakoche was already an elder. Having worked long enough, he now married Jessie Ngoma, twenty-five years
his younger. "Kakoche manages by having a young wife. Jessie is the one
in the household who does everything. She does all the fieldwork and
pays laborers to repair her house and granary," people commented. She
was helped by Kakoche's last born, Wickson, who worked with the Game
Department.

Kefa also assisted his father as he became a very old man. He visited
him and attended him when he was ill, although he rarely helped with
money. But Jessie made pots and also brewed beer to raise money.

In 1978 Kakoche was the oldest man in the village. We all knew that
he would die soon. We saw him sitting daily in his old deck-chair. He

had passed ninety and could hardly see, yet he still handled the sewing needle and mended his old trousers.

When Kakoche died he left behind nine living children borne him by three different wives, and more than fifty grandchildren. "He could have made his own village," said the people. His funeral drew friends and relatives from near and far. Among the mourners were two chiefs. One thousand people participated in the funeral procession that set out from the village on a hot, sunny day in the middle of March. Lamenting women and men, relatives and friends, young and old accompanied the frail body of Kakoche Mwale through the twisted lane that would take Kefa village residents to their final abode, the Kefa village burial ground.

Like other Zambians born at the end of last century, Kakoche Mwale lived through a time of radical change. Though too young to remember the agonizing battles between the Ngoni and Chewa people, he suffered under the disruptive and exploitative taxation system established by the colonizers. Because of it every adult man, Kakoche included, was forced to break away from home and go looking for cash, or to sign a slave contract with the hangmen of the colonialists, the unscrupulous contractors. There was the long-term and shattering impact of European traders, missionaries, and settlers. There was also the lasting lure and unfilled promise of rapidly growing towns, relentlessly devouring men and maize. There was the establishment of an educational system that taught that knowledge is found in imported, strange-languaged books, rather than in the mature, ancestral wisdom of the elders. And there was and is the growing shadow of international markets seeking raw materials and profit, yet giving little or nothing to the primary producers in return. Most of these forces are still actively shaping rural Zambia. When the transformation is complete, traditional Chewa wisdom is likely to be lost forever.

Thus, with Kakoche Mwale and his generation a historical epoch is disappearing, irrevocably and forever. As the elders die, what is lost are not only ancestors, relatives, and friends, but also the true last bearers of ceremony and tradition. With them will vanish a way of thinking and living in which the village is the core of the universe, and togetherness the ultimate purpose of life. As we shall see in the chapters that follow, village living still links up with the past, but less and less so, as whole generations of people come to distrust their roots and the culture that shaped them.

Notes

1. Two authors provide us with descriptions of the Chewa village in 1950. In the quotes from Bruwer (1955) and Marwick (1952) rendered below, the descriptions fit the present-day situation just as well and indicate that structure and administration have encountered little change since the colonial era.

"The basic local unit as far as residence and social organization are concerned is the village (MU/DZI). Cewa villages vary to a great extent in regard to number of huts as well as population. A village may consist of a few huts only or it may include as many as a hundred or even more. Generally however the Cewa village is of fair size with up to a hundred or more inhabitants. The village has no stereotyped form. The internal structural composition does however follow a regular pattern and is based upon the matrilineage as a localized unit. Analysis of villages shows that they are mainly occupied by members of a dominant or senior matrilineal core providing the village headman and one or more alien matrilineage groups linked to the founding matrilineage by conjugal bonds. Sometimes individuals alien to the village composing matrilineages attach themselves to a village and form part of its population." (Bruwer, 1955:114.)

"The unit of the social organization is a village (*mudzi*) of from about 40 to upwards of 200 huts. An average-sized village has about 60 huts and a population of just over 100. There is generally no pattern of hut-grouping, but socially most villages comprise sections (*vigawo*, sing. *cigawo*) the spatial limits of which may or may not be clear. The section is usually a kinship unit, though it may include a few biological families who are not related to the majority of the section inhabitants. The kinship group comprising the core of the section is a matrilineage with a depth of three or four generations, to which are appended the spouses and seminal children of certain of its members." (Marwick, 1952:120.)

2. The Chewa people are a division of the Maravi people, one of four Bantu groups that migrated south about 1500 and came to live in a region enclosed by Zambesi River in the south, Lake Nyasa in the north, and Luangwa River in the west. Today the Chewa are one of the biggest language groups in Zambia. Their homeland is the Eastern Province adjoining Ngoni country. Kefa village is 30 km west of Chipata town on the road to Malambo in Luangwa Valley. It is well within the boundary of Chipata District.

3. "South of the Bemba plateau was dominated by chiefs of the Mushroom clan. Their subjects all came to be known as Bisa. There was never any one Bisa kingdom, but three Bisa chiefs were especially important by the later eighteenth century. . . The chiefs of the Senga people, on the upper Luangwa, trace their origins to the Bisa. . ." (Roberts, 1976:90.)

4. "In 1941 a program of resettlement was started to relieve pressure on the reserve and to introduce soil conservation. Much of the land held by the North Charterland Exploration Company in Fort Jameson District was purchased by the government and some of the unalienated Crown lands were opened for resettlement. . . It was estimated that 98,300 Chewa and Ngoni should be moved but this was impossible since there was sufficient land only for 35,000."

As part of the resettlement scheme "an elementary system of soil conservation was applied. Before the people were allowed to move into the settlement area, they had to agree to practice contour cultivation. They were allowed four or five years to adapt themselves to it. The land for cultivation was demarcated in contour strips separated by untouched belts of grass. An attempt was made to replace the traditional mound system by cultivation on ridges approximately on the contour. Contours were laid off by trained African assistants of the Ministry of Agriculture." (Tuthill et. al., 1968:4-5.)

5. "A village headman is the headman of the founding section, i.e., he is the senior surety of the founding matrilineage. Of the factors binding subordinate sections to the founding one, kinship sometimes plays a part, as when the children of the headman, who live patrilocally, form a matrilineage under the wardenship of the village headman's son. Other village sections may be bound to that of the headman, because they believe that they belong to the same matriclan (*Pfuko*, plur. *Mafuko*). . . . Other sections have attached themselves to the founding one because in the past there was a need for security or because, more recently, the Administration has demanded that villages be of a certain minimum size. Finally, some matrilineages and/or biological families have attached themselves to the headman's section because the headman or his village is popular." (Marwick, 1952:132.)

6. ". . . the relationship that the section headman typically bears to the inhabitants of his section are those of brother, mother's brother, or mother's mother's brother. Looking at it the other way, and remembering that Cewa marriage is predominantly uxorilocal, we may say that the matrilineal members of the section usually consist of the headman, his sisters, his sisters' children, his sisters' daughters' children, and so on. Residentially, then, the matrilineage is the basic group in Chewa social organization. It is a basic group in another way, too, in that it is the unit for litigation and for other formal social arrangement such as marriage. The headman and one of his sisters' sons—usually but not invariably his eldest sister's eldest son—are the *Ankhoswe* (sing. *Nkhoswe*) or 'sureties' in formal transactions." (Marwick, 1952:132.)

7. Bruwer, 1955:115.

8. Most of the proverbs quoted in the book are taken from Milimo,1972.

9. Matrilineal: "A principle of descent from an ancestress through her daughter, her daughter's daughter, etc. (in the female line)." (Keesing, 1981:514.)

10. Brideprice: "Marriage payments from the husband and his kin to the bride's kin. Characteristically these payments balance a transfer of rights over the wife's sexuality, work service, residence, fertility etc." (Keesing, 1981:508.)

11. Ngoni (sometimes spelled Nguni): A patrilineal people, primarily herders and warriors who moved northward from South Africa in the nineteenth century and settled in the Eastern part of Zambia.

12. The mild sentence Lubinda got for manslaughter was reduced even further because of his age and poor health. On returning to Kefa village after only one year, Lubinda immediately slaughtered a fine cow to mark his return and to give a gift of meat to the headman and the headman's wives. Some meat was also sold to people passing by on the road. But no Kefa residents came forward to buy, even though their hunger for meat was great. They did not know how to approach the man who slayed their kinsman.

   Particularly the close family of the deceased Kwezekani Mbewe were uneasy about seeing Lubinda back in the village. They came to the headman saying that they could not remain in the village if every day they would see the face of the person who killed their beloved family member.

   Kefa, not knowing how to solve this problem, was advised by Chief Chikuwe to sit with the two families and sort out their problems through discussions. And so they did. But the Kwezekani family was adamant, and Kefa ended by appealing to Lubinda: "Please, Mr. Lubinda, my villagers used to love you very much, but since you killed one of them, some fear that you may kill again while others cannot see you without crying for the deceased Kwezekani. That is why we ask you now to leave this village and go elsewhere." And Lubinda was old and tired and agreed to leave. He had no fighting spirit left.

   When the Deputy Chief came to hear that Lubinda and also his family were about to leave Kefa village, he called Headman Kefa and told him he had no right to expel a village member without the permission of the Chief. Thus a new meeting was held and this one was presided over by the Deputy Chief. Many villagers were present. The Deputy pointed out that Lubinda had already received his punishment. He had been in prison, away from family and friends and, as everybody present could see, he had suffered. Lubinda was now an old and sick man. He was certainly no threat to anyone. Yet, the Deputy Chief fully recognized the pain of Kwezekani's family. Kwezekani's children were without a parent and they had no one to help them. So, said the deputy, to solve this case once and for all, let Lubinda and the family stay on in Kefa village where they had lived ever since it was founded. But let them also repent the evil deed and help the family of the deceased. Lubinda is a rich man with plenty of cattle. Let him pay three cows so that the Kwezekani Mbewe family can eat well and also have money for school fees.

   And thus the case was resolved.

13. "Sitting high": To be seated more elevated than others is an indication of a higher status. Consequently it is impolite for juniors to be seated above their elders, or women above

men. It is also impolite to remain standing if somebody of a higher status is seated, or to squat, if an elder is sitting on the ground.

14. A "youngman" is a young man who is member of a special social category. From the time he is about sixteen years, until he is married and with children (preferably more than one) of his own, a youngman is important particularly to the labor pool of a village. As a not yet adult a youngman's demeanor is supposed to be softspoken and modest.

15. "In the years between 1840 and 1880 or thereabouts, large parts of Zambia, Malawi and Tanzania were conquered and settled by various groups of Ngoni. . . It was Mpezeni who created the principal permanent Ngoni settlement in Zambia. By 1880 he had crossed the Luangwa into Nsenga country. During the next twenty years he gradually encroached on the northern Chewa kingdom of Mkanda. By 1880 Mpezeni had killed Mkanda and overrun his kingdom. Mpezani's Ngoni formed a small state of their own, organized on the basis of segments within the chiefly family. The state expanded as the segments increased their numbers by recruiting prisoners of war." (Roberts, 1976:118, 119, 168.)

16. "Zikomo" is the polite way of greeting a person, getting his attention before one enters a conversation. In English "zikomo" is usually translated as "thank you" or "please," and it is also used in that way.

17. The British South Africa Company that then ruled over Northern Rhodesia was "anxious to see that mines both in Southern Rhodesia and Katanga obtained African labour as cheaply as possible. In Northern Rhodesia it was well placed to do this for there it ruled over about one million people, and these could be compelled to pay taxes in cash. For nearly all Africans in Northern Rhodesia the only way to obtaining cash was to engage in wage-labour outside the territory . . .

    "African labour migrants were by no means passive victims of the new cash economy. So far as possible, they chose their employers, for both wages and working conditions varied considerably. . . . It was not enough simply to induce Africans to work for wages, they had to be forced to go where they did not want to go and to stay when they wished to leave. This was the purpose of recruiting agents who collected groups of men in or near their home district and bound them by contract to one employer for a fixed time. Such agents from both Southern Rhodesia and Katanga were active in Northern Rhodesia from the early 1900s." (Roberts, 1976:177, 178.)

18. "Of far greater significance than the actual fighting was the effect on Northern Rhodesia of the forced recruitment of porters from all districts. It has been estimated that for a large part of the war, one-third of adult African males in the country were impressed to take food and equipment to the front. Women were also employed and an unknown number—at least several thousand—succumbed . . . the majority of Africans who returned from service in the Lundazi subdivision of the East Luangwa district arrived in a pitiable state of emaciation due to starvation and dysentery." (Hall, 1976:49.)

19. "Under Northern Rhodesia's first Governor, Sir Herbert Stanley, the government sought to encourage further European immigration, and it was therefore decided to set aside blocks of land which would in effect be available for exclusive European use . . . a distinction was made between Crown land which could be sold, and African reserves which could not . . . In all 60,000 people were moved . . ." (Roberts, 1976:183.)

CHAPTER 2   LAND AND LAND USES

Mbeu Mpoyamba
The Harvest Depends on the Beginning

*I see farming as a good occupation. It is plenty of
hard work during the rainy season, but at harvest
time benefits are reaped when crops are sold at the
market. Even those who do not grow cash crops
benefit from farming as they earn the food they eat.*

A villager's view

"Since we came to Kefa village, we have not known hunger," headman
Kefa has said. *Njala*—hunger—the greatest of all threats, the scourge that
has forced people after people to cross plains and mountains in search
of fertile lands, has never visited Kefa village. Kefa village lands are still
abundant and fertile.[1]

All the land in a chiefdom belongs to the Chief, and through him to
his deputies, the village headmen. But ordinary villagers also have rights
to land. As a member of a village community a person is entitled to
cultivate if a vacant land is available. If not, the age-old strategy is to break
away, either individually or as a family, and go where land is available.
Most headmen will welcome newcomers, as they want their villages to
grow. And only people can make a village grow and give fame to its leader.

Like all other villagers, the chief and headmen also farm the land.
In addition, they administer the land and serve as arbitrators if disputes
over access arise. This power gives them a definite advantage compared
to ordinary villagers. A bad headman can give the least attractive plots
to those residents whom he wants to punish and reserve the most fertile
land for himself and his relatives. Village land cannot be bought or sold.
It existed before money.[2]

In Kefa, village land is usually allocated without much problem. A
person can acquire a field in many different ways. And once a field is
cleared, the person who did so, or who was instrumental to its being done
by paying others for the job has rights to what grows in it. He or she is
responsible for developing and looking after the field, and, at the right
time, for letting it rest or handing it over to somebody else, as Brighton
Lungu reported about the field of Emelia Mbao.

Being a "youngman" Simon Sakala was still eating from his mothers'
fields, from that of Mtole Mbao (his mother's sister) and his proper mother
Emelia. Because when he got married he had no field of his own, Emelia

decided to help him. She gave Simon her own field and she herself went to live with the[3] husband who worked in Luangwa Valley.

The field Simon got from Emelia was old. When he found that he could not harvest enough he decided to clear a new garden.[4] He consulted with his friend James Phiri and together they selected the land next to James' field as the most attractive site for a new field for Simon. Only then did Simon go to the headman to tell him that he wanted to cultivate next to James. And the headman said: "Chabwino—Okay, Mr. Sakala, that land is not used by anybody and you can keep it as long as you want. Besides, it is a good field. I have watched the way the grass grows, and I think this year it will give you plenty of maize."

It is not only by inheriting land or clearing new ground that villagers acquire a garden. People also borrow fields from each other. Sometimes the ownership becomes quite confusing, but people are usually able to sort out who has what rights to which plots without having to appeal to the headman to decide whose rights are more valid than others.

Lucia Manda cultivates a plot lent her by Soka Tembo, and part of this plot she has lent to Maximina Banda. Originally the plot belonged to Soka's husband, but now he is in Chipata. This particular field was next to Lucia's field, and Lucia used to cultivate there, but now she cultivates beans in her own maize plot, and that is why she has permitted Maximina to use it.

However long a garden is used by a cultivator, whoever cleared the field first is considered the owner unless it is formally handed back to the headman, who is the caretaker of all village land. To advise and pass judgment concerning land is one of the headman's responsibilities and he does so on behalf of the chief. Thus, if a villager refuses to accept a headman's ruling, the case will be referred to the chief for final judgment. A wise headman rarely encounters this situation; instead he allocates "his" land well aware that next to labor land is the most important of resources. Thus, when Kefa Mwale received the news that the uncle of Prison Njobvu had died in Lusaka, Kefa called Prison, who cultivated maize in the uncle's field, and said: "Please, Mr. Njobvu, stop cultivating this garden that you have enjoyed now for so many years. Our relative has died, and I do not want his children to say that headman Kefa took our father's land and gave it to his own kinsman." And Prison Njobvu accepted and said he would grow his maize elsewhere. And Kefa suggested that he choose between three different sites, all vacant because the owners had gone to Lusaka and the Copperbelt.

Because large parts of the village land lie fallow at any time, and because people lend their land to others but still retain a claim in it, it takes an expert to know what land is without claimants. The headman knows the land better than anybody else. The power to allocate land gives the headman an advantage over other village residents. Kefa Mwale has more (and probably better) land than they. Kefa says that the village land was given him by his former boss, the Englishman, and Chief Chikuwe agrees with him and supports him.

A border dispute erupted between headman Kefa and headman Nyanthani and Kefa summoned headman Nyanthani to the Chief's court, accusing him of impinging on his land. When the Chief passed judgment, he said: "Historically, Kefa was the first village in the area. When headman Nyanthani came to form his own village, he sat with Kefa Mwale, and they decided where Nyanthani village land should be. Because headman Nyanthani then submitted himself to headman Kefa, he must do so, also today." In this way the Chief confirmed that the land belonged to Kefa.

Kefa Mwale also took Blush Ngoma to the Chief's court when Blush, in spite of Kefa's objections, went ahead and cultivated land left by the Phiri family, when they were expelled from the village. And Blush had to leave the land. When Limited Banda asked if he could cultivate land left by Chaluka Banda, Kefa said no; he wanted to keep this land for his own use.

Blackson Zulu from Chiwayo village came to Kefa Mwale and asked for land. He wanted to go into cash crop farming and hire a tractor to help him. The land he was cultivating already bordered Kefa village lands, but it was no longer enough. As Mr. Zulu came from outside Kefa village, it was easy for the headman to refuse him. He did so saying that such an arrangement could cause problems in the future "because my grandson Gilbert plans to buy a tractor and come back and farm here in three years time." When James Kamaswanda Njobvu, the basket-maker from Petauke, asked the headman permission to settle in the village to make and sell baskets, he also asked for a field so that he could cultivate food. This Kefa accepted. One day James will go elsewhere to sell his baskets, and the land will revert to the headman.

Sylvester reported:

> "From 1942 until this day Kefa Mwale's land has expanded steadily. This is how Kefa can afford to marry five wives. All the wives have their own fields and they also weed in the headman's field. Now Kefa wants to reserve land for his grandchildren, and particularly for Gilbert Zulu. He seems to know that land will be scarce in the future, not plentiful like now, and that ownership of land is a key to future riches."

There are many reasons why people want a new field. Youngmen like Simon Sakala need land to settle down as heads of household. Some fields have been cultivated for so long that the soil is exhausted and yields become too small. Some shift lands because of animals. Cows, goats, and pigs cause a lot of trouble in fields that lie near village grazing grounds. On the outskirts of village land monkeys and birds are a nuisance. And some shift because of disagreement over ownership or quarrels with neighbors.

Once a field has been acquired, the tough job of clearing it begins. Clearing land is a man's job, and one obvious consequence is that women depend on men to increase their acreage. "I am the husband, and when I want more land I inform my wife about my decision and then ask the headman because he has plenty of land. It is my decision because I am the man and my job is to cut trees and clear the field," said Micheck Phiri, who had become a Kefa village resident through his wife Mwada Simba, fifteen years his elder.

To clear a field large trees are cut one or two yards above ground. The trunks are piled together and left to dry for a few months, and then burned with smaller trees and shrub. The very large trees are usually left intact to provide shade and shelter. Ash patches are sought out when finger-millet, pumpkins and sweet stalks are planted, and maize too is fertilized with ash when it is available.

Many people pay friends and relatives to clear land for them. Thus Simon hired Kabanda Nyuni, his cousin, and Pensulani Njobvu, a young neighbor, to help him to clear the new garden next to James Phiri's field. The trees were left to dry while Simon harvested in his mother's old field. Then he burned them, and in August he was ready to cultivate in the new field.

Simon himself did piecework for his kinswoman Zelipa Banda, now divorced. He cut down the large trees in her maize field to prevent monkeys from eating her crop. Simon had already paid 12 kwacha to Kabanda and Pensulani for their job, and now he received 6 kwacha from Zelipa. He asked: "Please Zelipa, do not give your money to anybody else, give it to me and I shall work for you."

A newly opened field is called *mphanje* and the hard work of breaking the soil is usually rewarded at harvest time when grains are fuller and vegetables bigger from the *mphanje* than from the *mphindule*, fields that have already produced for a year or two.[5] Most people cultivate their fields until the fertility decreases markedly. Then they leave them, usually only for a few years so that the bush does not take over altogether. In this way, if the soil is good and crops are rotated, a field can be cultivated for a very long time. In fact, some villagers claim to have cultivated their fields more or less continuously for the past two and even three decades. When land is abandoned altogether, it is said to take from twenty to thirty years for a field to regain its full fertility, but such long fallows are rare, at least for the more centrally placed of the village land.

The size of a family, the age of the household members, and their willingness and ability to work hard determine how much land a household can and will cultivate.[6] Yet older people tend to have larger fields than younger ones, even when they have few or no children to help them. It seems that a cultivator hesitates to leave a garden fallow, even when he or she clears new land.[7]

Of the sixteen people in the sample whom we came to know so well, Tilele Zulu and her husband Lemekani Mbao, the headman's half brother, have the largest acreage under cultivation. Both belong to the group of village elders who were around fifty years old. Altogether they cultivate on 8 acres, all in one place. Tilele grows cotton on 1.5 acres all by herself and makes considerable profit by it, and groundnuts on 1 acre for home use. Lemekani has his own groundnut garden of 0.25 acre; he grows local maize on 3 acres, and hybrid maize on 2 acres of which only 0.5 acre is any good. To plough the hybrid maize field Lemekani hires oxen from neighboring Kamanga village. Tilele does most of the other weeding and harvesting, although Lemekani considers the hybrid maize as his and keeps most of the money he gets when marketing it. Tilele is the most hardworking woman in our sample. On average she worked more than 3 hours every day during the year that we recorded her activities. Because her two adolescent daughters help her cook and keep house, she does not have to hurry home, like so many of her female relatives.

Mwanishupa Phiri and Sandikonda Daka have two children at home, and both children help their parents cultivate. The family has 5.6 acres under cultivation and another 7 acres lying fallow. Sandikonda Daka, who is about forty years old, explains:

"In the past I used to be the best of farmers. I cultivated tobacco and became prosperous. But people were jealous because I produced so much and bewitched me. Since then I have great pains in my right leg. I could no longer work hard on the tobacco so I came home to Kefa village. The headman gave me land. I hired a few people to help me clear the land with money I had found from the tobacco, and I ploughed by hand with only a hoe. My fields expanded slowly until this day they measure 13 acres. The land has been divided into four plots because it provides me with a good timetable for my work. I cultivate maize together with the mother of Custom [Mwanishupa, his wife], but we have separate groundnut plots. Just now I grow only maize for food and groundnuts for sale. This year I have cut trees because I want to extend the field by 0.2 acre. After ploughing the new field by hand I shall grow fingermillet. But first of all I want to concentrate on groundnuts so that they grow well. Part of my land lies fallow and I am glad to know that it will grow strong again."

Sandikonda also has a small plot of virginia tobacco for his personal consumption, and Mwanishupa has a small field of sweet potatoes.

Both Tilele and Mwanishupa cultivate groundnuts separate from their husbands.

"When they are newly married and for some time afterwards, a husband and wife usually grow their crops together. It is when a husband and a wife start to disagree because one does not approve of the working style of the other, that the wife starts to think that she wants her own field. It is the one who has to work alone who starts to complain. It may be that the man drinks so much beer that he forgets about his work in the field. Or that both partners work hard, but when crops are sold one uses the money carelessly without sharing it with his friend [his wife]. Tilele Zulu cultivates her own plot because of the character of her husband Lemekani who loves gambling and tends to spend too much money playing cards," Tyford explains.

With his new field, Simon Sakala has extended his total acreage by 2.2 acres. He and his wife cultivate groundnuts in the old field of Simon's mother which only measured 0.5 acre. In addition, they have 1 acre with local maize and 1 acre with hybrid. Simon also has a *dimba*—a small vegetable garden in the *dambo*—wetland by the river—where he grows rape, tomatoes, and onions.

Many men have a *dimba*, but few work as hard as Simon. A *dimba* is cultivated intensively as the soil in the *dambo* is fertile and water can be dug from the nearby riverbed in the dry season. The men seem to have monopolized the *dambo* area for their own cash crops cultivation, and the vegetables from the *dimba* are mostly sold, while vegetables that are eaten by the family are mostly cultivated by women in the *minda*.

Tisauke Phiri is a hard working cultivator with 5.5 acres divided in three plots. She cultivates local maize, groundnuts, cotton, and small crops like peas, beans, cucumbers, and pumpkins, but only to eat and never to sell as the men do. She is the only person in the village with a half-acre field of sunflowers. Tisauke manages her fields alone. The husband works outside the village and comes to see his two Kefa wives during weekends. Although Tisauke keeps hoping that the husband will help her cultivate, he never does. When he comes home he wants to rest.

Fields are marked by paths, contour ridges, or bush. James Phiri has three plots, each in a different place. The groundnut plot he has borrowed from his mother and at any time he may be asked to return it to her. The hybrid maize field on the other side of Mtewe river he cleared by himself three years ago. His plot of local maize near the *dambo* was given him freely by Kwezekani Mbewe. And he has a vegetable garden by the river. James is a very hard worker. Because his vegetable garden provides him with a steady income and he frequently helps the family members with money, his family treats him with much respect, almost as if he, and not Kabanda, were the elder son.

When a male cultivator dies the land goes to his brothers and sons, and they become responsible for the widow and children. It is the custom that a man marries his brother's widow, if she so wishes. In that way the loss of a family member creates the least disturbance from the point of view both of the family and of agricultural production. But if the widow does not want to marry, she goes back to her own village (if she came from someplace else), leaving the children with the husband's brother, unless the children are very young. These are the general rules. But, as we shall see time and again, the Chewa are a pragmatic people and rules are adapted to situations as well as to personal wishes. If a wife dies, husband and children continue cultivating as they did before, and after mourning the husband will start looking for a new wife. (More about this in Chapter 7.)

Food Crops

Of all crops *cimanga*—maize—is cultivated on the largest acreage. It is the first crop to be sown after the rain starts. It is the first to be weeded, the first to be weeded a second time, and the first to be harvested. More than any other crop, maize is food. Thus the main concern of every cultivator is to fill up the granary bin with enough of the golden corn to feed family and visitors until next harvest. Only the most destitute do not plan for at least some surplus, in case the harvest will be poor.[8] In good years such surplus can be used to brew beer, or to barter and to sell. Or to give to friends and relations who for some reason have failed to grow enough for themselves.

Because maize is so vitally important, the opportunity to rotate crops is limited. Most cultivators grow maize in a given field until the yield is severely reduced. They switch over to groundnuts for a season and then revert to maize once more. The two staples, maize and groundnuts, thrive in each other's company, and maize in particular grows willingly in a groundnut field.

To a villager maize is only *one* thing, *the local variety* that they and their kin and ancestors have stored, graded, planted, and stored again and again for the past hundred years or so. For this reason local maize is a very different crop from the new high yielding S-52 variety, or "hybrid," as is its local name for short. Hybrid is a cash crop and cultivated accordingly. One major difference (others will be described shortly) is that hybrid maize demands and receives cash inputs like fertilizers, pesticides, and even ploughing by oxen or tractor, expenses that rarely are tolerated for the food crops. The general philosophy is clear: money must be spent only where it can come back (that is, for cash crops). Still, as of late some youngmen have a different view.

Kabanda Nyuni, who earns from his vegetable garden, and Simon Sakala were squatting in Kabanda's *ndinda*—field shelter—waiting for the rain to pass. Simon commented:

> "Now that I have married and am about to form my own family, I shall take more care over farming than before. I do not want my family to run out of food like an old man's family. As I work hard in the vegetable garden, I have money to buy fertilizers and if I am lucky, also Rogor [an insecticide], even for food crops. These days it is only old men who think that money must be spent just where money can be found. They remember when they had to walk for weeks to earn 20 ngwee a month" [U.S. 25 cents]. And he added: "At that time money was really hard to come by. You could not sell vegetables like now. You had to sell yourself [go away and sell your labor] and leave your wife behind to weed alone." Kabanda nodded and said: "Yes, fertilizers are good even for food crops."

Not everybody agrees. Some people think that the maize will get used to fertilizers and refuse to grow without them. Nor do they want to change age-old cultivation methods that have proved right in the past. *Cimanga*—the daily food—is too important to be experimented on. "Even if yields improve this year and the next who knows what will happen in the future? And if you try out new practices and fail whom to blame but yourself? The elders will shake their heads and say, 'Who keeps close to his mother does not fall in the trap.'" So most villagers cultivate local maize the way their mothers did and ignore new advice concerning fertilizers, winter ploughing, and spacing.

Nshawa—groundnuts—are the second most important crop. In every village the groundnut granaries, stilted and smeared with mud to protect the precious contents from insects and rodents, stand side by side with the bulky maize granaries. Everybody grows groundnuts except Square Banda, who has cultivated only one major crop this year. Groundnuts are important because they add flavor, protein, and fat to the everyday maize meal. Groundnuts are the most used of all relishes. They are also delicious as a snack, raw or toasted. But groundnuts demand a lot of work, and people mostly cultivate them on one-half acre or less.[9]

Many people sell at least some groundnuts, not necessarily because they have surplus, but because they prefer the money, and whatever it can buy, to eating the nuts themselves. A woman might need money for her child's schooling. One sack of groundnuts sells for about four times the price of a sack of maize, but it takes about four times as long to produce them. Most people sell groundnuts by the tin, and even by the handful. A few cultivators, like Lubinda Mwale, have made groundnuts their main cash crop. Most of them are people with sufficient cash to hire others to do the hardest work in the field.

Groundnuts are planted on ridges. Because they grow underground and are harvested when the soil is dry and hard, the ridges not only increase the yield but make harvesting easier. Like maize, groundnuts should be weeded twice but people rarely have the time. Unlike maize, the seeds are planted close together so that the ground is covered as the plants grow down the rows if not between rows. In April nuts are dug out from under the ground and left to dry in the sun. Both *chalimbana*, the refined confectionary type, and the local varieties are grown by Kefa village residents.

Kacamba—sweet potatoes—are another much cherished food crop. They are usually grown in a separate field, like maize and groundnuts. The leaves are used as relish, and the tuber, which is the main food, constitutes a whole meal by itself. So does pumpkin, which is usually intercropped with the maize. Pumpkin leaves are used like spinach. As long as they are grown for local consumption, tomatoes, beans, onions, gourds, cowpeas, and leafy vegetables like okra and rape are also intercropped, or given a small plot by themselves. The vegetable production carried out by some of the young men in the *dambo* wetland is a different matter altogether. The minor food crops are rarely grown in any quantity, and though they are stored by drying, few households eat dried vegetable relish more than three months after harvest. Not even *mawele*, or fingermillet, an important ingredient when beer is brewed, is grown in large quantity.

Fruits do not grow very willingly on the Zambian plateau, where Kefa is situated about 1,200 meters above sea level. A few residents have planted and tended pawpaw trees to maturity, warding off constant attacks from pigs and goats. Zindikani Miti has both a "plantation" banana garden and a guava garden and often shares these fruits with friends and relatives. Other people have banana gardens and fruit trees, but not in the large quantities of Zindi Miti.

Tobacco is grown only for local consumption. Sandikonda Daka has four ridges each about six yards long. He cures the tobacco himself. If he feels like it, he sells or gives some freely to friends who beg tobacco from him.

Wife and husband usually discuss what crops to grow. Sometimes, the one who is the most active goes ahead and plants. Being responsible for the daily meal, women may be more concerned with relish crops than are men, that is, at least in Micheck Phiri's view.

"In a family, husband and wife talk together and plan together. The wife may make suggestions and so does the husband. A wife wants to plant plenty of small crops, but I am most concerned with our African maize. So she decides about beans, pumpkins, and millet, though I may also decide. The point is to make up your mind, because if you don't, a wife uses the opportunity and starts to rule not only in the house but in the field too. In our house we decide everything together."

Mwada Simba, the wife, has her own views:

"I confide in you privately that Mr. Phiri is too young in many ways
[Mwada is fifteen years his elder], so I feed him with knowledge. I do so
without insulting him. Because I am really old [she is forty-five], I have more
experience in life than he, and so I decide many things. Sometimes I discuss
these with him, sometimes I do things on my own, but I always obey his
orders. At a house there are duties for the man and for the woman. When
I know that I have to cook, there is no need for me to wait until I am told.
When I know I shall need relish, I do not need to be told to grow groundnuts, okra, or rape. I have taken to deciding many things because Kefa village
is more my home than Phiri's [Micheck moved into the village when he married Mwada] and for this reason his objections are less powerful. Phiri has
no children with me, so what I decide concerning the children I just tell
him. But, as he loves me, he looks after my children as if they were his own.
This is why he always helps me in the field." [And so he does. Mwada and
Micheck are inseparable, except when they fight each other because of
jealousy.]

Although food crops are mainly the women's job, a good husband
helps and some do more than just help. Mwanishupa, the wife, confided
to us: "Though Mr. Daka does not eat sweet potatoes himself, he grows
plenty for me. He helps me collect firewood, too. Many a time when he
goes into the bush or comes home from the garden he brings me firewood."
Mwanishupa spoke very softly as if afraid that the husband might change
his good ways and stop helping her if he heard her praise.

Cash Crops

These days everybody needs at least some money. However poor, a
person will want to buy salt and sugar, and paraffin to light the lamp at
night, and to take maize to the local mill. There are major expenses like
clothes, a blanket to cover oneself during the cold season, pots and pans,
and school fees. And of course luxuries like beer from a beer hall, shoes,
transport costs, and more clothes than one really needs.

The most common and basic needs can be acquired doing piecework
for 1 kwacha a day, or by selling surplus maize and groundnuts. Those
who go into the cash crop production have greater ambitions than to light
their lamps every evening. These are people who want to change their
way of life. They work not for next season or next year, but for the future.
To them money means self-reliance and they are ready to work hard to
achieve it. Their ambition is not to consume but to invest—in a new way
of life. (Chapter 8 discusses this new way of life in greater detail).

Tisauke Phiri is one of those set on improving their lot. She works
alone as the husband is a wage earner with the government in Bouleya,

a small town some 50 kilometers away. Tisauke is thirty-four years old and the mother of several children. One day, we overheard this conversation when Tisauke was winnowing maize and her neighbor Nyokase Ngoma came to her to beg green leaves. As Tisauke gave her some leaves, she said,

"I have plenty of beans but my mind is on cash crops—on the cotton I am growing and the sunflowers. I have educated all my children by my own effort. I divorced my first husband because he never helped me, and the money to do so I earned from my groundnuts. Mr. Phiri is just as lazy as my first husband, but I am reluctant to divorce him. I do not want my children to remain without a father.

"Yesterday I worked in the field all day and when I came home I brewed beer. My mind is set on making money because my daughter will need it if she passes her exam. That is why I have refused to stay with Mr. Phiri at Bouleya. I cannot earn any money there and food is a problem. Here I grow my own food. I send K. 20 for my children's school fund. I ask my relatives to help me, but I do not rely on them. I rely on myself and on my cash crops."

Sylvester Miti filed this report:

"People choose different crops for different reasons. Some consider themselves too weak for certain crops and fit for others. Those who decide to grow hybrid think they have escaped the hard work of growing cotton, groundnuts, or tobacco, but they need money to buy fertilizers. For those who have no cash groundnuts or vegetables are best."

Vegetables are not generally considered cash crop, but a few young men grow tomatoes, cabbage, rape, and onions primarily to raise money, and expend a lot of effort to make their vegetable cultivation profitable. One of them, Kabanda, comments:

"Many Kefa village residents started their *dimba* [vegetable garden] long ago, but because they did not work hard transplanting and watering they do not find any profit. They keep the *dimba* to eat and are satisfied when they have harvested once, and when they run out of relish they start buying or begging green leaves from their friends again. But some of us grow tomatoes, bananas, cassava, rape, sugar canes, and onions. We make a business out of our gardens by selling crops and earning well."

To establish a vegetable garden the grass mat of the *dambo*—swamp area—has to be broken or cleared. Beds are built to prevent the plants from becoming waterlogged. Seedlings must be protected against the sun, watered carefully, and transplanted. Pig manure and cow dung are applied to give a good harvest. And when the crop is ripe one needs a bicycle to go from village to village to sell, and selling too is a tough job. As vegetables need neither too little nor too much water, the serious growers cultivate vegetables during the dry season and rely on watering the plants.

The great advantage of cash crops like vegetables, groundnuts, and bananas is that they can be sold locally. To sell hybrid maize, cotton, and sunflowers the grower depends on cooperative bodies which are not always very efficient and on national and even international markets over which he or she has no control. A grower is not even paid in cash when delivering produce to the local marketing cooperatives. All he or she gets is a receipt that may be transformed into money at some later stage. As many cultivators are not that familiar with arithmetic, transactions where money is involved lend themselves easily to misconduct.

The really serious cultivator of cash crops chooses hybrid maize or cotton as his or her cash crop. The reason is simply that this is what the agricultural extension service advocates. In fact, for these crops it offers all kinds of loan arrangements and supportive services (see below).[10]

Hybrid maize has the advantage of being maize, and as such it is familiar. But it is hybrid, too, and thus it demands some special attention that sets it apart from local maize—in particular, its need for fertilizers.

If it is properly tended, the hybrid variety SR-52, recommended by the agricultural authorities, yields about four times as much as the local variety, or twenty-seven bags rather than seven bags to an acre. That is a very big difference. Instead of cultivating 4 acres to fill her granary, a woman might make do with hoeing, weeding, and harvesting only 1 acre. Unfortunately there are drawbacks attached to hybrid maize other than its need for cash inputs like fertilizers. It does not store well under local storage methods. The hybrid grain is softer and less flinty than local maize and unless it is properly treated, it is quickly infested by insects. And villagers have no storage facilities other than the traditional bamboo bin.

As a consequence, even successful hybrid maize growers also cultivate local maize, as it is only by having sufficient local maize that a villager can be sure that her family will eat well until next harvest. Of course, if better storage methods were available locally, or if villagers were sure they could buy maize flour (the so-called mealiemeal) at the local store throughout the year, the poorer grain quality of the SR-52 would be no problem. As this is not the case, most village residents concentrate all their effort on local maize and do not find the time to grow hybrid at all.

The two youngmen James Phiri and Simon Sakala, both fathers of small children and ardent vegetable growers, were discussing what and how to cultivate during the next year. James asserts:

"I shall never grow cotton because I cannot eat it. With cotton all you can do is to sell it for money. Hybrid is better, because I can eat it. I can eat it when it is green and I can roast it on the fire. I can grind it to mealiemeal and cook *nsima* [the local staple]. But cotton—can you grind it and make *nsima* or porridge? I tell you, Mr. Sakala, cotton is useless." And Simon Sakala agreed with him strongly: "Cotton is useless. I too do not want to grow cotton. My mind is set on hybrid [maize] and *mbatatice*—Irish potatoes, vegetables and bananas. But cotton—never." James agreed that he too would grow hybrid the following year.

Cotton is a 100 percent cash crop. There is no local demand for it and the cultivator depends entirely on the Cooperative Union to sell it. Both production and marketing entail definite risks; insects and pests are constant threats. No wonder James and Simon hesitate to grow cotton. But others do not and in Kefa village the women have been the most innovative about cotton. Tilele Zulu, the mother of six and the wife of Lemekani Mbao, was the most successful and Tisauke Phiri, eager to earn enough to send her daughter to secondary school, was among those who saw Tilele's success and cleared a field for cotton the following year. She was well aware that the price of cotton had doubled in only four years, making cotton the most profitable of all crops—*provided* nothing went wrong during its production. She also knew that the agricultural extension service provided a credit "packet" for people like herself and helped with pest control.[11]

Sunflowers are a traditional crop recently promoted as cash crop for their oil and for the flour that can be made from the plants. Only Tisauke grew sunflowers in Kefa village. Her sunflower plot was only one-half acre and the profits she made were limited. Maybe this is why she followed Tilele's cotton success with so much concern.

Extension Services

Agriculture is given a lot of importance in Zambia. According to the Third National Development Plan (1979–83) subsistence producers and small-scale peasants hold a key position when it comes to increased production.[12] Tilele Zulu, James Phiri, Simon Sakala, Tisauke Phiri, Kabanda Nyuni, even headman Kefa, and the other Kefa village residents are small-scale farmers. In national agricultural politics they are an important target group. The country needs them, or rather whatever they can produce over and above what their families eat. In the national economy peasant surpluses become national income. But most subsistence cultivators do not produce a surplus. Some do not find the time. Some do not have the strength. Some prefer to spend their energy on other activities and adjust their ambitions to produce just enough to cover their own needs.

One way to increase small-scale peasant production is to increase productivity. Agricultural methods have to be "modernized." Peasants too should have a share in new scientific know-how and technical improve-ments. Partly for this purpose the agricultural extension service has been formed and spread throughout the Zambian countryside. Kefa village residents are privileged to have an agricultural extension camp only 3 kilometers away. But the camp is small and the area it serves is big. In-stead of an extension service that goes out to cultivators, people are at times summoned to the camp.[13]

Sylvester Miti reported:

"Micheck was resting when Jenelani Khosa, the new deputy headman, came to his house and said: 'You, Micheck Phiri and Thomase Banda, you should go to the Agricultural Officer for a meeting on farming. Go before breakfast and you will find something to eat there.' So Micheck and Thomase washed and prepared themselves for the journey, and the deputy went to choose two women to attend the meeting. But Mr. Khosa did not do his job well. He just approached a group of women and said, 'You and you must go to the meeting.' Shoes Zulu and Sandikonda Daka saw the way it happened and went to headman Kefa to complain. They did not like the way people were ordered around by the *induna*. But Kefa supported his deputy and said that those who had been chosen must go. If not, their names will be written down and handed over to the Chief and they will be charged a fine because of their lack of cooperation. Shoes still protested: 'I can only agree to go to a meeting if first I am asked if I have any other business to attend to. Then, if I say no, you can ask me to help you by attending this meeting. If people are forced to go it is wrong.'

"In the end Micheck, Thomase, Rosemary, and Mulembenji went. When they arrived at the agricultural station, they were told that they had come with too few people and that they should go home and get another man and another woman. So before midday they were already back in the village, looking for two more people to join them and for food before they returned to Kalichero."

Whether a villager meets with the agricultural extension people or not depends partly on what crops he or she grows. A cotton grower is almost sure to be visited by the commodity demonstrator (the most specialized and least educated of the extension personnel) at least once. Hybrid maize growers are less likely to get a visit, and those who grow neither cotton nor hybrid have little or no contact with the service, partic-ularly if they are women. Of twenty-five women cultivators only five had ever been visited by an extension agent and only three had been visited during the last two years. Tilele Zulu, the cotton grower, was one of them. She had attended a meeting at the extension camp where a cotton demonstrator talked about cotton and the Agricultural Assistant explained how to apply for loans. After the meeting they had helped her fill in her loan application. Five months later she received the Agricultural Finance

Corporation (AFC) loan-packet of cotton seeds and chemicals. Later on, when her cotton plants were 2 feet high, she was visited by the commodity demonstrator. She was pleased with the extension service and when we asked her she said they ought to visit all cultivators.

Other women complained: "They only visit people who cultivate for the market," and "they never visit us and they never talk to us so we cannot know whether their work is good or bad." Agnes Sakala and Tikambenji suggested: "We are old so we are not useful to them" and "they stopped visiting us when Welensky[14] left. I don't know why. Maybe the government told them not to visit us because we have no strength to grow crops for the market?"

Of fifteen male growers, seven had been visited by an agent, but only three during the last two years. Opinions among the men differed widely. Simon Sakala said: "They do nothing for us and they never visit us. When I want to know the right way of farming I get advice by asking the people around here who are known to be the best farmers." James Phiri, who had just got a K. 38 loan-packet to grow hybrid, said: "They are too good to us," but only a few weeks earlier he had complained that "extension people are of no use. They only visit people with big farms like Mr. G. Nyirenda and Luciano Tembo. People like us in Kefa village have to grow cotton, hybrid, and sunflowers on our own." While Lemekani Mbao claimed that "they teach us true ways of producing more", Micheck mumbled "they are just cheating." Sandikonda added: "I have never been visited since I came to Kefa village. As I have stopped growing tobacco for the market years ago, I consider my chances for ever receiving any advice from them as exhausted." And Square Banda said that he would never apply for a loan for only rich people get loans from Kalichero.

It is the ward committee[15] that guarantees the loans and approves or disapproves of applicants. Among small-scale peasants the best known loans are given in "packets." A loan packet includes the cash input needed for production of the specified crop—hybrid maize, cotton, sunflowers, or tobacco. A first-time applicant will get a "one-packet" loan, which provides him or her with seeds, fertilizers, and pesticides necessary to grow the chosen crop on one acre.

When the loan is repaid, and most loans are, the cultivator can apply for a "two-packet" loan and ultimately for a "three-packet" loan. There are several loan systems: seasonal loans, medium-term loans, and long-term loans. But the "packet" loans are probably best suited for village residents, because they are tailored to their needs as minor producers depending primarily on hand labor.

Tilele Zulu and James Phiri were the only people in the village who had applied and taken loans from the Agricultural Finance Corporation. Most villagers hesitate to borrow from AFC. When we asked why, the men said that they had not yet made up their mind what to grow, or that they planned to raise money in some other way, or that they did not want to cultivate cash crops at all. The women said that they had not time to cultivate for the market, or that they had no strength, or that they were married and their husbands did not want them to apply, or that they were not married and had no men to help them clear land and help them cultivate it.

In most people's minds the extension service equals fertilizers, and different people see fertilizers differently. It is of course well known that fertilizers increase yields, but they cost money and money is scarce. For that reason some of the more innovative cultivators have worked out their own formula for how to apply this precious stuff, minimizing costs and—they hope—maximizing returns. One of them, James Phiri, explains his very personal approach:

> "It is well known by now that I have this special fertilizer that I call 'planting fertilizer.' My planting fertilizer consists of five *nsima* plates with top dressing which I mix carefully with five *nsima* plates with basal dressing. This I apply when the maize is one foot tall. This system I started long ago and I tell you in truth, this is a way of cultivating from which I find much profit. The fact is that, whatever other people tell me, I shall never use fertilizers in any other way."

Extensions agents who have been in the service for along time, regret the heavy emphasis on fertilizers.[16] They say it makes people forget about the importance of manure. In the 1950s the extension service recommended that people renew the grass in the cattle kraal every two months and plough old grass into the fields in September. It meant hard work, but plants thrived and it did not cost any money. Today, few people talk about manure from a public stance, although village residents who cultivate vegetables for sale use manure regularly. Those who do not have domestic animals beg manure from friends and relatives. Sandikonda often provides Jackson with chicken manure, Kabanda collects manure from his brother's chicken pen, and James and Kabanda go to Robert Manda for cow dung.

Village residents help each other in matters other than manure. To seek and give help or advice is to underline the communal nature of village living, and to the villagers extension agents are strangers. In a social and economic setting where the dividing line between plenty and hunger, health and disease, friends and enemies often is precarious, people seek what they perceive is safe. And the extension service is not always safe. Often cultivation is seen in isolation from the many other needs according to which the villagers administer their resources. Winter ploughing is a good example. The agricultural service recommends that people plough immediately after harvest in May or June, or, if the field has been fallow, in March. Such early ploughing (winter ploughing) prevents weeds from spreading for plants are ploughed into the ground before they bear seeds. Early ploughing is also easier than later ploughing because the earth is still soft. And if more people ploughed after harvest there would be less demand for tractors in October and November, which is the time when most people do plough. From the point of view of the extension service, the case is clear. But not from that of the cultivator, for he or she has other considerations. Says headman Kefa: "How can I plough the vegetation into the ground when my cattle go hungry for food?"

It is crops like local maize, groundnuts, onions, beans, cowpeas, rape gourds, tomatoes, pumpkins, sweet potatoes, cassava, fingermillet, sugarcane, okra, pumpkins, bananas, pawpaws, oranges, and mangoes that are the main concern of the subsistence cultivator. These are gifts of nature that people know, cherish, eat, and want to eat more of. They are generously provided by nature's own larder only if the cultivator fulfills her part of the bargain, loosening the earth when the rain comes at the end of November, clearing weeds and grass so that the plants can thrive, and taking fruits and leaves home in the fullness of time.

It is difficult for villagers to understand why the extension service gives no attention to food crops. Surely, it is not people who should be useful to the service, but the service that should be useful to people, to the hard working, poorly-equipped, struggling small-scale producer. Perhaps if villagers came to view the agricultural extension as a service that had something to offer to *them*, inefficient cultivation methods could be turned to a lasting and profitable surplus production for the cultivators. At least a first step would be taken to eradicate *njala*—hunger—not only from the countryside but from each peasant household too.

Many older people feel deep insecurity these days, because of outside penetration into the usual way of things. One of them, Ketherina Daka, expresses it this way: "Before, farming was not such a problem as it is now when you have to find money to buy seeds and fertilizers and to hire tractors or oxen for ploughing. Even the rain falls differently now and the signs in nature which indicate when to do things are no longer the ones we were used to. It seems that our old ways of cultivating are perishing as the government teaches us new ways of doing things."

Notes

1. The soil in Kalichero subdistrict in Chipata District has good agricultural potential. It is typified by a red clay-loam topsoil with a structured clay subsoil. Soil pH ($CaCl_2$) is good (falling in the 5.1–5.4 range) as are essential plant nutrient supplies. The Kalichero subdistrict is almost 1,000 meters above sea level.

2. When a large part of the most central and most fertile land in Zambia was declared Crown Land in the 1920s, it was turned into a commodity that could be bought and sold. Some of this land (State Land) still is.

3. In Nyanja, the language of the Chewa, the possessive pronoun is carefully used. For that reason the definite article will be found in many places throughout the book when one may have expected the possessive pronoun in English (*the* rather than *his* or *her*). The implication is that emphasis is first and foremost on roles (here: that of husband) rather than on relationship (Emelia's husband). Such emphasis is more in tune with Chewa thinking.

4. The words "field" and "garden" are here used interchangeably. Like "garden," the Nyanja word *munda* (pl. *minda*) indicates a more personalized relationship and is usually translated as "garden." It does, however, not cover a garden of flowers, or a field of grass.

5. According to a agricultural survey carried out in Kalichero subdistrict in 1970-71, the yields did not necessarily decline with the number of years a field had been cultivated. In fact, it appeared that maize yields tended to be higher on older land and on newly cleared land than on land that had been cropped from 1 to 5 years. New land is enriched through ash and partly sterilized by the recent burning of timber, but why land cropped for more than 10 years should have a rather high yield was not clear. (Harvey, 1973.)

6. In the 1930s Audrey Richards studied the Bembas in the northern part of Zambia. Though 50 years have passed and the Chewas live in a very different part of Zambia and have a very different history from the Bemba people, when it comes to everyday life of agriculture and also food habits there are so many similarities that it is well worth noting. The quotation below is included to link the Chewa presence to the (Bemba) past:
   "Where land is as plentiful as it is in this area, the amount of ground a man can cultivate obviously depends on the labour he can command, the annual sequence of his different activities, and the whole system of economic cooperation by which garden and other work is carried out. Less obviously, but equally certainly, production also depends on the people's economic rhythm, their habits of work, and their methods of reckoning time." (Richards, 1939:380.)

7. In 1976 the Ministry of Agriculture decided that all cultivators should be registered in terms of acreage, major crops, and use of fertilizers. Before this date, only cash crop farmers had been included in the Farm Register. Needless to say, this decision meant a lot of extra work for the Agricultural Assistants (AA). While registration work increased, the agricultural staff did not increase. That is why we decided to do our own registration.
   According to the Farm Register of 1977, 31 growers were registered from Kefa village, 11 of whom were women. In fact, more than 80 people cultivate in Kefa and more than half of them are women. According to the Register 6 people including 2 women were registered as hybrid maize growers and most of them with 2 acres. The average acreage of local maize was 4 acres and this number tallies with the average household acreage in our census. 28 to 31 growers in the Register grew groundnuts—most of them on 1 acre—and the mean was 1.7 acres. If we assume that most households consist of two adult growers (a dubious assumption as we shall see later on), the Register data tally with ours in regard to acreage.

8. In a survey done by Harvey of agricultural productivity of rural households in Kalichero subdistrict, the average sample family produced 1,192 kg local maize per hectare (S.D. ±466). An average of 349 kg of maize was retained for consumption for each household member over 9 years, or 1,360 kg per household. There was a close relationship between total local maize production and household size. However, the sample was stratified with an overrepresentation of households with above average involvement in cultivating cash crops. (Harvey, 1973.)

9. In a comprehensive study in 1973-74 of two Chief Areas in Chipata District, one of which was Chief Chikuwe, 79 percent of all households cultivated groundnuts. The average groundnut acreage was 0.7 acre per household. (Hedlund, 1980.) Harvey (1973) estimated that a total of 2.426 hours was needed to cultivate one hectare of groundnuts compared

to 6.09 hours for one hectare of local maize. The average yield of one hectare of ground-nuts was 15 bags, each of which fetched between K 22 and 25 in 1977 depending on the quality of the nuts. Of the total number of hours needed to cultivate one hectare of ground nuts, 950 hours were spent on shelling the nuts, while shelling maize from one hectare took about 70 hours.

According to the survey an average of 47 kg of shelled nuts was retained for eating by each family member over 9 years, but the amount retained related less closely to household size than was the case for local maize (r=0.61). In kilograms the yield of one hectare ranges from 124 to 959 kg with a mean of 542 kg (S.D. ±222 kg). (Harvey, 1973.)

10. According to a survey carried out in Chief Chikuwe area in 1973–74, 10 percent of the households cultivated hybrid maize and the average acreage was 1.7 acres. According to Harvey's survey in 1970–71, hybrid yields were high as crop value averaged K 114 per hectare with a range of K 0-220 per hectare. Production cost averaged K 38 per hectare. High yields were obtained for mid-December plantings, tractor ploughing, fertilizers, and use of measured intrarow spacing. But by missing out some of the essential ingredients, a cultivator might produce worse results than if he or she had grown local maize in the traditional manner. In order to be a successful hybrid maize grower the cultivator must have access to working capital and the purchased inputs, but little expertise is required to produce the crop except for following the recipe. (Harvey, 1973.)

11. Cotton has been grown for a very long time in Zambia. In the sixteenth century cotton was even exported. In the twentieth century the pattern for cotton has been a build-up of production to a peak approximately every 10 years, with a decline then occurring as insect populations grow and destroy the crop. In 1961 cotton was successfully reintroduced to African farmers and by 1971 almost all the market cotton came from Zambians. Zambian cotton is of a very high quality as it is mainly picked by hand. In Chipata there is a ginnery that in 1971 handled 1.5 million pounds of seed cotton, the capacity being 7 million pounds. For 1978 estimated cotton yield was 12,000 tons, which exceeds the capacity of Kafue textile mill. Now there are plans to expand the Zambian milling capacity. (Tuthill et al., 1978.)

An IDZ survey from 1973–74 found 46 cotton-growing households (3 percent) in Chief Chikuwe and Chief Sayiri, based on data from 1.871 households. Cotton was grown on an average of 1.1 acre per household. Fourteen out of the 46 cotton growers experienced total crop failure. (Hedlund, 1980:15.) Harvey had 19 cotton growers in his sample and he too found that their average cotton yield was not good. Two of the 19 growers made a cash loss on their crop. (Harvey, 1973:24.)

12. "The Objectives and Strategy of the Third National Development Plan is i.e., "to give the highest priority to rural development in order to create a strong rural economy, with major emphasis," i.e. on "adopting of investment and production programmes and creating of marketing and extensions facilities which will benefit directly subsistence producers and small-scale farmers." (Third National Development Plan 1973–88. Government of Zambia, 1973:21.)

13. The district headquarters of the Department of Agriculture Extension Branch is situated at the Kalichero Agricultural Station, where the District Agricultural Officer, responsible for all extension personnel and activities in the district, resides. The district is divided into 17 agricultural areas, each serviced by staff working from a centrally placed camp. The Kalichero Camp is staffed by an Agricultural Assistant and two commodity demonstrators. While the AA has been educated at the Zambia College of Agriculture, the commodity demonstrators usually have taken a three-month course in which they specialize in one commodity such as cotton, hybrid maize, or tobacco.

14. Roy Welensky was prime minister of the Central African Federation, an amalgamation of Malawi, Zimbabwe, and Zambia that lasted from 1953 to 1963, when Zambia finally became independent under the leadership of Kenneth Kaunda.

15. It is the ward committee that decides who shall get loans through the Agricultural Finance Corporation as the AFCZ usually follows the ward's recommendations. In Kalichero the wards reject only one or two out of a hundred applicants. In 1976, 101 cultivators got

money in the Kalichero subdistrict. Applications are handed in between May and July and the loan packets effectuated in September. Almost all pay back the loan and if they do not manage the first year they are given a second chance the following year. In the past, AFCZ depended on the Eastern Cooperation Union (ECU) market officer to get its money, which was subtracted from the pay handed over to the cultivator. However, as officers embezzled funds, this practice has been changed. In fact, growers refused to pay their loans back this way because they do not trust the officers. AFCZ has been in the area since the beginning of the 1970s.

16. Harvey found that 7 out of his stratified sample of 85 households used fertilizers on their local maize and that the average yield for those using fertilizers was 1506 kg per hectare as compared to 1163 kg per hectare for those who did not. These data were for 1971. It is likely that cultivators' involvement in the cash economy and the number who use fertilizers have increased since then (Harvey, 1973.)

CHAPTER 3　　THE AGRICULTURAL CYCLE

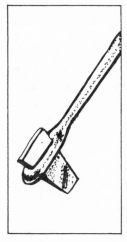

Kanthu ndi khama
Success Presupposes Effort

Before farming was not such a problem as it is now when you have to find money to buy seeds and fertilizers and to hire tractor or oxen for ploughing. Even the rain falls differently now and the signs in nature which indicate when to do things are no longer the same as before. Now we see old ways of cultivating perish and the government teaches us new ways of doing things.

A villager's view

The Farmer's Calendar

Like all other living things, plants have different needs at different stages of their growth, and each variety demands special care. Local maize must be looked after so that it is not strangled by weeds; groundnuts need ridges if they are to thrive. Sweet potatoes demand a field of their own where they can freely unfold their foliage. Vegetables do not like either too much or too little water, cotton must be sprayed to keep pests away, and hybrid does not grow well without fertilizer.

It is the job of the cultivator to see to it that each crop has what it needs to thrive. In return the plants feed the family. It is as if a silent partnership has been struck up between plants and people.

In September and October, well in advance of the rain, the time comes to loosen the earth in the fields. With the first rain local maize and groundnuts are planted and then minor crops like beans, sweet stalk, millet, pumpkins, and cucumbers. Cotton and hybrid can wait until December when the rainy season is well under way, and sunflowers until January when weeding is mostly finished.

With the rain everything grows fast, and the villagers must weed the fields so that plants are not suffocated by weeds and grass. As people wait for the maize to ripen, the young men have time to turn to their *dimba* gardens, where they sow, transplant, thin and weed the vegetables and, as the rain subsides, water and weed again and again.

The harvest starts, slowly at first, then hurriedly, as all nature suddenly seems to bear fruit. And just as nature turns back upon herself to rest and get ready for a new cycle of generous growth, so do the people. In the cold months of July and August, and also in September when the days get hotter again, villagers have the time they need to repair their houses and their tools, to meet with friends and exchange news and views, to visit relatives in other parts of Zambia, and to make plans for the coming season.

Then, once more, the rain approaches as the heat grows, and hoeing and planting can begin. It all fits, or the cultivators make it fit, into a timetable carefully drawn up by the sun and the rain for villagers and everything else alive in their environment.

Hoeing and Planting

Most cultivators start the season in September or October when they clear and burn weeds and debris in the field; and they then hoe the earth to loosen it for planting. Some people prefer to hoe in August to avoid the heat of October, but if you hoe in August you have to harrow before you plant. Other cultivators, who feel they do not have the strength to hoe a surface hardened by a sun that shines without any break from May to October or November, wait "for the weeds to get out from under the soil"—that is, after the first rain has fallen—before they hoe. But to hoe after the rain has started means to spew weed seeds, so that though less work is spent hoeing more will be needed to weed.

To break soil that has not seen rain for up to six months with no tool other than a hoe is tough.[1] Yet hoeing is primarily considered a woman's work. Zuwaila Zulu, a man of three wives, explained:

> "Hoeing is a simple job and that is why it is suitable for women. Women are not good workers like us men. The man is the head of the family and he is involved in heavy and important jobs like stumping trees and deciding what and when to plant. Women are too weak for certain jobs and for a man to practice women's work is for him to practice weakness."

Like most other "sex specific" jobs in Kefa village, hoeing is nevertheless done dexterously both by men and women. Kabanda Nyuni seems to be responsible for most agricultural work in his household. People say that his wife, Evelinar, is a very lazy women, but as we shall see in Chapter 7 she is also not very well.

One morning on his way to the field we heard Kabanda tell his wife: "Please, do not stay in the village. Today you should come to the field." And the wife answered: "When I have bought salt I shall come provided it does not rain." And Kabanda said: "If you do not come, do not expect me to do all the work." But that day she never arrived and Kabanda hoed alone. One day when she did come, she sat down to rest in the *ndinda* field shelter. When Kabanda told her to hoe, she got annoyed and went back home, saying that there was no mealiemeal in the house and that she had to pound.

Square Banda has no wife to depend on. He is a cripple with no strength in his legs and with one lame hand. Though he has only a small field, it is difficult for him to work it. When he hoes, his hands and legs pain him. When sowing, he clutches his walking stick and hoes with one hand, and with the same hand he takes maize seeds from his pocket. Because of his handicap Square has been provided with a field very close to the village; it belonged to Muchoke Soko who gave it to Square because they are distantly related. But goats kept troubling Square in this field, and Muchoke felt pity for him and gave him another field further away from the village. Robby Phiri, Square's cousin, has promised to make a fence around the field and to build a *ndinda* shelter where Square can rest while watching over his crops.

Many cultivators have built themselves a *ndinda*, a thatched roof resting on poles which provides protection against the scorching sun and the rain. Men and women leave the village in the early morning and will return only as the sun sends its last rays over the undulating lands around Kefa village. Between those times, in the heat of the day it is good to have a field shelter where one can rest and cook. Sandikonda Daka has equipped his *ndinda* with a cow's skin that he got as a free gift from his sister. When he gets tired, and he often does because his leg pains him, he lies down on the skin to rest. When Mr. Mbao feels like a rest, he goes to his neighbor in the field, Nyokase Mulumbenji, to relax and chat and spend the hottest hour of the day.

Most people keep their hoes tucked away somewhere in the field. When a man goes to work, he is usually empty handed while a woman carries half her kitchen. One day we saw Tisauke on her way to work carrying mealimeal and a few maize cobs, a pot, and on her back her last born son. Simon is four years and walks but not fast enough for Tisauke on her way to cultivate. Other women bring more, depending on how many people they have to cater for in the field. During the most busy time women cook *nsima* for themselves and their field helpers and whatever they need they have brought from home. Square Banda, the cripple, also carries provisions. Depending on a walking stick is not easy, but Square has adapted to the situation. We have seen him with sweet potatoes and beans in one pot and a frying pan with embers on his head.

When people go home in the evening, the women carry firewood and relish (vegetables, mushrooms, or whatever they have found in the field or on the way). And they may pass by the water hole to fill up a bucket. Only rarely does a woman go empty-handed or -headed. Once back in the village, the men sit down to rest after a busy day, while women hurry to prepare the evening meal.

Most cultivators, struggling under the burning October sun to break the earth in their field, dream of the day when a tractor will speed across their plots, to leave them in a cloud of dust, the earth ploughed open to receive the rain and seeds. Tractor ploughing has many advantages. Firstly, it reduces the hard work of hoeing by hand. What takes a woman or man two weeks to accomplish, the tractor does in a few hours. Yields also increase because the tractor ploughs the richer surface soil deeper into the earth than does the cultivator. Because land preparation by hand takes more time, tractor ploughing enables people to cultivate more land.

But money is not sufficient to hire one of the tractors stationed at the agricultural services camp. In many fields tractor ploughing is impossible because large trees have been left along with roots from smaller trees that have been cut, and tractor drivers fear that their plough shares may get stuck in combat with roots and stones. Even cultivators with adequately cleared fields cannot be sure that they will get a tractor to come. From September to November the demand for tractor ploughing generally far exceeds the supply. Breakdowns are frequent and spare parts are often out of stock. Furthermore, as the service operates according to the principle "first come, first served," valuable tractor time is lost as a tractor goes from one village or area to another to plough for its customers. Another problem is that the service is paid for when booked. As a result a cultivator who has already paid for tractor ploughing hesitates to hoe by hand, even when planting time approaches and the tractor is still nowhere to be seen.

Thus a tractor offers not only new possibilities, but also new hazards. Brighton Lungu recalls:

"Adona Lelia Mbewe is the wife headman Kefa loves the most. The name Adona [from *Dona*, lady] has been given her because of her brown skin and fair complexion. Lelia Mbewe is very beautiful.

"At the time when other village residents were preparing their fields, Adona Lelia did not because the headman had promised her that she would have a tractor to plough for her. She kept waiting, but the tractor never came. Others who hoed by hand worked on their fields every day, and by the end of October most of them had finished ploughing. But Adona Lelia still waited for the tractor. As the days grew hotter and the rain approached she became increasingly worried. One day she got up early and walked to Kalichero where the tractors are stationed. The man in charge reassured her by saying: 'the tractor will come to you when it is your turn. All the names to whom we shall go are on this list and the list is our timetable.' So Lelia went home and waited. And she waited and waited. The rain came, but not the tractor. Adona Lelia waited until the grass had reached the size that made hoeing by hand very difficult, and now she was really very worried about her cultivation.

"Finally she went to Kazembe Mwale, Lubinda's son, who ploughs with his father's oxen for money.[2] She begged him to help her to plough her field so that she could plant before it was too late. And Kazembe came. But by now Lelia was so upset, that she kept telling Kazembe that he must plough properly so that no grass be left. All of a sudden he became so annoyed that he left the job altogether, saying that she would have to find somebody else to do such impossible work. By then it was long past the first rain and Lelia lost all hope of growing maize.

"So this year she has no maize field of her own separate from that of the husband. But the other wives who hoed their fields by hand will soon have maize, pumpkins, and sweet stalks sprouting."

Like so many other village stories this one exists in a different version. According to it the tractor did come, but Lelia's field was so full of trees and stones the driver refused to plough. And Lelia Mbewe did nothing more but left the field fallow, for she is planning to divorce Kefa Mwale because he took a fifth wife.

The rainy season has its vanguards. Excessive heat and humidity proclaim that the rain is about to start. And the cultivator is ready for it. Local maize is the first crop to be planted, just before or just after the first rain, usually in the beginning of November. When a man and a woman cultivate together, the man makes the holes—three feet apart according to extension service instructions—and the woman drops three seeds into each and covers them up.

Some villagers have their own methods. For example, Evelinar always puts four seeds in a hole. Lemekani says that "to plant nine inches apart as the extension people advise, is not good. It does not increase the yield. According to my experience, seeds must be planted five inches apart. Only then will the harvest be really good. That is my experience based upon my fifty years as a maize grower. The extension staff may think differently, but for how many seasons have they been cultivating maize?"

To plant the usual food crops takes a household about four weeks.[3] Although planting is supposed to be women's work, as villagers are in a hurry to get the seeds into the earth the men, if they are present, will help. Nobody wants to give the weeds a headstart, and when the rain starts all forms of vegetation unfold with amazing speed.

Not everybody manages to plant in due time. There are those who are ill, who have been away, or who for some reason have been unable to clear their fields. Schuzi (Shoes) Zulu is an example of one of those who decided not to rely on agricultural performance, but to try their luck elsewhere. This is what happened to him:

Shuzi considered himself very fortunate when in September he was offered a job as a driver to an Indian wholesaler. However, in December the business closed down because of a misfortune that fell upon the wholesaler. Shuzi did not look for a new job, nor did he go home to Kefa village, for he was led to believe that the wholesale shop would reopen shortly. It did not. As time passed Shuzi and his wife Jenifa spent for food all the money that he had earned being in business for three months. When there was no money left and no food, only then did Shuzi and Jenifa decide to go home.

In the village people had cautioned Shuzi before he went, saying: "The best thing to do is to leave your wife here at home so that she can cultivate. If you are to depend on food from there, your job may finish, and you will find that you have nothing to eat." But Shuzi refused to listen. He was so confident about his job that he did not worry about the future. He felt so certain that he would find sufficient money to buy whatever his family needed to eat and live well that both of them had gone. Now they are back, just as the wise elder villagers had predicted they would be, and they have no field to rely on. Very soon the other village residents will eat green maize, groundnuts, and sweet stalks and take pride in their cash crops like hybrid and cotton. But Shuzi and Jenifa have to eat with relatives. Now Shuzi plans to work hard in the *dimba* vegetable garden to raise enough money to buy the food that the other people grow.

Most villagers use charms to increase yields and to prevent people from stealing the crops. (More will be said of this in Chapter 7.) "Some people steal from others by the help of magic," headman Kefa explained.

"But if a cultivator knows how to protect himself [by using charms], nobody will be able to touch that crop, not even a cob, however clever he may be. In this art of using charms we elders know more. For that reason you will see that our maize stands taller. As a village resident grows up he will learn how to go about to protect himself and also his crops and animals. For that reason we, the elders, can give advice and help our friends."

Seeds are kept from one year to the next. Those who have enough seeds will grade them carefully before they sow. Cultivators who have run out of seeds beg, borrow, barter, or buy what they need from friends and relatives. Kabanda Nyuni has planted groundnuts that he got from Tiku Banda, Kwezekani's widow, and in return he will weed Tiku's maize field; he has planted beans he received from his mother Sonile. Simon Sakala got eight cobs of maize as a free gift from Fatness Manda to use for seeds. Sandikonda Daka has planted sweet potatoes he received from Tisauke Phiri and tobacco seedlings that came from Thomase Banda.

For hybrid maize, cotton, and Irish potatoes villagers must buy seeds from the National Agricultural Marketing Board (NAMBOARD). Some people (mostly farmers cultivating crops on a large scale and selling them) prefer to buy all their seeds from NAMBOARD.[4] They say NAMBOARD seeds are "certified by the government and treated with charms so that they cannot be spoiled." But again, certain individuals store even hybrid maize seeds at home, treating them with insecticides such as DDT and Rogor.

Weeding

Rain is the elixir of life. Almost everywhere in Africa rain is the deter-
mining factor between sufficiency and want. Never far from the people's
thoughts, rain is the subject of daily conversation. One of the most polite
ways of thanking a person is to say, "I make it rain for you." And to someone who leaves one says "Go with the rain" or "Come back with the rain."
A child born in a good year may be called "One-who-comes-with-rain,"
and another born in a bad year, "One-who-comes-from-waterless-valley."[5]

Once the rain arrives, everything grows fast. What used to be
yellowish-brown and seemingly lifeless, suddenly sprouts with a
wonderous vitality. One can almost see plants, grass, and shrubs grow.
In the short span of a few weeks dusty plains become undulating
meadows, sandy village floors light green carpets, parched river beds
gurgling streams and even roaring rivers. *Dambos* are conjured into
bottomless swamps, and paths and even roads disappear in grass that
rises higher and higher.

Rain means prosperity provided that the seeds have been planted at
the right time and the weeds are kept under control. How well people
cope with weeding depends on the size of their fields and the labor they
can draw upon. As with planting and harvesting, weeding demands a
lot of work, so that to have a large family is particularly important at this
time of the year. Still, a big family does not necessarily mean a large labor
pool. Lemekani Mbao is the father of many, but he mostly weeds alone.
Some of his children stay away in town, but even his daughters in Kefa
village are not always willing to help their father in the field.

> One day while Lemekani is weeding the father asks the twelve-year-
> old Esnaya what her sister, sixteen-year-old Alines, is up to. Esnaya answers:
> "Alines says that she has finished her job, that she has completed the ridges
> she was supposed to weed, so now she has gone home. She says she has
> jobs to do in the house."
>
> But Lemekani does not agree: "Alines must come back and weed some
> more," he insists. "I want her to work here with me. I do not trust her unless
> I see that she works hard. You, Esnaya, you are not like your sister. I trust
> you." And Esnaya stays with the father and weeds until evening comes.
>
> Lemekani is coughing badly and we ask why his wife and daughter are
> not helping him to weed. Lemekani says: "Alines is my daughter, but she
> is a very lazy girl. She forgets that the money I spend on her schooling comes
> from this field. When I tell her to do something for me she does not listen.
> When I tell her to weed she says: 'Did you start growing hybrid because
> of me? I do not want to be forced to do such work. I have duties at home.'
> This is what she tells me every time I want her to help me. About Alines'
> mother [Tilele Zulu, Lemekani's wife] I do not mind if she does not help
> me, because she has her own fields with cotton and local maize."

And he adds: "Alines is fond of playing about. She does not like to work, either in the home or in the field. Only when I am dead will she understand me. Then she will cry and cry until she learns to work hard. Obviously, as long as I am alive and help her with food she will never learn. When she marries she will run into problems with her husband. He may even beat her hard because she is so lazy."

December and January are the months of *milochi*—the rain that keeps pouring all day. On *milochi* days people remain in the village, sitting around the fire to keep warm and dry, chatting quietly with friends, waiting for the rain to pass, so that they can get on with the weeding. The long-lasting rain prevents people not only from working, but also from going to the forest to pick firewood and relish. So the villagers speak of *milochi* as *njala*—hunger. All the same, lazy people are said to welcome it, for it provides them with a break in the weeding. The hard-working are said to hate it. And there are those, like Zindikani Miti's deceased father, nicknamed *Intouya*, "the hard-working one," who get famous because they go to their field to work, in spite of *milochi*.

To weed an acre of local maize takes a woman three weeks, provided she works eight hours a day. So most village residents spend half of November, all of December, and even January weeding. *Palila*, the first weeding, must be done so that weeds do not suffocate the crop; as the crop continues to grow, it is time for *mbwelela*, the second weeding.[6] During *mbwelela* ridges are made and the last small crops are planted in between the maize. Now the youngmen with some cash apply their fertilizers, determined that they will not allow their families to starve. How well a cultivator weeds depends on his or her strength. Some people never finish the *palila* weeding. They work hard but the weeds defy their effort.

In January Sylvester Miti reports:

"Most village residents are now weeding for the second time, but those with large fields have not yet finished *palila*, and have started worrying about their crops. Sandikonda Daka is one of them. Mwanishupa and he divided the work between themselves, so that he weeds the hybrid and she the local maize. He has left part of his hybrid unweeded while he helps the wife weed the local maize for the second time [as it is the more important crop]. Simon Sakala has weeded only once. Rather than weed a second time, he has decided to make ridges and plant sweet potatoes, beans, and tobacco for his own private use. He has also applied fertilizers on his hybrid, mixing top and basal dressing into his special 'planting fertilizer.' Kabanda Nyuni, who mostly works alone, has finished weeding his local maize twice and is now planting onions in the *dimba*."

January and particularly February are the hunger months. In many households last year's maize is already finished, and those who still have something in their granary bin may cut down on their meals to make whatever they have left last until the green maize ripens in March. Those who have neither food nor money may have to sell their labor or barter it in order to be able to eat. By doing so they enter a vicious circle. As they weed in other people's fields rather than their own, their harvest suffers and at this time next year their granary bins may well be empty again, so that once more they will have to weed for others.

Sylvester continues:

"Headman Kefa Mwale uses paid labor for almost every hard job he has. He has sons but they are not willing to work for his wives. Instead, Kefa employs people whenever his wives ask him for assistance. Since July Kefa has hired a fellow villager to plaster the rooms in his house, to extend his and his wives' fields, to assist in carrying mud for Gilbert Zulu's new brick house [see Chapter 8], to have a tractor plough his hybrid field, and to repair his maize and groundnut bins. He has also hired Micheck Phiri to weed his hybrid field and has paid him with a pair of trousers given him for this purpose by his grandson Gilbert Zulu. Micheck Phiri is a man ever wrking for Kefa. But yesterday, when Kefa asked Micheck to weed for him, he answered ''Pepani—I am very sorry—but today we are going to Ezidon's field to weed because we took meat from him yesterday.''"

Simon Sakala and Tilele Zulu are among those who sometimes buy and sometimes sell labor. Many people do both because to work for others is a way not only to earn food or cash, but also to emphasize fellowship and reciprocity. Piecework is also an occasion for enjoyment. It is a means to raise money for groups like Dynamo, the Kefa village football team, or for church groups. Through piecework at Mr. Ngoma's farm, the Caritas group raised K. 70; ten women and three men, including Simon and Tilele from Kefa village, weeded for several days and were invited to Mr. Ngoma's house for food by the end of each day, and there was much talking and joking.

Beer parties are a popular way of mobilizing labor.[7] They are used for all kinds of jobs, and men and women participate. When Jessie Tonga made sweet beer to give to the people who would clear her maize field, ten persons, most of them women, came. On another occasion Jessie sold a goat to an Asian trader. Some of the money she spent paying her sons Alick and Kambula, as well as (Kefa's sons) David and Pascale and a few other youngmen from the Dynamo football team, to weed her maize.

Mwada Simba and her much younger husband Michek Phiri are among those who never seem to be able to afford to pay others to work for them, but who themselves frequently work for other people. It is said that they spend too much time on beer, and that there is no proper planning in their house. Faides Phiri, with five children and no husband, frequently gets maize, groundnuts, and money on credit from her neighbors and repays them with work. Tyford expains to us:

> "Faides Phiri is making ridges in Angripina's field because she has taken meat from Angripina on credit. She made six long ridges. Last week she and Joseph [her son, who is fifteen years old] weeded in Mwanizing's field, paying her back with work for the groundnuts she had given them. They also weeded in Ezidon's field as Ezidon had slaughtered a pig to pay people to help him. Mwada Simba and Micheck Phiri were also weeding in Ezidon's field, so altogether they were four people, and Ezidon occasionally came to see that they all worked hard."

Fortunately it is not only money and meat that moves villagers to work for each other. Betina Tembo weeded in Square Banda's field "according to the Christian custom of doing good towards others," we were told. And when Jenelani Khosa killed a pig to pay people to weed his groundnuts, he took a piece to Square, even though Square, the cripple, will never be able to repay him by work.

Watching and Waiting

Whatever nature offers is not intended for humans alone. So many other creatures are waiting for it, eager to get their share. The very moment the maize starts to ripen, mischievious monkeys are on the spot ready to revel in row upon row of green delight. Villagers whose fields border on the forest are particularly troubled by them, and constant vigilance is needed to protect the crops.

Tisauke Phiri and Simon Sakala are among those who have had their crops greatly reduced because of monkeys. Now they wonder if they should quit growing hybrid altogether. Simon is deliberating whether to make vegetables rather than hybrid his cash crop, because monkeys do not like tomatoes and rape. But they do eat pumpkins. Last year Mwada Simba's pumpkin crop was badly damaged by monkeys. She and Micheck had gone to Lundazi (150 kilometers away) to see a relative who was ill, and while they were away the monkeys descended onto their field.

James Phiri, too, has been troubled by monkeys. One day he took his two-year-old daughter Unice on his bike to the health center, as she had been coughing badly. While waiting in line, he got the message that his maize had been spoiled by monkeys. He left the daughter with a relative from Kefa village, who was also waiting in the line and rushed home to find his maize eaten.

To protect the crops most fields are constantly guarded from December to the end of February. Monkeys are one of the main problems, but there are also birds, rats, bush pigs, goats, and cattle. Throughout the rainy season cattle are herded to protect the crops, but every now and then stray animals find their way into somebody's field.

One day in March headman Kefa called a village meeting. Cattle had strayed into Eliza Phiri's maize field and destroyed a lot of her crop. Eliza stood before her fellow village residents with a half-eaten maize stalk in her hand. She wanted to give it to the owner of the stray cattle so that he could repay her with unspoiled maize after the harvest. "Unless the owner pays me back for the damage caused, I shall summon every cattle owner in this village before the Chief, because the tracks clearly show that the animals came from this village!" she said.

The elders discussed the matter and Lemekani Mbao talked for them all when he said: "Because a case of trespassing last week involved head-man Kefa's cattle, this time Robert Manda and Lubinda Mwale [two other big cattle owners in the village] will be held responsible, and you, Eliza Phiri, when harvest time comes, these are the friends you will turn to." And Robert and Lubinda promised Eliza to give her maize. Eliza Phiri was very happy with the decision. She had been worried because she had taken a loan from the Roman Catholic Church Group to buy fertilizers. She had planned to repay the loan by selling her hybrid, as she had no other means.

In March the maize starts drying up, and the different predators stop preying. All of a sudden there is a brief spell of leisure for the villagers. The rain does not fall as frequently as before, and the air is pleasantly warm. There is enough food everywhere, for green maize and bush plants can be eaten. After months of very hard work, most villagers are happy to be able to drift about, preparing snacks for themselves by roasting green maize on the cob, visiting friends, chatting, and making sure that their granary bins are large enough and strong enough to keep the year's harvest unspoiled throughout the next year.

Not everybody can afford to relax at this time. Hardworking vegetable growers like Simon Sakala, James Phiri, and Jackson Phiri still have much to do. All of them make money from their gardens and with the money they buy fertilizers, hire oxen and even a tractor to carry their maize home from the field, and buy seeds for next year, or tools, clothes, paraffin, and soap.

Simon starts going regularly to his *dimba* in February when he has finished most of the work on his food crops and hybrid maize and when the monkeys are no longer a problem. He had already planted tomatoes in a small nursery down by the river, and when the seedlings were four inches high he transplanted them into the *dimba*. By April he has twenty-nine beds of rape and seven of tomatoes. While harvesting and selling rape, he weeds and waters the tomatoes.

Harvesting

"It was April, the month when women ask you to help lift the heavy loads from their heads."[8]

Maize is a wonder of creation. Only three months after the golden grains have been planted, the fields are ablaze with plants taller than the cultivator who depends on them for food. Each plant carries cobs in its folds, hidden in protective foliage. As early as February maize is available, fresh and juicy, as "green maize." Because this is the time when many a household is desperately short of food, green maize is most welcome, often not as a delicious luxury, but as a basic necessity. As the first important supplement to a meager diet, it signifies that a new season is rapidly approaching, a time of plenty when food can be picked almost everywhere.

Days pass by, with sunshine and an occasional shower, and nature generously starts releasing one vegetable delight after another: those that grow to ripeness without human involvement, and those that have been carefully nurtured. Maize is among the latter, the first important crop to mature.

Green maize is not only the herald of plenty and a delicacy, it of course has an economic value. Early planters who have succeeded in tending their maize crop to ripeness before others may praise themselves lucky. Even the poor, crippled Square Banda with his limited financial resources buys green maize before his own is ready, reluctantly paying his relative Danga Banda to savor the first maize of the season. "Danga has no sense of right and wrong," Square complains afterwards. "How can he *sell* green maize to me, as if I were not his father? [Square is Danga's extended father] I am very sorry Danga sells me maize, as if he was not of my own family. It is not right. Am I not his father? What about when he was young? Was I selling him food then? And if I had sold him food, would he have been able to grow up at all?"

Green maize cannot be stored. Only after all the juicy freshness has been concentrated in the fruit and the entire plant has turned golden will the grains become sufficiently impenetrable to keep for a long time. By then it is already the middle of April.

Before the harvest proper starts, every household must have its granary bins ready, so that the year's harvest can be adequately stored and kept. Like beads on a string, the *nkhokwe*—the granary bins—encircle the village. (See the map at the opening of Chapter 1.) Each household has at least two: a small one for groundnuts and a large one for maize. When spouses cultivate separately, as do Kefa Mwale and his five wives and Lemekani and Tilele, the household usually has several bins.

The *nkhokwe* is made of bamboo woven into a cylinder; it is set on a wooden platform supported by tree trunks dug firmly into the ground and covered with a conical roof. The larger maize bin is some two meters across and two meters high. The bins for groundnuts are lined on the inside with mud from an anthill, which becomes almost as hard as cement once it dries. Because groundnuts are more popular than maize with termites, rats, and insects, the bins are raised higher above the ground than the maize bins. Small crops like sweet stalks, dried leaves, and gourds are kept on top of the main crop in the groundnut or maize bin, while sorghum may get a bin of its own. To prevent stored food from disappearing, most people use charms. Unwanted creatures lie in wait for the treasures that a well-stocked *nkhokwe* contains—whether they be ordinary human thieves, or witchpeople and their companions the hyenas—and the right charms can guarantee that a year's hard work, the harvest, will not be eroded with unnatural speed.

To make and repair granary bins is a man's job. Because one in four village households have to make do without adult male members, and a granary bin has to be repaired annually and renewed every second year, John Ngoma, Goefe Zulu, and Jones Mwale have decided to make granary bins their business. Their prospects seem good. Sylvester tells us:

"Obadirya Shawa was employed by White Nyirenda, a commercial farmer, to make a granary bin, and was paid K. 2.90 in advance. On the day that Obadirya was supposed to start work, he went to drink beer with his friends in Kefa village instead. White, coming to see how the job was getting on, could not find his man anywhere until he was led to Kefa village. Here he pushed Obadirya aside to talk to him and insisted that he must go to the forest right away to start cutting bamboo for the *nkhokwe*. Obadirya, who was drunk with beer, tried to apologize. The other beer drinkers persuaded White not to beat Obadirya, but only to talk firmly to him.

The next morning Obadirya again went for beer at Timeke's house. When White found out, he followed him. Finding him drinking again, he got so angry that he rushed at Obadirya and pulled his beard so hard that some of it came off the chin, pushed him and wanted to beat him. But the people present intervened. They caught White by the arm and managed to separate the two. White then abused Obadirya with words, saying he would beat him terribly unless he went right away to cut bamboo, so that the bin would be ready the following day when he was expecting a tractor to come with his maize."

While March is a month of leisure, in April and particularly in May and June everybody has to work very hard. Hands are needed in every field to dig, pick, and carry. Soon the cattle will be let loose to graze wherever they want. Then the bushfires start indiscriminately to devour everything on their way. So everybody is in a hurry. Only when the *nkhokwe* are filled up can the village residents relax once more.

Maize is the main concern. First, the cobs are wrung from the stalk and graded so that the less healthy ones can be eaten first. To complete the drying process, which starts as early as February, the cobs in their shield are placed in the open to dry. Some cultivators have made a bamboo platform in their fields where they put the maize to prevent termites from feasting on the drying maize. While their cobs are basking in the sun, cultivators hurry to their groundnut field to dig. Groundnuts, too, are left on the ground to dry for as long as it takes to carry the maize crop to the village. Then the groundnut pods are removed from the vine and taken home and stored (unshelled) in the groundnut bin.

The subsistence crops grown by a household weigh about one ton. Within a few weeks they must all be brought from fields to the village. Whether transport is done by tractor, by oxen, or by women depends on the cash situation of the family, and on availability. Cash crops are carried mostly by tractor and oxen, food crops mainly by women. Women in households without adult men can rarely afford to pay others to carry their crops. Being alone, they have enough problems to earn cash to keep children in school and grind maize at the mill. In Kefa village, as in most other villages, men and money go together.

In the beginning of May Sylvester made the following entry in his diary:

"Maize is now being delivered to the *nkhokwe* in the village. Transport is mainly done through cooperation of women. Anyone who has finished separating cobs from stalks and piled them, tells her workmates so that they all come and carry her maize. Today women have been carrying Doris Mbewe's maize.

"Though women are physically weaker than men, their necks are stronger, so carrying headloads is women's work. Men carry headloads, too, but it is not their job. They only do so to help the women."

It is only headload transport that is women's work. The moment oxen, combustion engines, or even bicycles enter the rural scene, transport is no longer considered a woman's affair but that of men. But in Kefa village headloads still dominate. Each afternoon women come in from the field, alone or in a group carrying basketfuls of pumpkins, green maize, roots, and leaves.

In order to make the best out of their many tasks and limited resources, women work harder and cooperate better than men, from necessity as well as sociability. Two persons are needed to lift a headload from the ground. When a group of women carry maize, trotting in a line, encouraging each other to endure and shortening distances by shouts and even laughter, even a load of 50 kilograms seems bearable.

Sometimes such cooperation is organized. When Fatnes Manda and Betina Tembo went for a two-week course in how to run a Women's Club at Kalichero Agricultural Centre, the headman told the other village women to harvest their fields, and nine women joined in and carried Fatnes' and Betina's maize.

There is a tacit agreement that favors are to be returned. The agreement can also be an explicit one and even married couples sometimes keep accounts with each other: Sandikonda Daka and Mwanishupa Phiri cultivated groundnuts separately, but they grew maize together. From April to May they harvested the groundnuts separately. When in the middle of May Mwanishupa started harvesting the maize, Sandikonda was busy at home making new granary bins. Mwanishupa worked hard in the maize field, separating the cobs from the stalks and putting them in a heap. But when she finished half the field she stopped, as the agreement was that she and her husband Sandikonda would harvest half a field each.

Square Banda depends for his harvest on the good will of others. Because of his handicap it is impossible for him to carry heavy loads. Last year his relatives Rosemary and Rachel loaded his maize onto a tractor, which took his harvest to his house free of charge. This year Muchoke Soko carried Square's maize by headload. All the same, as everybody is so busy at harvest time, Square is usually the last village resident to see his *nkhokwe* filled up. To be dependent on others is always a disadvantage, and more so at harvest time. This year he only just started harvesting when cattle settled in his field and ate a lot of his maize. Tyford tells us:

"Square Banda has reported the damage in his field to the owners of the cattle who have been identified as Robert Manda and Kefa Mwale. But nothing has happened. Now Square is crying about his lost maize and all his other problems. Having no wife, he has nobody to cultivate for him and to look after and feed him, and now even his maize is lost. He is very sad and cannot talk happily or show a happy face. Instead he says: 'God must help me. Nobody in this village does, not even my sons. Danga and Jackson [his relatives] are very unkind. Unless the owners of the cattle give me maize back, I shall ask the Chief to help me regain it.'

"Instead of talking to people who pass by his house, Square Banda only sits quietly, warming himself by the fire, singing sorry songs to himself. He is even thinking of becoming a bad man, using charms to harm those who have harmed him. But Sandikonda Daka advises him strongly against using his powers, because Square Banda is a well-known witch doctor not only in Kefa village but in the entire area. He knows charms and medicines that others do not. And Mr. Daka reminds Square of the old saying: *Ukasauka usamagwira nyanga*—'When you are poor, do not take hold of the horn,' which means do not harm others through medicines and sorcery."

How very busy people are during harvest time we can realize only with a few figures. A woman who works as a cultivator seven hours per day will need about ten days to cut, strip, and stack cobs from one acre of local maize, thirty-three days to stack groundnuts from one-half acre on tripods and clean and strip them, and three days to harvest beans from one-quarter acre—a total of forty-six working days. If she consistently works seven hours per day, six days per week, the job will be done in seven-and-one-half weeks. This is all the time she has, as the harvest starts around the middle of April and finishes by the middle of June.[9]

These estimates says nothing about transporting crops from field to village. Two acres of maize, groundnuts, and minor crops is the least that a family with only one adult needs to feed itself. If the figures are right, and they are based on studies carried out by an agricultural research station in the district, it is amazing that some people, single or married, manage to grow cash crops in addition to their subsistence ones.

Tisauke Phiri is a good example. Tisauke's husband Kwerekani comes to Kefa village only to relax during weekends. Tisauke's ten-year-old daughter Nyawa provides the mother with the most regular help she has in the field. Tisauke tells us that she cultivates three acres of local maize, one acre of groundnuts, one acre of cotton, and one-half acre of sunflowers. According to the estimate Tisauke should work 168 days from the middle of April until the end of June, a period of only seventy-five days. How does she do it? She certainly cannot afford to pay someone to work for her all the time. Let us say that she manages to raise labor by hiring the Dynamo football boys for ten days (five boys for two days). It will cost her K. 30 and she still has 158 workdays left. Little Nyawa may help her a bit every day, but more than 120 working days still remain for Tisauke, who even when she is harvesting, occasionally has to pound the maize and take it to the hammer mill so that she and Nyawa can eat.

Maybe Tisauke has exaggerated the acreage she cultivates; perhaps her cultivation is not particularly intensive. Even if her workload between April and June amounts to only half the remaining 120 days, she will be very busy. And so are most of the other villagers. No wonder villages seem deserted at this time of the year. Except for the very young, the very old, and the seriously ill, every adult is busy in the field.

Every household needs grass to thatch and repair roofs, whether it is that of the dwelling hut, the animal shelters, the granary bins, or the field shelter. Grass too must be harvested before the bushfires are released. Grass cutting is another women's job. "But there are a few men who do not mind doing this job," Lemekani explained to us.

Bushfires mark the definite end of the harvesting season. By the middle of June, the fires illuminate the darkness of night, leaping toward the sky as they eat their way through bush, fields, and meadows engulfing whatever moves and grows. June is the time of "early burning" when the fires, though they look fearful, are still under human control. There are many reasons for burning dried grass: The most important is that early burning, also called "controlled burning," prevents late and uncontrolled fires, fires that may become disastrous not only for insects and reptiles, but also for people and their settlements. Between June and October one is not likely to see a drop of rain, and as the months go by not only the grass but bush and trees become highly flammable.

Early burning does not threaten the trees. Furthermore, cattle owners are eager to see the fresh green grass sprout from under the ashes, as if rain had fallen already. Mouse hunters of every age, but particularly the youngsters, want the ground cleared to track the delicious forest mouse down to her underground home. Villagers are glad to see that insects and reptiles disappear in the flames. And every rural resident prefers an open countryside to the jungle of tall, yellowish, unruly grass that grows up during each rainy season. So, though the agricultural extension advises against burning, once the villagers have brought their crops home youngsters and others will set the dry grass afire.

In July the Cooperative Union market opens up. For a few weeks tons and tons of maize, groundnuts, cotton, tobacco, and sunflowers leave the villages for centers like Lusaka and the Copper Belt. Twenty-three Kefa village residents, eight of them women, sold maize to the Cooperative Union market.[10] With 46 bags (90 kg each) headman Kefa was the biggest maize seller. His income from the maize amounted to K. 290. Four men and three women sold only groundnuts at the market. Lubinda Mwale with one bag (80 kg) earned the most: K. 24.30. One man and two women sold only cotton. In all there were thirty-three surplus producers out of a total of 117 adult village residents. The Cooperative Union is a sure buyer of cash crops. But there is one major drawback in selling to the Union: the cultivator is not paid upon delivery. Having handed over the goods, he or she can never be quite sure when, or if at all, money will follow. Those who have taken loans are particularly insecure. Debts are deducted from the pay by the ECU and suspicion regularly arises as to whether the deductions are correct. Often they have turned out not to be.

For such reasons many people prefer to sell to local traders or to other villagers who pay cash on delivery. Such sales usually of small quantities take place throughout the year at varying prices. Measurements are no longer in bags, but in tins and handfuls. Even Square Banda sold five buckets of maize this way and earned K. 4.75.

To prepare crops for sale takes time. To shell ten bags of maize is estimated to take two full working days while shelling a bag of groundnuts takes four days. To pick and bale an acre of cotton takes fifty-two days, according to the estimates from the provincial agricultural research station.

Planning for the Future

Good living depends on many things: the fertility of the fields, the strength of available labor, the skills of the cultivator, and the risk that the rain falls when expected and in sufficient quantity. Some of these things are outside the control of villagers, but how the cultivator uses his or her land and labor is largely an individual decision.

Once the harvest is secured and leisure time increases as the weather grows colder, the time has come to think of the future. In only a few months a new agricultural season will start, demanding decisions on crops and fields, on the use of capital inputs like fertilizers and pesticides, or on whether to turn one's back to Kefa village altogether and look for paid work in town.

Simon Sakala's plans for next year are to work harder and to concentrate on hybrid maize. He wants to clear new land and extend his fields. As he has no money to spare he will do the job himself. The following year he hopes to earn sufficient money to pay others to extend his fields still farther. His aim is to grow enough maize to buy work oxen. But he will grow neither cotton not tobacco. "My only interest is food crops, that is, local maize, hybrid, and possibly Irish potatoes, but as to the potatoes I have not quite decided."

Kabanda Nyuni declares: "This year I had no chance of growing hybrid because I had no fertilizers, but next year I shall grow more groundnuts and the money I find from the nuts I shall use to buy fertilizers, and in the following year I shall start growing hybrid." And Jackson, his friend says: "I have started growing cotton. Next year I shall try hybrid if I do not make much money from my cotton this year." Kabanda replies: "You, my friend, you are lucky because your wife helps you cultivating. My wife is too lazy. She spends all her time chatting with other women. She utterly refuses to help me in the field so I have to cultivate alone."

Square Banda too is drawing up plans as he sits by the fire one cold evening in July savoring beer that Jessie Tonga has given him free of charge: "My plans for the future are that next year, if God permits, I shall plant cowpeas and, if I have any groundnut seeds, I shall plant groundnuts too."

Mwada Simba and Faides Phiri talk about their future plans. Mwada says: "Let us share the uncultivated land that lies between our fields and that of Hundred Banda. If we extend our acreage both of us can grow more food and earn money to send our children to school." But Faides takes offense at the idea. Unlike Mwada, Faides has no husband to help her clear and cultivate new land. She begins an argument with Mwada. After some time Micheck, Mwada's husband, and Joseph, Faides' son, join them in a long discussion about the working style of different people and about who has a right to the land Mwada wants to annex. Mwada wins the argument and concludes the discussion: "Our president Kaunda says that those who have the strength must hoe as much as they can. This is the only way through which our Zambia can prosper, and being a Zambian I at least will follow the advice of Kaunda, our leader."

A popular way of turning surplus production into money is to brew beer. (We learn more about beer production in Chapter 5.) When the harvest is over, the granaries are full, and surplus produce has been sold, money, as well as spare time is readily available in the village. Many people use it around the beer pot. As the weather grows colder, villagers congregate to sit around the fire and enjoy the good days. Those with money pay for the beer and pass it around for their friends to savor. As hours and days pass, they exchange views, review the events of the past season, and plan for the coming season. In only a few months a new agricultural cycle will begin again for the cultivators.

Notes

1. "Land preparation time . . . varies enormously depending on previous cropping, time of the year, method used, etc. It is so difficult to hand-cultivate in the dry season that there is a tendency to do a minimum of weed and crop residue clearance and reconstruct old ridges. Time required for ridging under these circumstances ranges from 200–300 manhours or 29–43 mandays per hectare. For later planted crops, e.g., beans and sunflowers, it is necessary to clear weed growth from the start of rains. This may take up to 500 manhours, or 72 mandays per hectare." (Heney, 1973:34.)

2. In the 1950s ox power promised people relief from the hard work of hoeing by hand. Many people had their oxen trained. But by the end of the 1960s the tractor arrived on the scene, becoming increasingly more common during the 1970s. As a result ox-drawn equipment was suddenly no longer available either locally or in Chipata, and as the old equipment wore down oxen could no longer be used for ploughing—unfortunate because a tractor at K. 7000 is hardly a substitute for an ox plough at K. 40. In the 1980s, however, trends are reversing again. Ox power is once more on its way in, and the agricultural extension service now includes the training of oxen.

3. To plant various crops on 1 acre of land takes an estimate of 5 work days (7 hours) for local maize, 7 days for groundnuts, 8 days for beans, 7 days for cotton, 4 days for hybrid maize, and 11 days for sunflowers. (Heney, 1973:32.)

4. NAMBOARD—National Agricultural Marketing Board—is a major marketing organization in Zambia. NAMBOARD buys and sells crops such as maize, groundnuts, and sunflowers. It has the responsibilities of supplying inputs to farmers, too, such as seeds, fertilizers, pesticides, and the like. NAMBOARD is parastatal and has long suffered from serious coordination problems with other units in the rural areas.

5. Watson, 1982:178.

6. Heney estimates that it takes 136 hours to weed 1 acre of maize, 125 hours to weed 1 acre of groundnuts, 100 hours for 1 acre of beans, 115 hours for 1 acre of hybrid, 160 hours for 1 acre of cotton, and 70 hours for 1 acre of sunflowers. (Heney, 1973:32)

7. "A drum of beer, costing some K. 5 to produce, could be converted into about 150 man hours, or enough labour to weed 2.5 acres or hoe a field of 1.5 acres. It is difficult to make an exact cost comparison between various ways of paying for labour, but it is estimated that if a field of 2.5 acres were to be weeded by casual labourers on piece work basis during one day, the employer would need 21 workers working for 7 hours

and this would cost at least K. 12, or 6 times as much as through a beer party . . . Compared to labour obtained through beer parties, labour paid in kind in maize would appear to cost more . . . However, it is estimated that a household able to employ labour, paid directly in baskets of maize per man-day for all the operations involved in growing a crop would still be able to obtain a substantial profit at average yields and prices." (Hedlund, 1980:42–43.)

8. Watson, 1982:130.

9. The estimates are those quoted by Heney (1973:32–33). The *actual* time people use on various activities depends on the quality of their labor and on skills. Concerning cotton, for instance, Harvey (1973:22) wrote that "cultivators have little idea of picking methods and as a result spent perhaps three or four times longer harvesting the crop than is necessary."

10. The estimates are based on observations carried out at Msekera Regional Research Station by the Farm Management Research Officer.

CHAPTER 4   FOOD AND GOOD HOUSEKEEPING

Adye zabwino adadya zowawa
Not All Food Tastes Good

Pophika nsima	Our mother is cooking *nsima*
Pophika nsima maiwa	Our mother is cooking *nsima*
Cedwa	So late
	It is good to eat

Meals

People cultivate to be able to eat well. Food is necessary to live and to work, and the right food often can prevent illnesses. Yet nutrition is only a part of the picture. When it is well prepared, food is a source of pleasure and contentment to whoever makes it and those who eat it. To share food is to emphasize togetherness and reciprocity, and to eat in the company of others may signal friendship and love. Furthermore, food is the subject of endless conversations and discussions, the focal point at ceremonies, a messenger of care and concern, and, first and foremost, the major task around which most of women's lives are centered.

"Cooking and everything that goes with it is my job," says Regina Shawa, the headman's third wife. "I decide everything concerning cooking unless he [the husband] is hungry or busy and wants to eat before our usual eating time. When it comes to items like salt and salad oil that are bought for money, I report to Mr. Kefa what we need, so that he can buy if he has money. As a wife must earn a man's respect, I give the man of my house the opportunity to decide everything for himself. Only if he needs my help do we discuss the matter."

Brighton believes women to be less subservient: "Women cook so that we all can eat well," he says, "and they also prepare and store food to share with their friends who happen not to have anything to eat. Women are always so helpful to each other. When somebody comes to beg relish [see below], they always share and they even cook extra to give away. Doing so, they never consult with their husband, asking for his permission or whether he is hungry."

It is part of a man's birthright, or so it seems, to have a woman cook for him. "If food is not ready when a husband wants to eat, he has a good reason for beating you," Regina explains, yet we never heard of any such case. Men who do not have a wife (at home), eat with a sister, mother, or daughter. Square Banda is an exception. Usually he cooks alone and for himself, though kind women like Muchoke, Rosemary, and Fatnes occasionally send him *nsima* and relish. (Relish is a sauce or stew served with any starchy staple like maize or cassava to make it a meal.)

"Since we came to Kefa village we have never experienced *njala*—hunger," headman Kefa used to say. But many people go hungry occasionally, and particularly during the lean season, when granary bins are depleted and there is nothing to be found in the bush. During planting, weeding, and harvesting time, when women work in the field from sunrise to sunset, many families do not have a proper meal before nighttime. The children are the worst off; time and again the recorders reported that a child "was crying from hunger." But when staple and relish crops mature, in March and more so in April, food is cooked several times a day and generously shared with whoever happens to be around. For this reason, meal patterns vary according to season and villagers as they grow older get used to irregular eating hours.

The main Chewa meal is eaten around midday, but can also be eaten in the evening. It invariably consists of the maize staple *nsima*, made from maize meal cooked into a soft paste, and relish. The relish is made from green leaves, vegetables and/or groundnuts, and, occasionally, fish, meat, termites, or mice. A vegetable relish is most common. Cherished condiments are groundnut powder, tomatoes, onions, red pepper, and chillies. If available, salt is added.

Breakfast is not part of the village meal pattern. Food early in the morning is considered fitting only for children and for ill people. Yet, if there are leftovers from yesterday's supper, "*nsima* that has slept" may be eaten as a morning meal by adult men. But we never observed women eating early in the morning. It is only in the more affluent homes, like that of Tilele Zulu, the cotton grower, that children are likely to get a morning meal on a regular basis. Porridge with salt, sugar, and margarine is a real delicacy that most people cannot afford, even when the ingredients are available at the local store. Morning "tea" is less demanding, consisting merely of hot water poured over a spoon of sugar that has been burned over the fire. Tea leaves are rarely available at the store, but the "morning tea" is hot and sweet, and has the right tea color. Still, as sugar is a luxury, so is any hot, sweet beverage.

Utensils

"As far as I have observed, our kitchen equipment these days does not look very African. Elders tell us that in the past, all food was cooked in self-made clay pots and eaten from self-made shallow bamboo plates. But nowadays clay pots are mostly used by the older village residents only. They say food is more tasty when it is cooked in a clay pot. Young women use metal pots and eat on English plates using spoons. They prefer metal pots because they do not break," Sylvester reported.

Every household has a set of wicker baskets made from woven bamboo. The large and deep baskets, *chitundu* and *dengo*, are used to store maize, millet, and mealiemeal. The shallow *licelo* and *lwang* baskets are used to sieve maize and to carry small amounts of flour and groundnut powder. To make baskets and carve cooking sticks used to be the men's job. Whenever they weave or carve men usually sit together. They have a song:

Kalicelo kanga mcopepete	I am making a basket.
Tungika iwe	You will be for sieving.
Kalicelo kanga mcopepete	I am making a beautiful
Tungika iwe	basket for sieving.

These days, rather then weave baskets, carve handles, and make pots, people with money prefer to buy the tools they need from itinerant craftsmen. James Kamaswanda Njobvu is such an itinerant craftsman who has come to live for some time in the Kefa village to sell his baskets. *Kamaswanda* means basket in Nyanja. Though he works to sell baskets, James Njobvu still has to cultivate to live.

To make pots is a traditional women's craft. Jessie Ngoma, Kakoche Mwale's widow, is one of the best pot-makers in the village. She makes all kinds of clay pots, both to use herself and to sell to those with money to buy. The clay she takes from a nearby anthill. To make the pots strong she burns them on the fire, and some she decorates with a special stone to make them especially beautiful. Potters also have a song to sing:

Mbiya umbika umbika	Pot, be made
Ukapita pa moto usaka	When you go on fire.
Pwanyike	Do not break.

Most large households have a separate kitchen house, made from mud-and-wattle just like the dwelling hut itself. The kitchens often serve as sleeping quarters for the bigger children, thus leaving more privacy for the parents at night. Inside the kitchen, or the dwelling hut for those who have no separate kitchen, pots, pans, and other kitchen equipment are neatly stacked at the back or along walls: wicker baskets for maize, millet, and flour; big clay pots for beer making; small clay pots for a variety of purposes; one or two metal pots, some metal dishes, a few gourds for drinking, a cooking stick and a knife, one or two debe-cans for carrying water, and, in some households, a mortar and one or two pestles.

Mortar and pestle are tools no woman can do without, yet they are found only in half of the homes in the village. It is mostly the younger women who borrow from the elders, but not exclusively; Tilele Zulu is among those who do not have a mortar of their own.[1]

Some people seem to share in other people's possessions almost continuously. Evelinar Njobvu is one of them. On one and the same day we saw her borrow plates and a dish from her mother-in-law, Sonile Ngoma, a sieve from Mwada Simba, Sonile's sister, ochra leaves from her friend, Timeke Daka, a pot and a knife from her sister-in-law, Dorothy Banda, and mealiemeal from her friend Fatnes Mbewe. Simon's wife, Tisalire Banda, borrows a broom every time she sweeps her house and front yard, which she may do several times a day. People mostly use the possessions of their close kin. It may be that the term "borrow" is a misnomer altogether. Most people seem to share their belongings with relatives without much ado, while a few with a more "modern outlook" make the lack of private property a reason for moving away from the village and close relatives. (See Chapter 5.)

As most food is harvested only once a year, storage technology contributes to the quality and quantity of food at the end of the agricultural season. How long different foods can be stored depends on the season and on the insect and rat population. Wicker baskets, clay pots, and cans are used to store maize flour, millet, green leaves, and smoked meat and fish.

Tyford reports:

> "Food is stored according to different methods. To store food like maize and groundnuts in large quantities, a good storehouse or granary bin is required. Sorghum, pumpkins, millet, and gourds are also stored in the maize granary—nkhokwe—on top of the maize. To store unboiled sweet potatoes one digs a deep hole in the ground and covers the potatoes with earth. Green leaves and vegetables are sundried, or boiled first and sundried afterward for four or five days. Green leaves are wrapped up in the chikwati [a big basket]. At the end of the rainy season every housewife has several vikwati [pl.] hanging from her roof poles, as it is the women's job to store food to last the family throughout the year."

A villager has few and simple tools to prepare and preserve food. To compensate for the lack of equipment there is little a woman can do, but to work hard. And she does. According to the time allocation we made throughout the survey year, a woman spends on average between four and five hours *every* day to prepare the food her family eats. This is about twice the time it takes the villagers to grow and gather food- and cash-crops. As we shall see shortly, there is no chain of activities that is more time consuming than to convert the golden maize grain into the daily nsima—maize mash.

From Maize to Nsima

Food preparation provides a good example of women's ingenuity. It was in the middle of the last century that the Chewa in Zambia replaced their staple crop millet with maize, which had come from the Portuguese of lower Zambezi.[2] Today women utilize the intrinsic qualities of the maize plant to an amazing degree: Maize can be boiled and roasted when it is fresh and when it has dried in the field, and flour can be made from both green and dried maize. There is *nsima*, the everyday staple made from flour and water; *chimbala*—"*nsima* that has slept," which is leftover from the night before; *phala*—porridge made from the water in which maize has been soaked for a couple of days; *masewa*—maize bran, which is used to make porridge; *chibwabwa*—pounded roasted maize eaten by people with poor or no teeth; *mowa*—beer made from germinated maize; *fushala*—boiled dried maize; *vingowe*—unpounded cooked maize; and *msele*, made from the very small grains that are left when the maize has been pounded twice and cooked with salt, sugar, and mashed groundnuts. The maize stalk is eaten too, almost like the sugar cane, and also used for animal fodder. The husk is used to make *kacasu*—liquor. It is also fed to goats and pigs, and cooked and given to dogs and puppies. Husks can also be boiled into a sticky substance that is used to mend cracks in pots and pans. A versatile plant indeed!

It is not only because it takes just three months to mature, or that it can be used for such a variety of recipes and purposes, or its storability, that makes maize so special. It also has another less attractive quality; it is a very time-consuming process to transform the grain to the daily *nsima* meal, at least for a villager with little or no access to modern technology. The process can be divided in eleven stages and together they make the preparation of the daily *nsima* the most time-consuming group of activities that village women undertake: one hour and twenty minutes daily is the average time spent and this includes:

- shelling the maize by removing the grains from the cob,
- pounding the grains to loosen the outer coat,
- winnowing to separate grain and husk,
- soaking the maize in water to start the germination process,
- washing the submerged grains,
- drying the kernels on a mat in the sun,
- taking it to the mill for grinding,
- carrying the ground maize back home,
- spreading the flour out in the sun to dry once more, and
- storing it away.

Only then is it ready to be cooked as *nsima*, the daily staple.

Pounding is too heavy a job to be done well by girls, though they often help their mothers. But adult women must pound, whether they have the strength or not. Elena Ngoma has a lame leg and can hardly walk, but she pounds; so does Brandine Kamanga whose right hand is deformed through polio. Brandine uses only her left arm when pounding. Both women have specially made mortars and pestles, smaller in size than the ordinary ones.

During the hot season, women occasionally take advantage of the cooler night air and rise hours before dawn to do their pounding. Whenever death touches a village, the pounding rhythm is everywhere. The women are busy preparing food for the many hundred visitors that will come to pay their respect to the family of the deceased and mourn with the villagers. On such occasions every village woman is called upon to contribute maize and labor. Pounding is done in groups, and the pulsating beats that soon envelope the village seem to announce that even in the shadow of death life must go on.

Because pounding is so tiresome, women often help each other also on a private basis. On a very hot November day we observed Marin, Faides, Livines, Chanda, and Jessie helping Mwanishupa to pound: "not out of love, but because we want her to help us in return," Jessie explained. It is well known that togetherness makes hard work easier and more enjoyable. So do the rhythms of a pounding song:

Bamuna akakopanda	When your husband beats you
Usalilila pabwalo	Do not cry outside
Pita in nyumba	Go into the house
Nulilila mumwemo	Cry there
Tenga msako	Get a pot
Phika nsima	Cook nsima
Pita nayo mapinda	Take it into the bedroom
Funsa amuna ako	Then ask your husband
Cimene akupandila	Why has he beaten you.

Once kernel and husk have been separated, the maize is winnowed. By the skillful use of the *licelo* basket, the husk is on the ground in no time. The kernels are safely stored in the *citundu* basket. Winnowing too is women's work, but when Evelinar Njobvu was recovering from having given birth two months too early, Kabanda, her husband, dexterously manipulated the winnowing basket.

Next, the grains are soaked in large earthen pots for two to four days. Submerged in water, the maize germinates and develops valuable vitamin B. How women came to enrich their staple in this simple but ingenious way is a mystery. But they thereby make the maize more nutritious and easier to digest. The water, *mteteka,* is used to make porridge or soup, to brew beer, or to feed animals.

Once the maize has been retrieved and dried in the sun, it is ready for the mill. Most women make the trip once or every two weeks. Usually they go in a group, each woman carrying between twenty kilograms and forty kilograms. With such a headload no one tarries on the road. By walking fast, they make the journey in about one hour each way. At the mill there is often a line. No wonder women at times try to persuade their men to take the maize for grinding.

Kabanda is a quiet man and because of his timidity his family seems to think he can be sent everywhere. But Kabanda is now getting increasingly annoyed at being treated as the errand boy of the family. So one day, when Sonile, his mother, asks him to go to the mill, he refuses saying: "Mother, all the time you keep sending me to the grinding mill. I have to sell things for you and do all kinds of jobs. I work hard for our family but you do not even thank me. Since I was young, I have been working for this family, but nobody considers my wants and now I am getting tired." And he adds: "You have got a last born in our family, your son James, but you do not give him jobs like me, and you do not send him to the mill."

And Sonile answers: "James has his own family and his own house." But Kabanda replies: "What about me! Do I sleep in your house? Don't I have my own children? Who is older, James Phiri or I? When will you teach my younger brother to help his family like I do? James is younger than I and has more strength."

Sonile reflects upon what Kabanda has said and finds that he is right. She is wrong to send her older son to do her errands when she has a younger son in the village. She admits: "James is proud, that is why we come to you and ask for help." Kabanda answers: "*Chabwino*—okay, from today don't send me to the grinding mill. I shall do other jobs like making granary bins and selling your tomatoes, but I will not go to the mill. So stop telling the women of the family that they need not go to the mill because Kabanda will go for them. From now on I will not be troubled as long as my younger brother is here, even if he too is married. Our wives can go to the mill themselves and not always rely on us men."

Sonile and Hundred, the husband, agree with what Kabanda has said. And Sonile tells James that from now on he will have to take over jobs that Kabanda used to do. Hundred says: "You, James, when you eat with Kabanda and when you finish the meal, who takes the plates and puts them inside the house?" James answers: "It is I who take the plates because I am young and he is my elder brother. As long as I am here, he cannot take the plates away after eating."

Kabanda asks: "Then why don't you take the maize to the grinding mill, as you are my younger brother?" James answers: "To take maize to the grinding mill is the work of women. It is not our job. If they are ill I can help them, but otherwise it is a job for women." And Kabanda agrees: "James, you are right, when they are busy or sick we can help them, but not otherwise." He turns to the women and announces: "You women, do not always ask my help. If you want to be helped, it is James the youngman of the family you must ask. From now on he will take my place." And Hundred: "Yes, this is proper. You, Kabanda, should have some rest. Let us try to send James as he is the youngman."

But from then on, Sonile tells Evelinar, Kabanda's wife, to go to the Asiba grinding mill.

Though grinding the maize at the mill means a capital outlay of about K. 2 a month, women cultivate surpluses or brew beer to earn the money rather than pounding the maize at home, for pounding is very hard work. They carry the maize ten kilometers and wait for hours in the line. When, occasionally, they grind maize at home, they first soak it in water for a week to soften the grain.

Back from the mill, the women spread the mealiemeal out on a mat to dry. Somebody has to watch the meal lest goats, pigs, and hens help themselves to a treat. Men and children often do this job, recognizing that a woman returning after having walked ten kilometers with a twenty- or thirty-kilogram load on her head is too tired.

The ultimate purpose of all the activities is the *nsima*, the maize mash staple that people eat at least once and preferably two and even three times daily, depending on availability. The actual cooking is simple, once the flour is there. A few handfuls of flour are stirred into heated water, brought to a boil, kept boiling for a few minutes while more flour is added under constant stirring until the paste has the desired thickness. Then it is kept on the fire for a few more minutes, and that is it: *nsima* is ready.

To transform grain to gruel takes a lot of time, but what can a woman do? *Nsima* is the food that sustains people, and as long as industrially processed flour is not available on a *permanent* basis, rural women will continue to spend so much of their time preparing food. They will also continue to cultivate the local maize variety, and not the hybrid recommended by the extension service, because the hybrid cannot be stored with traditional storage methods. It is a vicious circle, and a tremendous challenge to rural development efforts: if industrially processed flour could be bought in rural shops on a *permanent* basis, women would not have to spend so many hours each day converting grain into flour. They could concentrate on growing hybrid maize as they need not store any grain. Their yield would increase many times, not only because the hybrid variety is so much more productive, but also because they could spend more time cultivating. And with a large increase in yield, women's earning capacity could improve radically. But there are dangers involved. If women were to cultivate *only* the hybrid variety and industrially processed flour were suddenly *not* available, people would starve.

And it was to escape hunger that Kefa village was started in the first place. Development is a double-edged sword; it promises relief from hard work and new opportunities, but often at the cost of a new dependency.

Relishes and Other Delicacies

To eat *nsima* means to eat maize paste and relish, that is, a sauce or stew. Only Square Banda and a few others have to be content to eat *nsima* with no other relish but salt, a poor man's food indeed. Others, if they have no relish, are likely to postpone their meal until they can find, beg, borrow, or barter some.

While the *nsima* staple is always the same, there are many relishes. Each has its season, its special properties, and its recipes determined by tradition and by personal taste. Groundnuts are the only relish that is stored in large quantities; in fact, every family and sometimes each spouse has a groundnut bin from which they eat throughout the year (if the harvest was satisfactory). Just like maize, groundnuts are eaten in a variety of ways. Most commonly they are cooked with cooking oil and salt into a stew. And they are eaten fresh, dried, boiled, roasted, or fried, with *nsima* or as a snack in between meals, to relieve hunger or just for pleasure because they are so good. A crying child is easily comforted with a handful of nuts. The groundnut, roasted and pounded into peanut butter, can be stored for months, and groundnut powder, *ntwilo*, is a favorite condiment with a lot of different dishes, meat, fish, and caterpillars included.

A common stew or sauce is made of green leaves or vegetables. During the rainy season women pick leaves in the field, gather whatever they find on their way home from work, and make frequent detours into the bush or fields lying fallow in search for edibles. To gather relish is definitely a woman's job, so much so that Tyford made a special point of it when Micheck Phiri went with his wife to collect *ndelele*—ochra leaves—in a neighboring field. Other men too may pick relish when they come across some; most of them want to help their wives and they also want to eat well. But during *milochi*, when rain pours continuously all day, Sylvester reports: "Most village residents stay at home. Only women are out. They are looking for relish."[3]

By March and April women switch from green leaves to vegetables. Now beans, cowpeas, cucumbers, pumpkins, cabbage, gourds, rape, and sweet potatoes are ripening. This is the time when green leaves and vegetables are dried and stored in the *vikwati*—bundles, to be eaten during the dry season when the earth slowly dries up and nothing grows except wild roots and fruits, and the ever-willing cassava with its leaves and tubers. From June to December women must rely on their own stocks, unless they want to depend on the all-year vegetable growers like Kabanda Nyuni and Simon Sakala.

Agnes reports:

"There is a fast way of cooking all vegetables called *kushola*. The vegetables are cleaned and cut and boiled in water with nothing added but salt or *chidulu* [ash water]. A more refined way to prepare relish is to add tomatoes and onions. This is considered English cooking or *dowi*. Here is how it is done: Tomatoes and onions are cleaned and boiled with very little water. If they are available, *ntwilo* [pounded groundnuts] are mixed into the water and stirred into a porridge, and then salt is added, if there is any in the house. The *dowi* dish is kept boiling for about twenty minutes. We like it a lot, but some older people never eat it because there are no tomatoes and onions in their house, ever."

Chidulu—ash water—is an alkaline solution that softens and gives flavor to leafy vegetables. Women have discovered that *chidulu* is the secret property of the groundnut leaves. To extract it, one needs only to burn the groundnut leaves to ashes, let water seep through the ashes, and there it is, *chidulu*, helping to make leaves from pumpkins, sweet potatoes, ochra, and beans become soft (and also rather slimy!).

Every now and then relish made of meat or fish turns a meal into a very special occasion. And there are special occasions that call for special foods: beef is the most typical ceremonial food, and reserved, almost exclusively, for weddings and funerals, particularly funerals, which are the village event that receives by far the most attention (more on this in Chapter 7). Meat is a real delicacy and most people keep a few goats, pigs, or at least some hens. Pigs and goats play an important role in the mobilization of labor; they can easily be converted into cash or "food for work." Hens are eaten to honor a visitor, assure a friendship, or just to eat well for a meal or two. For example, when Mwanizinga's son-in-law and Sandikonda's daughter came to visit their parents, a hen was slaughtered in both households.

"Whether to slaughter an animal is a matter usually discussed between husband and wife," Brighton reports. "Goats, cattle, sheep, and pigs are killed by the husband because he is strong. Chicken, ducks, and pigeons are slaughtered by the wife. The usual method is to cut the throat with a knife. To kill the cow a strong axe is used to make the cow fall down, and when it is faint the throat is cut with the knife to make it bleed. Fowls too can be slaughtered by us men, if we decide to, yet mostly women do so. But men can do all sorts of activities. People decide to slaughter their domestic animals because they need relish for a visitor, or money or labor to cultivate or do other jobs like making granary bins. Sometimes people slaughter too because they have no food for the animal."

Jessie Tonga consulted with Kwerekani Phiri, the husband, and they decided to slaughter one of their three pigs. Jessie wanted to buy mealiemeal from Chipata. She wanted to spend more time in her field and not have to think about pounding maize. Angripina Sakala slaughtered a pig to give the meat to Micheck Phiri and Esidon Mwale so that they could help her to weed. Zuwaila gave Mwada goat meat and got maize in return. And Mishael Phiri sold his goat when he wanted to go to Lusaka to see his daughter, who was seriously ill.

When an animal is slaughtered, many people come to buy or beg meat. Everything is eaten except hide, hooves, and bones. Lungs, liver, and stomach are cooked in the same way as is the rest of the animal. Blood is cooked into a pudding and eaten as a snack or with nsima. The meat is cut in pieces and boiled for hours to make it tender. Onions, tomatoes, and salt are added, as is oil, if these luxuries are available. The best meat is fried slightly and boiled. Boiling time may be three to four hours. Meat is roasted, too, in thin strips over the fire, or wrapped in leaves and buried in the embers.

Smoking is the usual preservation method. The longer the thin pieces of meat hang on the racks over the fire, the longer they last, and well-smoked meat can last for months during the dry season. But during the rains, meat is soon infested by maggots.

Hunting is a favorite pasttime for many, though from a nutrition point of view it does not amount to much. Kabanda is one who loves going into the bush whenever he has a chance. Usually he takes a dog along as he sets off to look for bush pigs, porcupines, mice or other rodents, and small deer. Shuzi Zulu is another hunter. Once he went to Luangwa Valley to hunt elephants with his uncle, who is a professional hunter with a hunting license, rifle, and Landrover. When Shuzi returned, he had more meat than he and the family could eat. Some was smoked, to be eaten later on, some was given away to friends and relatives, and some was bartered for groundnuts and maize, which Shuzi did not grow that year.

Mouse hunting is a cherished sport in July and August. It is not easy. "*Ziliko nkulinga utatokosa*," say the elders. "You can only know the mouse is there when you have checked by poking a stick into its hole." When the mice have been located they are forced out by smoke, and killed. Jackson Phiri and Livines Sakala, the wife, spent a whole day in August looking for mice, but they returned home with only four. Mice are boiled in a little water and dried before they are eaten.

Fish[4] is another much cherished relish. *Kapenta* can be bought from itinerant fishmongers, like the visitor who stayed in Sonile's house for two days in January. She had come from the Valley to sell dried fish in the area, and for a few days Sonile's house was turned into a fish stall. *Kapenta*, the most inexpensive fish, is also very tasty. For a handful Sonile's visitor charged only 20 ngwee, and two handfuls are enough to provide relish for an entire family. In return for her hospitality Sonile got *kapenta* and bream for free. Like almost all fish they were smoked.[5]

Mwaniyana Zulu is a Kefa resident business woman. Regularly she goes to Malambo and Malawi to buy smoked and dried fish, which she resells wherever she finds a profit.

In Kefa village and its surroundings the supply of fish is irregular. This is why when she went to Chipata, Mwanizinga Mbewe bought bream for K. 3.20. Mwanizinga comes from one of the richest households in the village, and she will store the fish to feed her family well.

Women often wash dried and smoked fish in hot water to rid it of sand and insects before it is cooked, or rub the fish between their hands to remove such unwanted additions. *Kapenta*, which is very small, is boiled for just five minutes, the bream much longer. Little water is used; cooking oil, salt, or *ntwilo* groundnut powder are added sometimes.

Milk is another commodity that people with money buy. Kefa Mwale, Robert Manda, and Kathontho Mwale, the three big cattle owners in Kefa village, sell milk daily. Dorothy Phiri, Faides Phiri, Livines Sakala, and some others are regular buyers. A bottle costs 30 ngwee. They buy it to make milk porridge, a favorite breakfast food for children among those who can afford it.

Special Foods

Certain foods are considered unsuitable for people who are ill or for pregnant women. Some such prohibitions may protect the eater, while others serve to protect whatever is not being eaten. There are no absolute rules against eating eggs, but most people don't. They prefer chicken meat.

But the practice that women must not eat the tail of a hen, *kateya-kateya*, benefits men and not the hen. The headman Kefa explains:

"The great-grandparents made this rule and it is a custom so that a wife can respect her husband. Men are not told they must not eat things, only women are, and this is natural. Women must also not eat *ng'ambwa* or *bwanda*, which is a 'mouse with a very fat taste.' It lives underground but not in groups like other mice. My opinion is that if women eat the tail-end of a hen, she will become too sexy for a man to handle, because hens are very sexy. And if they eat this mouse, they will be fat, and the man will lose all his powers when he sleeps with her.

"Other foods that women do not eat are determined by the tribe. Maybe their people were not used to that food, or used the food once to cure them of some disease.

"In the case of men, I have never heard that they must not eat things because of tradition. When men do not eat certain foods, they do not like the taste, or they have used it for medicine. Simon Tonga, for example, does not eat *nsima* because his doctor in the hospital advised him not to because of his ulcer."

Independence Day on October 25th, Christmas Day, and New Year's Day are celebrated with special foods, which according to Sylvester "are not very African."

This is what Sylvester wrote about such celebrations:

"In general it can be said that people like to make something out of the ordinary, or something special out of Christmas and New Year's. At Christmas the roads are full of people walking about in their best clothes. (You know, some few people in Kefa are *very* Christian. Some are at certain periods, or for Christmas, but not otherwise. Most people combine traditional and Christian religion. But still, if they have time and money, they will relax on December 25th.) They want to eat good food like *nsima* with relish like meat and rice. To be able to afford it, people save money little by little, brewing beer or selling groundnuts and vegetables. Some rush to the baker to buy scones, breads, and biscuits, and sugar to make tea. On such days people drink a lot of tea, and this causes problems because of the shortage of sugar. But people make the best of it. Those who drink alcohol want plenty of beer and *kacasu* (local liquor).

"Those who do not have any money just go on an excursion along the roads, while others visit their relatives, or stay at home drinking or dancing. For some people, Christmas is the day when Christ was born, and they spend the day in prayer.

"At Chikuwe village there were *Chimtali* dances this Christmas. *Chimtali* is a women's dance. Margret Banda and a few other ladies beat the drum. The men stood around watching the women. The dance started at 9 p.m. There was also a band playing and to that music everybody danced throughout the night until the next morning at 8 a.m. And dancing started again at noon.

"There was also plenty of food—pork was sold at 10 ngwee apiece and there were mangoes, tea, bread, and alcoholic drinks for sale. For mere relaxation cigarettes and gambling were available. Some people started fighting just out of drunkenness!

"The villagers celebrate Christmas more than New Year's Day. At Christmas people eat and drink a lot, but on New Year's they just sit idle on their porch. Some attend a dance. One reason why people celebrate Christmas more is that they have no money left when New Year's comes. Whatever they had is already spent. New Year's is not cheerful like Christmas."

Making and Sharing Beer

"There are three different types of beer," Tyford explains. "One is the beer that is for sale. Then there is the beer that is drunk at funerals and weddings. And there is the *kavinde*—the secret beer that is made in small quantities to attract and please husbands and best friends. *Kavinde* is drunk secretly inside a person's house without many people knowing about it. But all beers are made the same way, they are all *masese*—the seven-day's beer."

The *masese* has got its name because it takes five days to make and two days to drink it. But before the brewing can start maize must be pounded and submerged in water for a few days, kept in a wicker basket for a week or so to sprout, and then dried and pounded again, this time together with millet. Only when the maize and millet have been pounded, steel drum, clay pots, and containers have been found, and plenty of water and firewood have been brought to the village, is a woman ready to start her seven-day's beer.

On the first day the maize and millet flour is boiled for half a day in the steel drum. Then it is put back into clay pots for the residue to sink to the bottom. At this stage the beer is *mtawa*. It is sweet and can be drunk. On the second day it is put back in the steel drum and boiled once more for eight hours or so. Now it becomes *thobwa*, which can still be drunk. On the third day the brew rests and is no longer tasty. On the fourth day a little ground millet is added for reaction and the beer can be tasted. On the fifth day millet and water are boiled into a thick porridge that is stirred into the brew. Now it becomes *chinya*, a beer that is enjoyed very much by women and children who do not drink the regular beer. After half a day *chinya* becomes *mowa wapya*—new beer. Finally, on the sixth day it is *mowa*—beer, the most loved and cherished drink in thousands of villages and homesteads all over Africa. Now neighbors, friends, and passersby flock to the house of the beer maker to sample, buy, or beg beer. As the owner of the beer keeps adding water to her brew to stretch the supply, the alcoholic content, which at no point is very high, keeps going down. When the drum is about empty the residue is filtered through some old sack (like used fertilizer bags) and squeezed so that no drop is lost.[6]

The main beer "season" is just after harvest when there is plenty of maize and millet and money around and people have the time it takes to brew and enjoy beer. During the cold season, from the end of June throughout August, every village has one or more "beer houses," that is, houses temporarily turned into bars. But during the busy agricultural season this practice changes abruptly. From December to June only sixteen Kefa women brew beer and the most thirsty village residents have to go outside the village to drink. Some villagers grow such a thirst for beer that, when Mwanishupa Phiri started brewing in March, they refused to wait until the beer was properly matured but finished it all on the fifth day, at the *chinya* stage. Mwanishupa tried the best she could to stop people from drinking her beer at this stage, but ended up selling *mowa mwapya*. She even gave the headman his traditional gourd on the fifth day.

On very special days like weddings and funerals, and during the hair-cutting ceremony after a funeral, beer plays a central part. Headman Kefa put it this way:

> "Funeral beer is given away for free. It is mostly sweet beer, made by boiling millet and maize, and can be drunk on the second day. Children, everybody likes it. People like to drink at funerals and during the hair-cutting ceremony so that everyone can be happy and forget about their sorrow. In this way they regain their strength to go about their daily duties like before.
>
> "*Kavinde* is a beer that old people like. It is brewed when the husband asks his wife to do so, and he may also help the wife by cutting firewood. It is brewed in a clay pot and not in a drum, secretly inside the house. The husband tells his friends to come to his house and share in this beer so that it can be known among his friends that his wife loves him."

Not only old people cherish *kavinde*. One day we found Timeke Daka busy preparing *kavinde* for the youngman who intends to marry her daughter, and she did so to please him.

Beer has many functions. It underlines reciprocal feelings of love and obligations. It is the rallying point of days of festivity like Independence Day, Christmas, and other special days. It plays an important part at weddings and funerals. It enables people to mobilize labor during the peak agricultural season and provides women with the opportunity to channel male earnings into their own pockets. It enables people to rejoice and to mourn, to remember and to forget, to share and to sponge, and to earn and to waste.

Sharing Food

> "Women cook and then they share the food like this: one plate for the men, one plate for the children, one plate for the mother and grandmother and sister, one plate for the young children, and one plate for the wife. If a visitor comes, even if I, the husband, have eaten my share, we tell him to eat with us. And even if very little food is left, we eat with him. If there is a visitor and no food, we tell the wife to cook again. A visitor no matter when he comes will always join us eating. It is a wife's duty to see that there is food in the house, and the man helps her by cultivating or buying relish," Lemekani explains.

When it comes to meals, men are the most important persons. When food is scarce, many women eat very little or nothing at all. If the husband is away or eats in somebody else's house, many a time we found that the wife did not cook at all. Children are also important. We often observed that a mother cooked extra when a child asked her to or "was crying from hunger."

That a wife no longer cooks for a husband or the husband refuses to take food from his wife means that the marriage is facing a crisis.

In Jessie Tonga's household Kwerekani Phiri no longer eats *nsima*, not from Jessie Tonga or from Tisauke Phiri, his two Kefa village wives. Neither does he sleep in Jessie's house. When this had been going on for some time, Jessie decided to consult Mtunduwathu Kamanga, her *n'khoswe* or marriage counselor. (See Chapter 6.) She asked Mtundu to help her and the husband to come to terms. She stated the problem: "Mtunduwathu Kamanga, you are our *n'khoswe*—please help us as we have got some trouble in our house. And this is our problem; my husband does not sleep, nor does he eat *nsima*, in my house. So please advise us how to solve this problem."

And Mtundu said to Kwerekani: "Is this true, what your wife is saying?" Kwerekani answered: "Yes, it is true. And the reason is this: When I come to this place [Kwerekani has a job outside the village], my wife gives me neither water to wash nor *nsima* to eat, nor mealiemeal to take to my work camp. When I look for such help she says she cannot give it because I do not help her in the field. So the only thing I can do is to refuse to eat *nsima* from her and to sleep in her house, because she has told me not to."

And Mtunduwathu said, "You, Jessie Tonga, is it true what Kwerekani says?" And Jessie admitted: "It is true. But I forget, and I cook *nsima* for him when he comes here for the weekend and I boil water for him to wash, but he still refuses me."

Mtundu asked: "Did Kwerekani not help in the field by giving you money?" Jessie said: "He gives me money to employ people, but I want him himself to work in my field, I don't want his money."

But Mtundu said, "Please, Jessie Tonga, this is bad thinking on your behalf. Do not repeat it. Kwerekani is not wrong, but you yourself are. You are an old woman. You have lived too long to behave so stupidly. If Kwerekani gives you money so that you can pay others to work in the field and buy clothes, soap, and paraffin, he is not bad. So from today, Jessie Tonga, you must cook *nsima* and boil water for him to wash himself and make mealiemeal for him which he can take to his working place. If you do not, you are no longer to be trusted as a wife, and I will ask the headman to call a village meeting and you will be ashamed of your behavior in front of the young people who will gather to hear your problem."

And Mtundu said to Kwerekani: "You are the head of this family. Do not behave like a woman. You are a man, so do not follow the ways of women. You should have called people to advise you on this problem when it arose, rather than doing nothing the way you did. It was your wife only who came to me, your counselor, so that this trouble between you could be ended."

It is not only between spouses that food is a matter of trust or contention. At Kapale Health Center one day, we found a sad example of the latter. It was in January, when granary bins were being emptied in many households. The problem arose because of hunger. Brighton reports:

"Mr. Nyirenda had gone out for beer, and when he returned drunk and found his daughter-in-law cooking *nsima* he got very annoyed. And he said: 'Why do you cook *nsima* with the last mealiemeal we have, when I am away?' The daughter-in-law answered: 'It is my mother-in-law who told me to cook.' Mr. Nyirenda said: "Don't you know that you are wrong?" but she retorted: 'No, I don't know I am wrong, so you must ask your wife who told me to cook.' Nyirenda took the *nsima* porridge from the fire and poured it on his son's wife and said: 'You have finished all my food. I work hard for my own self, and not for you and your husband.' And he added: 'You great eater of a woman!' And then he beat her.

"When the husband came, he found the wife badly burned and beaten by the father. And the father said: "I have no mealiemeal to feed all of you." So the son took the wife to Kapala Health Center. He also brought a bag of mealiemeal along. Now he is waiting for the wife to get well so that he can go to the local court to ask for judgment against his own father."

In olden times all the men in the village used to eat together as did the women. Villages were smaller then and most people in the same village were closely related. These days men and women still eat separately most of the time, but today's eating groups rarely consist of more than eight people. Women are said to cook better when the food will be shared in a group. Each wants to show her friends that she is a good cook with more than enough food in the house. Children mostly prefer to eat with their mothers as it is the mother who decides who eats what. The men get the better and bigger shares, but how good and how big is up to the woman and she often leaves some extras for the children. But when boys grow up, they want to be with the men. There are no rules as to who eats with whom except that a son-in-law must not eat in company with the mother-in-law.

Spouses who enjoy each other's company, like Mwada and Micheck, usually eat together. But it may reflect badly on a woman if she eats with the husband (or other men) too often.

Some families are "more extended" than others. Brighton reports:

"Sonile Ng'uni and Hundred Banda have two sons, Kabanda Nyuni and James Phiri [their second names indicate that they are not Hundred Banda's sons]. Kabanda is the first-born and has a wife and two children. James Phiri has a wife and three children. And there is Mwada Simba, who is a younger [very extended] sister of Sonile. Mwada has one son, Henly, and her husband Micheck here in Kefa village. All of these people eat *nsima* together."

Dorothy Banda explains how the women of the family divide the cooking duties among themselves:

"No, we do not have a timetable. Each one knows that she must cook once a day. When we are busy, and Mrs. Hundred Banda cooks *nsima* in the afternoon, then we, the young women, know that when the sun sets one of us must go home and make food. Whoever cooks also cleans pots and plates at the same time. And when somebody has cooked, we all eat, and whoever has not cooked yet knows that the next meal is entirely up to her. But if one of us does not have relish, she goes to her friend or to the boss, Sonile [the mother-in-law], and begs relish. As she cooks also for Sonile and her husband, there are no problems. We also do not lack relish because Kabanda and James have their vegetable gardens."

And Brighton adds: "Because they are well off, this family works together without any problems."

Other families share food on a less regular basis. Particularly on occasions like childbirth, neighbors and relatives come with food gifts. When Tisalire had a baby, Simon the husband was observed eating *nsima* three times between midday and one o'clock. And Tisalire got cooked pumpkin from Janet Lungu and from Tilolele Banda, sweet beer cooked by Lelia Mbewe, and *nsima* by Christina Banda, all on the same day. Everybody was happy and wanted to congratulate them with food.

On other occasions too, women share food and help each other. It is as Brighton has said: "Women are too good to each other." When Faides ran out of mealiemeal, Mwanishinga gave her some, and when goats finished her relish on Christmas Day, Tisauke helped her. When Evelinar gave *nsima* to Dorothy, Dorothy passed it on to Tisalire, because she was not hungry. When Livines Sakala was away, her husband, Jackson, ate from Mwanishupa "because she is his sister." Some days later Jackson gave Mwanishupa cabbage and tomatoes from his vegetable garden. And when Livines had a baby, Mwanishupa sent her *nsima*, just as Jenifa, Nabien, and Agnes gave *nsima* to Tisalire when her baby was born. Tisauke was reported sending *nsima* to Jessie Tonga, the first wife of her husband, to Ida Lungu whose son died recently, and to Dorothy because she had a new baby.

When Faides was sick, Mwada drew water for her and pounded her maize. When Mwada's maize meal ran out, Dorothy helped her. Yegge Njbovu helped Dorothy draw water for brewing "because Yegge is the wife of the brother of Dorothy's mother-in-law."

Still, cooperation is certainly not always prevalent. Tyford reports:

"Kabanda Nyuni had been given pig meat by Mr. Munga whose pig Kabanda had been looking after for some time. When he smoked the meat, Kabanda used the wife's firewood, but Evelinar got annoyed and told him to use his own firewood. And Kabanda got annoyed too, but shifted the fire to far outside the porch, complaining angrily that 'It is the confusion I dislike, I do not understand a woman's mind. I will give her meat so why should I not use her firewood.'

"When he was busy smoking his pork, Rahaby Sakala came by and asked

Evelinar to lend her Kabanda's axe. But Kabanda got annoyed again: 'Women do not take proper care of axes when they chop wood, and I refuse entirely to give a woman my axe. You go and get somebody else's axe, as I will certainly not give a woman my axe.'

"Micheck supported Kabanda: 'I too would not lend my axe to a woman. The elders say it: *Nkhwangwa yobwereka sikhala kuguluka*—a borrowed axe easily flies off its handle. It is better if people have their own things, so that they do not depend on borrowing other people's belongings all the time.' And so Rahaby had to leave, having been refused an axe twice.

"It seems that Kabanda did not want to lend his axe to avenge the pain his wife had caused him by refusing him her firewood, and not because he did not want to help Rahaby."

Most people practice *kupatsa nkuika*—to give is to save, for everybody needs the help of others at some time or other. Mwada Simba cooked for Sandikonda Daka when Mwanishupa was in Chipata to see her relative who was ill, though Mwada and Sandikonda are not related. And, when Sandikonda was in the field, he passed by the outskirt of the forest and tied up a bundle with firewood, which he carried home and gave to Mwada, though she had not asked for it. When Mwada wanted to refuse the gift, Mwanishupa was the one who persuaded her to accept. So Sandikonda left the bundle at Mwada's door, just to make her happy.

Housekeeping

Firewood and water are women's responsibility. Men can and do, of course, help, but it is not their job. It is a woman's job, for "they have stronger necks than men."

Firewood is no problem. Kefa village is surrounded by bush and forest, and a fallen tree or branch is the property of whoever carries it home. It is a woman's job to see that there is firewood in the house, but men again help. As the three-stone fireplace consumes whole logs, it is not necessary to chop the wood except to start the fire.

Water must be brought home every day. People, goats, pigs, dogs, and chicks need to drink. Husbands want to wash their faces and hands in the morning or at night when the day's work is over. Children dirty themselves. Vegetables must be cleaned before they are boiled. Hands are washed before and after meals. And the women need water to cook *nsima*, relish, and porridge, to soak pounded maize, and to brew beer.

The water hole is only three-quarters of a kilometer away from the village, down by the *dambo*, the wetland. In the cold and dry season when people are not very busy, women usually go to the *dambo* in the early morning or late evening. By the end of the dry season in September and October, when it has not rained for four or five months, the women often have to dig for water as the water hole is empty. It is best that they bring drinking water from the lined well two kilometers down the road towards Kalichero. And the men have to take the cattle to the Rural Council Dam three kilometers away.

At this time of the year, water usage is reduced to an absolute minimum. Children and adults wash in the same bowl and feed the water to the pigs afterward. Beer is no longer brewed. Some women even get up in the middle of the night, provided there is a moon to light the way, hoping that some water has seeped into the waterhole.

In November the rain starts, but problems are not over. Everything overflows and the water becomes exceedingly dirty. On some days it is so dirty that the women may decide not to draw any at all. This is a time when everybody complains of stomach disorders.

How much water a woman carries in a day depends on how much water there is, the size of her family, her ambitions as to cleanliness, her strength, and the number of daughters who can help her. Nyawa, nine, Esnaya, twelve, and Alines, sixteen, draw water regularly and also wash pots and plates, clothes, and themselves down by the water hole. Water-carrying is heavy. A full debe can weighs twenty kilograms, but even small girls can carry some water home. Because water-carrying is a tough job women help each other "not for love, but because they want other women to help them in turn."

Clothes and utensils are washed by the water hole. If a household can afford it, soap is used. Clothes are dried on the ground or on a clothes line. Lubinda Mwale, the cattle owner, is the only one owning an iron. Because an iron is a prestigious possession, Lubinda usually does the ironing himself.[7] Washing clothes, utensils, and children is usually done by the women, though men wash their own clothes at times. Kabanda is a man who does all kinds of housekeeping jobs including carrying full debe cans of water home. His problem is that Evelinar, the wife, is not very hard-working.

In the rainy season both men and women prefer to bathe in the river. To most soap is a luxury. A favorite bathing spot is that where the path to the fields crosses Mtewe river. All who approach the river call out loudly that they are coming to give a bather the opportunity to cover him or herself. Nobody wants to take his mother-in-law at her bath by surprise.

To Square Banda water is a problem. In the rainy season he digs a hole by his house and collects rain water. In the dry season he begs, buys, and barters water. He does not use much. Even the customary hand wash before and after meals is something he rarely can afford; he usually skips the first and wipes his fingers on the grass after the meal. Sometimes Square negotiates with young children to carry water for him. Twaibu, who is eight, does so occasionally, particularly when Square needs water for his special business, which is hat-making. To be a cripple does not mean that people do not expect you to work. But when Sandikonda Daka came to Square Banda's house and begged him for drinking water, Square got annoyed: "Don't you feel sorry for me? I have hardly any water and yet you come and beg water from me!" And to himself he muttered: "People in this village are too proud. They are haughty when they see a poor fellow like me, yet they too go begging for water."

The provision of fuel and water is the most demanding housekeeping job, and the most regular. Sweeping too is done at least once and sometimes several times a day, but because it is not heavy work it is often done by grandmothers and daughters. A newly swept house and compound look very neat and nice.[8] It is the women's responsibility to keep the surroundings neat.[9] When the rain comes, the dusty village floor turns green overnight, but as the grass starts growing, women try hard to keep it down. When they do not, the headman or his deputy or some neighbors are likely to complain. The look of the village is everybody's concern and reflects the cleanliness and orderliness of all the village residents.

More than anything else the housing standards signal the well-being of a village. Mud-and-wattle houses with thatched grass roofs have to be maintained regularly and this too is mostly women's responsibility. When building a new house, the men put up the skeleton made of poles and bamboo, while the women cover the structure with mud. The women cut the grass needed for the roof and the men thatch the roof. As it stands, a house, whether round or square, big or small, is the result of a cooperative effort of both sexes, each has its specialty, each is indispensable. To map how the chain of cooperation links every man and every woman in the village presupposes a study of networks that we never ventured upon. But it exists and makes a village very different from an urban settlement.

But mud-and-wattle houses soon grow old. Roofs have to be renewed every second year, and the rest of the house about every ten years. Scorching sun, torrential rains, termites, and even the small biting ants make roofs rot, walls crack, houses fall down, and people move out. To make a new house means plenty of work, but a new house is always much better than the old one.

Headman Kefa is much concerned with the appearance of his village. Old houses are torn down and burned and village residents admonished and encouraged to keep their houses and the village neat. And it shows. To maintain the environment is a major obligation of any village resident. After all, it is the environment that keeps the villagers.

Notes

1. About mortars Whitby writes: The most common type in most parts of the country is tall, more or less tubular at the top but with the interior narrowing toward the base and finally rounded off. Large mortars of this type, 2 to 3 feet high, are used for separating finger-millet and other grains from the heads, or for pounding maize, rice, sorghum, and sometimes cassava. Smaller ones, about 1½ feet high, are used for groundnuts, leafy vegetables, and other relish ingredients." (Whitby, 1972:12.)

2. "By the mid-nineteenth century, if not before, the northern Chewa had largely replaced their staple crop, millet, with maize which reached them from the Portuguese on the lower Zambezi. This greatly increased the agricultural productivity of Mkanda's kingdom. Yet Mkanda's maize fields and cattle were also his undoing for they powerfully attracted the Ngoni." (Roberts, 1976:119.)

3. "Besides collecting wood and water the woman has to provide relish, and this takes up much of her time at certain seasons of the year. During the rainy months regular expeditions are made daily to look for mushrooms. Women and girls go out with carrying baskets and line up across the bush, each picking what she finds. Such an expedition might take two or three hours. Wild spinaches have also to be looked for, and in the hot weather the girls are sent to gather *Icikanda* orchids . . . or the different wild fruits. Even when garden vegetables are available it may be necessary to walk two or three miles to a distant field to pick them. This is specially so when the gourds and pumpkins ripen, and it is reckoned that every other day the housewife must go out to her gardens to pick them as they reach their prime. All these accessory activities have somehow to be fitted into the day besides the regular gardening and cooking," Richards writes of the Bemba women of the 1930s. (Richards, 1938:103.) It is also very much the life of Chewa women two generations later, except that in Kefa village most people have their fields and gardens closer at hand than did the Bembas.

4. *Kapenta* or *ndagaa* (*Limnothrissa* and *Stolothrissa*) are small herringlike fish of Lake Tanganyika, most abundantly caught between June and November. There are related genera, that are less commercially important in Lake Mweru. Like other herring family members, they have oily flesh that contains vitamin A.

5. Smoking is an old and much used conservation method. Now and again extension staff and others point out that fish should be smoked better to make it more resistant to insect attacks. When fishermen and traders do not follow the advice, it is not only because longer smoking means more firewood, but because it also reduces profits, as smoked fish is sold by weight and more smoking means reduced water content in the fish. Thus improved quality is likely to depend on a pricing system that is not weight-based.

6. "The process of beer-making is the longest and most skilled operation . . . the housewife can undertake. The brewing may take from four to seven days and the varying temperature and moisture of the air affect its success, so that with the most experienced brewer there is always an element of luck. No housewife could give me exact instructions as to the quantities of grain used and the time taken, but was apparently guided by a judgement based on long experience, or as she herself would express it, with vigour: 'Young girls can't make beer. Only we elders know how to brew.' " So Richards (1939:97) observed some fifty years ago among the Bemba people.

7. ". . . in particular, ironing is considered a fashionable employment and one that is a mark of wealth and status. As such, it is chiefly in the hands of the men . . ." (Richards, 1939:103.)

8. "The floor, used as kitchen table, chair, and cupboard, must be swept with a grass brush once or twice a day. Though it is not scrubbed, it is frequently mudded over afresh. This is done sometimes for ritual purposes before relighting a new fire ceremonially and sometimes for reasons of cleanliness only. Small babies are allowed to urinate all over the floor, but adults, even in the last stages of illness, demand to be carried outside for this purpose however cold the night. Sleeping mats are washed frequently and blankets put out to air in the sun. The washing of eating vessels is simplified by the Bemba custom of sharing from one dish." (Richards, 1939:101.)

9. Our time allocation study reveals that the average Kefa village woman spends an average of 40 minutes per day on jobs like sweeping, washing clothes and utensils, and keeping the home in good order. The men spent an average of 2 minutes per day on such activities.

CHAPTER 5   OTHER ECONOMIC ACTIVITIES

Wolinda citsime sakufa ndi ludzu
Who Looks After a Well Does Not Die of Thirst

It seems that Kefa village residents depend on money quite a lot. They participate in many happy activities when they have money.

A villager's view

Fertile fields and competent cooking are the main sources of well-being in Kefa village, but the villagers also pursue other activities in order to live well. Some own cattle and other livestock, some brew and sell beer and even illicit liquor, and some practice a craft or have a specialized skill. And off and on there are those who run a business, that is, buy things to sell them again. Just like cultivation, such activities provide people with money, depending on the wisdom, ability, and ambitions of the person who undertakes them. They also enable the villagers to eat and drink well, or in other ways enjoy the products involved. In a village like Kefa, the use of a product is still more important than its exchange value.

But money is important, too. Tools, clothes, blankets, pots, and pans must be acquired and renewed from time to time, and these take money. Every week or so a woman goes to the mill to grind maize. Children need school uniforms; occasionally anybody may want to ride on the bus; illnesses necessitate medicine and advice must be bought; and weddings and funerals entail expenses, particularly for the families most directly affected, but also for the others that participate. And there are luxuries like sugar, salt, soap, and paraffin that anybody with a bit of extra money would like to have in stock in their home.

Money is an insignia of success. If spent on consumers' goods or shared with others at parties or during ceremonies, it confers status and respect on the owner. However, as we shall see, money is also a source of tension and conflict.

Cattle and Other Domestic Animals

Next to cultivation, domestic animals generously contribute to the good village living. The cow is the most treasured of all animals. It can be used to acquire a wife for oneself (if you are a man) or for a relative, and as a *lobola* gift to compensate a wife's family of origin so that the children she bears belong to the husband's lineage. It produces a daily bottle of milk, or so, throughout most of the year. When there is death in the village, a cow can feed innumerable visitors and confer respect and honor upon the deceased as well as on the owner of the animal. It can produce more cows and oxen that can be trained as draught animals. Cow dung makes vegetables thrive and vegetable growers prosper. And, as member of a herd, a cow stirs the feeling of love and pride in the fortunate owner. It can even, if need be and there are no other means of raising money, be sold and thus meet expenses that could not otherwise have been met. And, when Lubinda Mwale was released from prison having served his sentence for manslaughter, it was when he had transferred some cattle to Kwezekani Mbewe's family that he reestablished his rights as a Kefa village resident.

The symbiosis between man and domestic animal is part of an old African tradition. It is a cooperation that gives much and asks comparatively little of both parties involved. Just like the people, the Zebu cattle are hardy and well adapted to local conditions.[1] Kefa Mwale, the owner of a herd of ten heads, explains to us:

> "Generally, there are not many problems involved in keeping cows. Every year the cattle *khola* [enclosure] must be rebuilt, and in the rainy season the animals must be herded so that they do not destroy crops, lest the owner have to pay damage. Some people share in looking after each others' animals, so that one goes with the herd in the morning, and the other in the afternoon. Those who have children send them to herd, while they themselves cultivate. Among the village residents, it is we, the cattle owners, who are the most respected.

The cattle enclosures are made of tree trunks interconnected with wire. The cattle *khola* are all at the outskirt of the village, close to their owners' house. At night the animals are closed in to protect them against leopards and hyenas that roam about and prey on the village.

Also here theory and practice may vary. Headman Kefa has two sons in the village: Pascale is sixteen and David is eighteen, but neither helps his father to herd. In fact, their refusal to cooperate has been so adamant that Kefa called his brother Lemekani and together the two elders admonished the boys, saying that they deserve no part in their father's herd unless they change their behavior and obey their father.

In the past, Simon Sakala used to herd for the headman, who is Simon's mother's brother. For his many years of service, Kefa gave Simon a cow and a bicycle. The cow served Simon as bride wealth payment and enabled him to marry on his own, without further support from his relatives. When Simon got his own household and started cultivating hybrid and vegetables, Kefa turned to his brother Lemekani and asked him to help with the cattle. Since Kefa's sons are "utterly useless," as Kefa himself tells us, Kefa and Lemekani have looked after the headman's herd during the rainy season.

Recently the two brothers had an argument:

> Lemekani says: "Everybody keeps their cattle in our *khola* and they pay
> you to look after their animals, but when do I get my pay? You told me I
> would get a cow from the herd if I would help you look after the animals
> during the rainy season, but the rains have long stopped, and I have got
> nothing. This is why I ask you. Where is my remuneration?"
>
> Kefa answered: "Yes, I said I would give you a cow, but you did not
> help me in the way I expected. You went away to build houses and I had
> to milk and herd alone, so do not ask me now for a cow. When I really needed
> your help, Mr. Zulu took you away for K. 100 [which Lemekani got to help
> Mr. Zulu build his house], so just forget about getting any cow from me.
> Maybe next year, when I need your help, if you stay with me and help me
> properly, I may give you a heifer. But not this year."

Lemekani Mbao already is the owner of two cows and a small bull
calf. He is one of five villagers who keep their cattle in Kefa's *khola*. Like
most people, Lemekani started with one cow, which he got long ago for
K. 36. That cow mothered his present three animals and two oxen, which
he sold for K. 80 and K. 60. This money he used to pay bridewealth for
his two sons.

Every morning Lemekani milks the cows in Kefa's *khola*. To do so he
ties the hind legs of the cow. Eight cows give about ten bottles of milk.
One bottle is kept by Lemekani as thanks for doing the job. One bottle
is for the headman's first wife; one for the fourth wife; one for Twaibu,
Kefa's grandson; and one for Morrisse, the great-grandson. The remaining five bottles are usually sold. Dorothy Banda and a few others are
among the regular buyers, provided they have the 12 ngwee that is the
price from the regular customers. Others pay 15 ngwee If there are no
buyers in the village, Kefa or somebody else takes the milk to sell it outside the village.

Milking takes place once each day so that the calves can also drink.
Only men milk, because they are strong and fearless of the cow. Lemekani
explains:

> "Women can only be involved in this difficult job by standing in front
> of the cow, threatening it with a stick so that it does not move all the time.
> But a woman must never enter the cattle *khola*. That will upset the regular
> order of things. You know, the women just like cows have their fertility cycle.
> If the two [women and cows] get mixed up, this may upset the cow's fertil-
> ity. A woman can milk if she is able, but I tell you, the job is very tough.
> But as long as she is still young [and fertile] she must never go into the *khola*,
> that is an absolute rule. And here nobody wants to challenge it. Cows are
> so important. Women can own cattle, that is all right, but it is better if the
> animals belong to us men."

Jessie Tonga is a woman who keeps and looks after her two cows herself, while Mwada Simba and Mtole Mbao have given their cattle to be looked after by their relatives who stay in other villages.

The system of keeping and looking after other people's animals, and having relatives or friends look after yours is widespread and ingenious. *Kuikijya*[2]—the "putting out system"—serves so many purposes. It is a way to show trust and love because an animal is a living treasure that is not handed over to just anybody. It is a way to protect one's property, because if disease were to wipe out an entire *khola* population, it is good to have at least one or two animals elsewhere. It promotes equal opportunities, as those who cannot afford to buy or barter can still acquire a herd of their own by looking after somebody's cow, pig, or goat and receiving offspring as thanks. And it permits women-headed households and other families short of male labor to invest or maintain their capital in cows, even if they do not have the labor it takes to herd and look after the animals.

In the 1950s, a number of cattle owners had their oxen trained as draught animals. With the arrival of the tractors in the end of the 1960s, however, it became increasingly difficult to get ox-drawn equipment. In Kefa, Lubinda is the only one who now owns trained oxen. Kazembe, Lubinda's son, and Kazembe's friend Ellain work with the oxen in other people's fields. James the basket-maker knows how to train oxen and to carve yokes for the animals. Sometimes he borrows Robert Manda's oxen and carries loads for people, for a fee.

In return for all it provides people, the cow asks only for a safe place to sleep at night. Robert Manda and Lubinda Mwale are the big cattle owners in Kefa village. Each of them has more than thirty heads, and each owns his own *khola*.

Occasionally Asian traders visit Kefa village in order to buy cattle. The average cow is worth three times the monthly salary of an unskilled government laborer, and a fine animal may fetch twice that amount. Still, money is transient, while a cow is a treasure that can be enjoyed for its beauty, strength, and productivity, and for the status is confers upon its owner. Thus, only rarely do the Asian traders go away with such a big animal as a cow or a heifer.[3]

Goats and pigs are also walking capital, but of lesser magnitude. On the other hand they are easier to invest in and easier to convert into money, whether they are sold to Asian traders or slaughtered and exchanged for labor. Most households in the village own a few goats or a few pigs, or both. The number varies from one day to the next because of the tran-siency of life and the varying needs of the owner and his or her family.

Zuwaila used to be the biggest goat owner in Kefa village, with a total of twenty-four animals. When he decided to divorce his wife and leave the village he sold them all. Micheck Phiri bought three of them with his wife Mwada's money. The investment was part of some very sound economic dispositions; when Mwada's daughter got married, the mother received K. 100 as part of the marriage payment. Rather than buy food with the money, Mwada bought a young cow, which since then has calved three times. Recently Mwada sold a heifer for K. 120. Another heifer she has given to her relatives who had been looking after the cow and calves in Lundazi town. So now, out of the initial K. 100 Mwada has one cow and a calf with her relatives in Lundazi and three goats here in Kefa village. The goats are kept in the same *khola* in which Micheck, Mwada's husband, keeps a pig for Alick Phiri. We shall learn more about the pig later.

"Goats are the most troublesome creatures in the village," Micheck Phiri says. "They break into people's houses and eat whatever they find, in fact they destroy just everything. The rules are such that the owner of the goat must pay for whatever his goat destroys. As the goats trouble so many innocent villagers, some people cannot refrain from casting insults upon the owner. For that reason a good animal keeper must not be short-tempered and answer back with insults to people abusing him because their possessions have been eaten. Earlier, goats used to be herded the same way cattle are, but nowadays they have the freedom to graze wherever they want. If anybody has a field close to the village, he will have to shift or build a fence; otherwise, the goats will trouble him to no end. Unlike cattle, goats have their own conscience to return home in the evening. It is the man's job to close them in at night, but if the husband has a pressing business, the woman can help him and do the job."

Robert Manda and Zindikani Miti have more than ten goats, and Muchoke Soko and John Scout Phiri more than five. A number of village residents own or care for just one or two. Goats certainly contribute to keeping the village meticulously clean. They eat almost anything on their way, rubbish as well as relish off a pot, growing pawpaw trees, blankets on a clothes line, a collapsing roof. We even lost some of our survey papers as goat fodder! So people take their precautions. Growing trees are fenced and relish tucked away.

Though sometimes a nuisance, domestic animals are quite undemanding. All they want from people is a place to sleep. In return they let themselves be converted into money, meat, and manpower. Yet they often fail to fulfill the hopes and expectations invested in them. They go astray, hurt themselves, fail to reproduce, grow ill and die.

Sandikonda Daka kept his goat in Muchoke Soko's care. One day Muchoke reported to Sandikonda that the goat was failing to give birth. Sandikonda hurried to see his goat, but could do nothing. As he, Muchoke, Micheck, and some children stood by, the goat died. Micheck helped him skin it, and they cut it up and all present were thanked for their help with a small piece of meat. Sandikonda also took a piece to the headman and had some brought to his daughter in Mcace village. The skin he decided to give to his granddaughter. Then he sat down to think about how he could get a new goat.

Some people share pigs by agreement. The customary reward for looking after other people's pigs is piglets. Pigs need not be watched closely because they never go very far. Still in some villages they are closed in during the rainy season and fed in the enclosure. But in the dry season they are free to roam about, to find food wherever they can.

Kabanda Nyuni had some bad luck with his pig. Although it gave birth to seven piglets, after only two days all the piglets died. Then Kabanda made an agreement with Angrippina Banda that he would look after her pig and be paid with a male and a female piglet when it produced children. His mother Sonile helps him feed the pigs, keeping husk for him whenever she pounds.

Sandikonda has two pigs called Tunganoshy and Vanganitaya. His wife, Mwanishupa, calls them by name or by saying *Kudya, Kudya, Kudya* ("eat, eat, eat") and they come running for something to eat. Tunganoshy had a litter of nine but three have died. Sandikonda has made an agreement with Shuzi Zulu that Shuzi keeps and feeds Vanganitaya and that he will be thanked with two piglets. Shuzi and Jenifa already have two pigs, which belong to Thomase Banda, Shuzi's father (married to his mother's sister). They will receive two piglets each from the offspring produced by Thomase's pigs.

Jenifa says:

"Pigs do not go far away, and one can call them by saying *Kudya*. The pigs know the word. When they hear it, they rush fast to their shed hoping for something to eat. The problem with pigs is that they must be fed, just like dogs. It is the woman's job to feed them, but if she is busy the man can do so. It is not his business, though, so when he is not there he need not worry about it. The usual food is maize husks mixed with water. During the rainy season, if there are no husks, pigs are given pumpkins and pumpkin leaves. All through the year pigs go about looking for human excrement, which is their favorite food."

Faides Phiri has an agreement with Liza Phiri to help feed her pigs. She will be thanked with piglets. Dorothy Banda has an agreement with Brighton to reserve husks for Brighton's pigs whenever she pounds.

Micheck had a pig that belonged to his cousin Alick Phiri at Dalala Stores. The agreement was that Micheck take care of the pig until it grows up and produces young. When the piglets were the right size, Micheck and Alick would divide the small pigs, slaughter the mother pig, and share the meat equally.

So Micheck took great care of the pig and eventually she got pregnant. But suddenly one day Alick sold the pig! Money was paid, the pig was slaughtered, Alick went home loaded with cash, and the buyer went away with his baskets full of pork. But Micheck had not been informed. Micheck was in the field at the time and he was also ill with malaria. When he heard a woman talk about a pig that had been slaughtered and that the name of the owner was Alick, he suspected Alick to have killed his pig and hurried home to get the full information. At Mtewe River he asked two boys bathing if they had heard about a pig that had been slaughtered at home. And one of the boys said: "You are right, Mr. Micheck, your pig has been slaughtered and sold by Alick."

Now, Micheck, upset and angry, rushed home to ask advice from people before he started to fight Alick. The village residents advised him not to fight. So he sat down to compose his mind. In the late afternoon, Micheck went to Dalala Stores to see Alick and ask him, without quarreling, what had happened. Once there, he found Alick asleep completely intoxicated, but people present told him that before he had got drunk, Alick had left him a message, saying that when Micheck comes, tell him not to worry because he would be given two other pigs. On hearing this Micheck was very glad and he returned home planning how the next morning he would borrow James' bicycle and go to Dalala Stores and collect his pigs.

The next morning Micheck went to see his cousin. By then Alick had changed his mind and refused entirely to give Micheck two pigs. "One is enough," he said. But Micheck did not worry if he did not get two pigs. He took the one pig and went home.[4]

With her ten pigs, Jessie Tonga is the biggest pig owner in the village. Micheck, Kabanda, and Sandikonda have five. Angrippina used to have three, but recently she gave one to James Njobvu so that he could make bricks for her new brick house. Faides used to look after two pigs belonging to Kandikani from Kamanga village, but within one week both died. Mr. Kandikani got the meat and there was no charge.

Cattle, goats, pigs, and hens are the common domestic animals, but a few people rear sheep, ducks, and pigeons. Kefa Mwale and John Scout Phiri keep pigeons. Most people think that special magic or medicine is needed to "bind the birds to the owner" so that they do not fly away into somebody else's house, but Kefa says that it is only when they are not adequately fed on grain and husk that pigeons fly away. Pigeons are not eaten but are kept for their liveliness and beauty and perhaps as a sign of rank, or so the Bembas have reported.[5]

In the face of catastrophe, whatever the magnitude, villagers seem better prepared and more able to cope than many a town dweller. The volatility of life and luck is so apparent in a village where life is lived out of doors and in constant contact with others, where resources are often marginal, and where neighbors and relatives constantly share each others' dreams and despair. As a result, the agony, but also the calm, may be greater when families and fortunes are decimated. When a domestic animal is lost, the entire savings of a family can be gone, but people make the best out of it, as some of the previous accounts have demonstrated.

Only the very poor, like Square Banda, own no domestic animals, but he is not alone to depend on generous relatives and neighbors when it comes to tasting meat. Yet, to keep smaller livestock is something virtually everybody does from time to time. Thanks to the "putting-out" system, any able-bodied individual can built him or herself a small herd, with a little bit of luck. Still, the profits that may accrue from livestock take time to materialize. If the need for money becomes acute, and a villager has no animal capital in store, he or she has to look into possibilities other than animal husbandry. If it is a woman, her choice is quite simple. Brewing beer is the most likely and probably the best investment she can make.

Brewing Beer

Brewing beer is one of the few means a woman has to make money quickly, and it is a means most women make use of at least a few times during a year, provided they have the strength and the maize and millet needed. Some women are more set on earning money by brewing than others. Considering the fifty-six Kefa village households, Brighton, who knows the village well, calculated that thirteen village women "had the tendency for making beer." Among them were Lelia Mbewe, Kefa's fourth wife, and Dorothy Banda, neither of whom drinks any beer herself.[6]

If we do not consider labor a cost, brewing is good business indeed. To make one (oil) drum of beer one needs:

1 basket (30 liter) germinated maize at a cost of	K. 1.00
1 basket ordinary maize	K. 1.00
½ basket fingermillet	K. 1.50
⅔ basket millet	K. 1.00
TOTAL COST	K. 4.50

Of the resulting one-and-one-half drums of beer, about one may be sold, while one-half drum will be given away freely for people to taste the quality of the brew, for thanks to those who have helped with labor, tools, or other inputs, and as a special gift to headman, husband, and friends who all expect to drink the beer at no cost.

From her brew Fatnes Mbewe earned a total of K. 28.60; Regina Shawa, who sold her beer on a particularly auspicious day, got K. 36. Tisate Daka sold three hundred units—or gourds full—each for 5 ngwee and got altogether K. 15. As each one of them invested about the same amount of millet, maize, and labor, profits from beer brewing vary considerably. The ultimate economic result depends upon how much of the brew is sold and how much given away for free.

As few households have the equipment needed to make beer, most women borrow whatever they do not have, and some even sell their beer in other women's houses when they feel their own is not adequate. Micheck Phiri is the fortunate owner of a steel drum, which is in frequent demand during the peak beer season. When he lent his drum to Nyakala he was thanked with a container full of beer, and when Mwada, Micheck's wife, gave the drum to Bvuniwe Sakala she got in return a *nongo*—a clay pot full of beer that she sold for K. 1.50. Women help each other in every way, including labor. When Regina and Lelia, Kefa's third and fourth wives, helped Eliza Phiri brew, they were thanked with enough beer for headman Kefa to make a small beer party of his own.

About a third of any brew meant for sale is given away for free. When Tisate Daka brewed her one-and-one-half drums, she gave two full *nongo* to Penelani Khosa, the husband; two clay pots to Mtole Mbao from whom she had borrowed the container; one gourd to each of Jesinawo's two wives; one gourd to Zindi Miti; and one to headman Kefa. She also gave *dyonkho*—a free taste—to every customer who came to her house. Her cash return was K. 15. The money she spent on buying a dress for herself and school uniforms for her two sons.

Fatnes Manda borrowed Nyokasa's house to sell her beer. As it was just after harvest, the height of the beer season, most of the male Kefa village residents had gone to neighboring Kamanga village to taste the beer of Edith Kamanga. So in Nyokasa's house most of the beer drinkers were women. We counted a total of forty persons present. Toward the evening, as there was a full moon and people were very happy, Margret Banda came with her drum and the women danced *chimtali*—a local dance— throughout the evening and early night. Many women came as they heard the drumming, and also some men, and the beer sale went very well. Dancing, drinking, and a full moon gave Fatnes a pleasing net profit of K. 28.60 from her beer sale.

Some of the villagers spend a great deal of money on beer and on liquor (see below), and those who do not have the cash flock around them knowing that with some tenacity they are bound to benefit from the riches of the better-off villagers.

Micheck Phiri is one of those who inspires the generosity of others. During one day in August when we observed his activities, he started drinking at midday and continued for a full twelve hours. Very soon his money was spent, but that did not prevent him from savoring beer first at a private beer house and later on at the beer hall at Kachenga. At least fifteen times did his friends buy him beer during that day, while Micheck himself paid for at least five rounds. Unlike many other beer drinkers, Micheck usually drinks together with his wife, Mwada, whom he loves dearly.

Micheck is a "master of beer," and so are many other men. The advantage is that most of what they spend becomes the income of a woman, who spends it on food and clothing, soap, paraffin, and schooling. Vanira Phiri is one of those whose schooling has been paid by her mother's brewing. Tisauke Phiri, the mother, explains:

> "Mr. Phiri [the husband] and I agreed that I should finance the boys' schooling and he the girls', because he preferred it that way. And I saved money selling groundnuts and was prepared to pay for the boys. The problem started when Vanira was sent home from school because she did not have a school uniform. That is when I decided to brew beer, and since then my husband does not eat from me neither does he drink my beer. I reported the problem to the headman to ask his advice, and Kefa Mwale went to Mr. Phiri to hear his version. When he reported back, the headman said: 'Mr. Phiri told me that he is angry because you brewed beer in your mother's village. He asks how you can brew beer in your [mother's] home as if there are no buyers of beer here in Kefa village, and as if you do not intend to give us beer for free.' And I answered: 'The problem is this. When I told him to buy a school uniform for Vanira he got annoyed, saying that his money was all finished. Then he went away to his job in Luangwa Valley. When he came back he found that I had been making kavinde—secret beer—but he refused to drink. After that I decided not to brew in his presence, but in my mother's village and only for sale. My mind was entirely on my daughter and how to earn to provide her with a uniform.' "

Kwerekani Phiri, the husband, is another "master of beer." Having a permanent job and a regular income, he has money to drink. According to our observations Kwerekani spent more time drinking than eating. But he came to Kefa village only during weekends, when people drink more than on weekdays.

Many women and some men do not drink at all. Simon Sakala and Lemekani Mbao are among them, as are James Phiri and Evelinar Njobvu. But even if a villager does not drink, he or she may be affected by other people's drinking habits. News Miti kept harassing James to buy him beer and James answered that he had no money. But News kept bothering him until Njamini gave 50 ngwee to James, who added 10 ngwee and bought a bottle of *kacasu* liquor for News. When News thanked Njamini and said James was a very good fellow, Njamini said "I gave you the money because you have been harassing James even though you know that James does not drink." James himself said nothing.

At a house of beer, sharing is the rule. Kwerekani does so often and willingly. One day he shared his beer with a baby that had been brought along by the grandmother. As the baby was crying Kwerekani tried to comfort it with a lullaby, but the baby went on crying until Kwerekani gave it some of his beer. Then it fell asleep.

Not all beer is brewed locally and by women. *Chibuku* beer, sold at licensed beer halls, and bottled beer sold at Gia's store, are brewed in Chipata and Lusaka. Such beer is about the only consumer item that is in regular supply in the rural areas. A pint of bottled beer costs 40 ngwee or almost as much as a bottle of *kacasu*, hard liquor that is illegally distilled in the villages. Only farmers and people with a lot of money can afford bottled beer. It is surprising, and disappointing, that the more money men earn, the more they spend on things imported into the rural areas, and the harder it becomes for local producers, including women, to find customers for their products.

When they lose their "beer market," what short-term income generating activities are still open to women, except prostitution and distilling? While development may promise new opportunities to men, women see theirs reduced. Today, even *kacasu* production is being prohibited by the government, and *kacasu* used to be the only way that women with some extra sugar could raise money in a few days.

Tyford reports:

> "Chief Chikuwe visited Kefa village yesterday to talk about *kacasu* distilling businesses. Kamanga, Mtolo, Chindola, Nyathan, and other neighboring village headmen were called to a meeting in headman Kefa's yard. The Chief wanted to make every villager aware that *kacasu* alcohol is prohibited by the government and also by him, and that whoever is found distilling *kacasu* will be arrested. And he said: 'I give the power to all you headman not to hesitate to bring to court or report any village resident distilling *kacasu*. I give you the power to do so, even if neither you, nor those caught red-handed, will be happy about it.'
>
> "At the meeting people said nothing, but afterward they muttered to themselves and each other: The Chief will grow tired, *kacasu* will never end. Now, when he says we must not make liquor, it is as if he reminds us to distill more and even more!"

Distilling is another example of female ingenuity. That someone developed the method is a wonder, as it is so simple, yet so effective.

Agnes describes it in this way:

"Husks are soaked in water for a few days and removed, and a lot of
sugar is added to the liquid. The mixture starts to 'boil.' After five or six
days the 'boiling' stops and the smell of *kacasu* starts. The brew is then put
in a clay pot that is sealed off completely except for a thin pipe. The pot
is put on the fire and the vapor starts going through the pipe. It is cooled
off as the pipe goes through a *goli* [trough] with water and led by a thin
straw into a bottle. Now it is ready to be sold. A bottle costs 70 ngwee and
there are always plenty of customers. Some people who like *kacasu* say it
is good for fevers, malaria, and headaches, but most people take it because
they like to get drunk."

More so than beer, liquor is the source of apathy and aggression, waste
and withdrawal. Women worry about their husbands and sons. Muchoke
Soko is one of them. One day, when she came to beg tobacco from Square
Banda, she found a bottle of liquor in his house. She asked him how it
had got there and who had been drinking. Square said: "It was bought
by Faindani for Sandikonda, and I keep it here only because I needed
to taste it." But Muchoke did not trust her relative and said: "I think you
have been giving liquor to my son. But I have told you not to give him
any. Why do you want to spoil him?" Square said: "Trust me, I did not
give any to your son. Many times you have told me not to, so I do not.
What I have drunk has been for me alone." But Muchoke did not believe
him and hurried home to ask her son if he had been drinking with Square.

Even Square, who is a habitual drinker, does not trust others when
it comes to *kacasu*. When he sent money to Chumba Yekeke to buy *kacasu*
and she came the following day with a bottle, he made her drink first,
thinking she may have put medicine in the bottle.[7]

Kacasu is not always of good quality. Hangovers are a well-known
phenomenon. Brighton reports:

"Sandikonda was unable to work hard today because yesterday he
became drunk. Going home this morning from the house of beer, he met
the wife on the way. Seeing how he was, she made him go with her to the
ndinda [field shelter], saying 'let us first go to the shelter, and I will cook
nsima there, and afterward you can go home and rest.' Sandikonda did not
argue, and said: 'Chabwino—Okay, let me wash in the river first, and I shall
come.' So he went to have a bath in Mtewe river. As he crossed Zindikani
Miti's garden calling *Zikomo* [which is a way to ask permission to trespass],
Zindi, who was weeding, stopped him and made him rest. He said: 'I see
that you are tired. Wait here in the shade and I will give you some mangoes.'
So Sandikonda wrapped the mangoes in his shirt and went to eat *nsima*
prepared by the wife."

It is good to have friends and an understanding wife. But prohibition may be good too, even if it does not work fully. In July once more the Chief strictly prohibited *kacasu* distilling. Reflecting on the consequences Sylvester said: "I have noticed that there are less temporary marriages now, which particularly drunkards used to establish."

According to Sandikonda it is money rather than beer which turns village residents into drunkards:

"These days a person will drink all kinds of beer and liquor, reel about and insult people, and create trouble because he is under the influence of alcohol. But when we tell him to stop drinking, he will answer back that he has got his own money and does not depend on anybody, that the beer he drinks is neither given him for free nor begged from anybody, but bought by himself. In colonial days it was easy to restrict a drunkard from over-drinking. At that time people obeyed customs and everybody listened to the advice of the headman and the village elders. But this is no longer so. These days a man with money does what he wants. There is no order any longer. And there are some people who only think of how to earn money so that they can drink more and more."

Local Crafts and Businesses

Cultivation, cattle keeping, and beer brewing are traditional skills. With changing economic conditions they have acquired new significance, yet to most villagers they retain most of their old flavor, for value of use is still paramount. Though economic diversification and specialization are not particularly prevalent in rural Zambia, among Kefa village residents there are always a few individualists who (doggedly) pursue economic activities that set them apart from their fellows. What moves them is not always obvious, as the profits derived from most local crafts and businesses are not particularly large. Yet, in Kefa, as elsewhere, individuals pattern their lives on some inner logic that often remains hidden to their neighbors.[8]

James Kamaswanda Njobvu is a stranger from the small Petauke town. Kamaswanda means "basket maker," and basket making is indeed his business. Upon his arrival two years ago, he asked headman Kefa for permission to settle temporarily in the village to make baskets for sale. Kamaswanda came with a wife, Grace Zulu, two children, and a brother, Jackson Njobvu, a youngman of twenty-two.

Jackson helps James Kamaswanda in his business. It is not so that the brothers come from a family of basket makers, not more than any other men, because in this area, as in so many other places, basket making is every man's job. We asked why only men make baskets, and James the basket maker answered that to make a basket takes a lot of skill and intelligence. When we asked if men are more intelligent and skilled than women, James said only that to make baskets had always been a man's job. He admitted also that his wife, Grace Zulu, knew how, but her job would be primarily to provide him with water so that he could extract colors from the right roots, and to soak the bamboo strips to make them soft and supple.

Kamaswanda taught himself how to make baskets. He usually makes two types, a large one and a small, but he knows how to make just about anything. When he got an order for a baby cot, he made a very beautiful one, though it was the first cot he had ever made.

Most of Kamaswanda's customers are satisfied with his products. Tisalire Manda is an exception, as the following story shows:

> Tisalire Manda from Kaliyoyo village bought a basket from the basket maker in Kefa village. Three weeks later she returned to complain about the price she had paid. She had bought the basket for K. 8.50, but now she insisted that she was only prepared to pay K. 5 for the basket she had already bought and used. James the basket maker refused to reduce the price and he also refused to take the basket back. Tisalire then went to Emeria Mbao, her grandmother, in Kefa village and complained, and Emeria brought the young woman and her problem to the headman.
>
> The very same evening Kefa Mwale sounded the bell and called the villagers to come and help him sort out the conflict that had arisen. When the villagers had gathered, Emeria and Tisalire stood up to explain what had happened and the basket was brought forward as the central piece of evidence. Then James Kamaswanda was asked to say how he saw it all. It was Mtunduwathu Kamanga who asked the important question: "Why had Tisalire kept the basket for as much as three weeks before she came back to complain about the price?"
>
> When headman Kefa passed judgment, he put Emeria and Tisalire to shame by saying they had troubled the villagers for nothing. How could they expect the basket maker to take back a basket that had been used for three weeks! And then he closed the meeting as he usually did, by saying that if the plaintiff did not agree with the decision taken by the meeting, she should bring the case before the Chief's court.
>
> Afterward, people said that the problem arose because James Kamaswanda makes two types of baskets, one that he sells for K. 8.50 and one for K. 5. Tisalire, it seems, really wanted to buy the cheaper one, and it was only after three weeks that she realized that she had got the more expensive one.

As it is not easy to depend on payment from other villagers to earn and to eat, shortly after his arrival James asked headman Kefa for a field where he and particularly his wife could cultivate maize. Having stayed in Kefa village for a year, the basket maker took a Kefa girl as his second wife. The basket maker is the only full time professional artisan in the village, but if his two wives did not work in the field he would probably starve.

Staff Mwanza is another stranger who came to headman Kefa and asked to be allowed to live in the village and open his shopkeeping business. Next to his brick house shop, Staff built a brick oven where he planned for his wives to make scones and bread for sale. But Staff's business was never very good. Though Staff had no relatives in the village, so many people asked him for credit that he found it hard to realize any profit at all. Now, Staff has a job with the Roads Department and comes to Kefa village only during weekends.

Occasionally, when he is in Chipata and has the needed cash, Staff buys some provisions for his shop and for a few days biscuits, mirrors, vaseline, pens and soap are for sale right inside the village. One problem faced by small traders like Mr. Mwanza is that a trading license costs K. 30 no matter how much or little he sells. To solve that problem Staff Mwanza only opens his shop on demand, that is, if he has anything to sell. In this way he avoids paying the license.

Since Staff took a second wife, the shop has served as her living quarters. When his first wife's hut was about to fall down, she too moved into the shop, so it seems that the shop is about to close altogether.

Serving as housing quarters for two wives, the shop is not likely to have any room for merchandise. And the women in Kefa are already grumbling. When the two elderly ladies Lelia Mbewe and Mwanishinga Zulu were walking together, Lelia was overheard saying: "Our grocery is too poor, there is nothing on the shelves; no salt, no sugar, no cooking oil. Even paraffin and matches are impossible to get these days.[9] If only we could rely on the bus to come when it is supposed to. Then we would go to the *boma* [the administrative center at Chiparamba ten kilometers from Kefa village] in the morning, buy what we need, and return before dark. But these days you never know if the bus will come at all." And Mwanishinga replied: "Even at the *boma* there is nothing in the stores. That is why I have stopped drinking tea altogether. There is no sugar and no salt. But that does not worry me. I am so short of money that I have not seen even one coin for weeks and weeks."

Sometimes, an enterprising villager makes full use of the poor performance of local shopkeepers. James Phiri is one of the young men in the village set on improving his standard of living, and his ambitions are not limited to what he can make out of his vegetable cultivation. Once, when he got a free lift home from Chipata town, he carried two 4-gallon tins filled with cooking oil. The oil he sold by the cup to his fellow villagers. But it was a once and only once affair. Possibly he too was persuaded to give more credit than he could afford. To be a good villager *and* a good businessman seems almost a contradiction in Kefa.

Square Banda, the cripple, is another village resident with a business of his own, and Squre's business is that of straw hat making. The raw material for his hats Square finds in the bush. The only problem is that Square walks with so much effort and pain, that he must depend on others to fetch the leaves and fiber he needs for his production.

Mostly Square asks village children for help. He also needs water to soften the plant material that he uses. One day we overheard Square bargaining with the young boy Twaibu, who is eight years old. "Twaibu, you know my problem. I need your help. I have an order for two hats, but I have nothing to make them from. Please remember that problems like mine can affect anyone, as life is a secret that is revealed only little by little. If you will draw me two gallons of water today and two gallons tomorrow and two also the day after, in return I shall make three straw hats and I shall give one of them to you." And Twaibu looked quite pleased and said *"Chabwino,* okay, Mr. Banda. You have asked me, and I shall help you. I can even go into the bush and find the fiber you need to make my hat strong."

Others too help Square when he asks them, but his hat production is not particularly large. The price for a hat, unless Square agrees to make it free of charge, is K. 0.75. Fortunately, as we shall see in Chapter 7, Square Banda has other skills that are sought after more than that of making straw hats. It is his fame as a local healer that accounts for most of the cash he ever touches.

Most villagers set on earning money leave the village in order to do so. Some leave and are gone forever, some stay away for a few years or many. But there are also those who go out in search of piecework and odd jobs, particularly during the cold season, and return home when growing crops and weeds are sorely in need of their labor. Lemekani Mbao is one of the latter. In his younger days he went all over Zambia and even to Southern Rhodesia (Zimbabwe) in search of work. As time passed he developed his skills as a builder of houses. Lemekani still builds houses occasionally. Recently he was booked by the rich businessman Mr. Simba to build a grocery in Chongolo village. No sooner had he finished the assignment when he was asked by Lucien Tembo, who lives on a farm close to Kefa village, to make an oven so that Mr. Tembo's wife could bake bread for sale. Usually Lemekani would work for cash only during the dry season, but sometimes he builds also during the rains. Although his cultivation may suffer, he does not worry as he earns more from building than from cultivating. It is the job of his wife, Tilele Zulu, to cultivate food. It is her responsibility that the family granaries are full, while his is to find cash for the family.

Stephen Phiri is another carpenter. He first learned his skills from headman Kefa. Being a youngman Stephen was determined to earn money so he would no longer live in Kefa village. But when the Kefa housing scheme which we shall learn about in Chapter 8 started, Stephen realized that he could make a good profit from making roofs and window- and door-frames for his fellow villagers. He moved home, because it was in Kefa village that he could earn a living.

Yanzulani Nkhoma is another Kefa builder. Because he has conducted his business so cleverly he has been able to afford to build a house also in Chipata town and now is rarely in Kefa village. His wife, Mwanyiana Zulu, is a trader with her own business. She deals mostly in dried and smoked fish, which she buys in Malawi or in Luangwa Valley (up to six hundred kilometers away) and sells wherever she can find a profit. Sometimes she has fish left when she comes home to Kefa and people with money buy from her. The wife stays in the village much more often than the husband, yet it is said that he has only one wife. Yanzulani and Mwanyiana are very well off and their wealth has enabled them to send all their children to school. One son was even enrolled in the University at Lusaka, but as we shall see in Chapter 6 this has been no blessing for the hard-working parents.

As in almost every other field, when it comes to earning, women's opportunities are more limited than men's. Fewer school places are available for girls and fewer jobs are open to them. Girls also get less encouragement from home and from the community and they are kept so busy helping their mothers, and later on growing food of their own, that it is surprising that women ever manage anything but their own families. Although many do, their uneasy choice when it comes to making money seems to be that between the hard work of cultivating and brewing beer with traditional methods, and the seemingly more profitable alternatives of distilling illicit liquor or making their bodies available to men for money.

Prostitution—or something like it—is not uncommon. Nor does it represent any major break with the cultural pattern that has linked female sexuality to men's money gifts. Once it was established that bride price and marriage gifts be paid in cash, and these days this practice is more common than not all over Zambia, the idea that short-lasting sexual encounters should entail some financial reward is not farfetched. The great difference is rather *who* keeps the cash. For short unions, it is invariably the woman herself; and so some seem to find frequent exchange of sex for money to be preferable to a contracted and lasting marriage where the money gifts are paid to the bride's male relatives.

Milicka Mwanza is one of those who people say work all over the district, not minding with whom she sleeps and whether she is related to them. It is said that she cares only that there is money and that through her business she earns enough to keep her three children in school. People also say that she is lazy by nature, that it all started when she was a child, and that her father is really spoiling her because, whenever she has nothing to eat, he feeds her from his granary. In the cold season, when there is beer and money around, so is Milicka. But at the time of the year when other women start going to the fields to clear their plots and to prepare for the planting season, Milicka packs her bag and goes to town where business is forever good for people like her. It is said that women hate her because of a tendency in their men to spend money on Milicka and other women like her.

Because women's earning powers are so limited, particularly for those who have no harvest to sell or no maize and millet to make beer from, many women are glad for any gift of money or kind offered by men who want their sexual and other services in return. We shall read more of this in the next chapter.

Modern Careers

Specialization is very difficult at village level. Those who depend on only one skill are no longer self-reliant but have to rely on others who cultivate. But because cultivators are largely self-reliant they often have neither the money nor the need to buy any specialized skills. Even if a specialist were to find sufficient income to enable him to afford to buy the necessary family food, there might not be sufficient grain and relish around to feed him and the family throughout the year. So the specialist is likely to decide to grow his own food, or to find a wife who can do so, and leave her behind while looking for customers and clients outside the village and even in town.

It is the ambition of every young Kefa resident to go to town for some time and sooner or later most of them do. It is the most resourceful and the most enterprising who succeed in finding a job or a place to learn and who stay there. The net result is that the village is systematically bled of it best young blood and those who stay behind are left worse off than before. To assume that those who move out support their rural relatives with money and goods is, unfortunately, a fallacy.[10]

Mary Mwale, the daughter of headman Kefa's brother, spent two years in Lusaka. When her husband whom she had accompanied divorced her, she decided to come home. Now she cultivates maize and cotton and advises young people of what town living is really like:

> "Town living is fine, but only if you have a good job, because in town everything must be bought for money. Things in town are cheaper than here in the rural areas, there is plenty of entertainment like the cinema and bars everywhere, and transport is no problem. There are also so many ways in which even women can earn. The fact is that in town men have money and they give it more easily to women than do the men in the villages.

"In town, people are in the habit of keeping cleaner than village people, but there is a lot of thieving. Everything you need must be bought for cash. Relish is very expensive and people are not allowed to keep livestock like pigs and cattle. I tell you, town life only suits those who have good jobs. If you are employed in town you are self-reliant and no one bothers you by telling you to cooperate traditionally or attend funerals when you do not want to. But if you are unemployed you depend entirely on relatives and nobody gives you any respect.

"When somebody is hated by his relatives, that is when he goes to town. In town everybody seems ever ready to practice hatred even the very first time they quarrel. The problem there is that there is no one in authority to administer the living habits of people who turn against each others, like the headmen and village elders do in the villages. Town life is good if you have money but village life is better than being penniless in town."

And yet it is to earn money that young people yearn for the town. Shuzi Zulu and Jackson Phiri were discussing their prospects, and Schuzi said: "Friend, let us try to make a future career." And when Jackson asked him how, he continued:

"My future career is that, after all the work this year, and after the harvest, we go to Kabwe [a town on the rich Copper Belt] for lessons in how to drive a vehicle. Or we can go to Lusaka, where there is also a very good driving school. You know, Phiri, we are still youngmen, but if we remain here cultivating, we will wear ourselves out. We shall not enjoy life, and our bodies will be exhausted. First we should try to get a job with the government, so that we can earn. As for me I am really eager to do this driving exam. This year I have already lost many opportunities to get a good job. At Kapasa there is some construction work going on and I understand there are plenty of vacancies for drivers with a licence."

And after a brief pause Shuzi added: "Our wives would also like to travel. They too want to enjoy their girlhood. If we stay here we shall definitely ruin our minds and bodies."

And the friend Jackson strongly agreed with him.

Gilbert Zulu, headman Kefa's grandson, is one of those who succeeded in making a career for himself in town, as a "form four man" and having spent eleven years in school. Kefa residents expected that Gilbert would be lost to village living. After working for ten years with the Zambian Railway in Ndola town on the Copper Belt Gilbert has however decided to come home to Kefa village. Perhaps he will be an example of a new career pattern where town dwellers of village origin answer to the call of the Zambian government, which in particular encourages young people to take up commercial agriculture. Gilbert explains:

"The government keeps telling us to go home and cultivate. In the rural areas the advantages are far greater than in town. In town there is no fertile land to farm. We have to buy whatever food we need and it is very expensive. Despite what we earn, we people of rural origin are despised for our rural lifestyle and considered inferior to our urban neighbors. Our children grow up with jealous hearts because they cannot compete with neighboring children in terms of clothing and toys. Of course, some people are better off in town, but the majority are not and the majority count.

"Now my ambition is to become a farmer. That is why I went to town in the first place. When I have earned enough here in Ndola to buy a tractor, I shall return home and become a commercial farmer. My mind is clear. Someday I shall be back in Kefa village. I am lucky that my grandfather [the headman] never begged me to build him a house in a squatter compound in town, just for him to be near me and share from my earnings. On the contrary, every time I see him he tells me that my home is there in Kefa village and that I work for government in town only temporarily and that one day he wants me to come back there. It is my conviction that if you have money and start going into commercial farming you can earn well and be respected by everybody."

Gilbert is not the only villager who dreams of how he will increase his fields and grow more and more cash crops to become a commercial farmer rather than a traditional village cultivator. But how to go about it? Money is a first prerequisite because money is needed to hire labor and tractor services, to buy seeds and fertilizers and pesticides. But a new approach to life is also necessary as the difference between commercial farmer and peasant cultivator concerns more than acreage and cash. It is also a matter of perspectives, priorities, and preferences.

To be a commercial farmer you have to opt for individualism and accumulation rather than communalism and sharing. A commercial farmer bases his economic decisions on signals from the market rather than on the community. To do so it may be necessary to withdraw from the social bonds of mutual obligations that are the warp and woof of village life.

Individualism and accumulation are not inventions of market forces, nor are they present only among commercial farmers. But in subsistence societies such qualities are actively prevented from becoming dominant by a series of social mechanisms. The widespread belief in witchcraft is one very effective way through which inequalities are prevented from developing into class distinctions.[11] Rather than risk that occult powers are used against them, the economically successful choose to share their surplus with less fortunate relatives. Or they take care not to show that they are better off than their kin. A third strategy is to move away from the village communalism altogether, to go to town or to settle on a solitary farm away from the expectations and social controls of others.

Commercial farmers invariably choose the latter. One of them, Lucien Tembo, explains his predicament:

"If you have a farm and live outside the village setting you are not bothered by other people. You are free to work steadily and to be self-reliant, and you have more possibilities to extend your cultivation than do ordinary villagers. On the other hand, a farmer is easily lonely. There are few people who care about your problems and who are willing to aid you if you need their advice or help in any way. When you are ill few visitors come to see how you are, and you are seldom called for beer."

At a time of transition like the present there is no longer one value system to guide people's action but several, and often they are contradictory. When some people stick to the old ways while others settle for the new, family and friends clash in their most deeply felt sense of what is right and wrong, and suspicion and hostility result. It is to minimize such problems that the commercial farmer leaves the village to build himself a farm on the outskirts of communal land. While the older generation may deplore the selfishness of those who opt for individual rather than communal self-reliance, to the young people such a farmer may appear as the embodiment of the freedom they silently dream of. Still, as Lubinda Mwale pointed out to his son, to live apart is not to earn people's respect as a man of the future.

"People move away from the village for different reasons, and some people on solitary farms live like ordinary villagers. They just move to get away from those whom they have come to hate and distrust. People like Nyirenda Phiri and Limited Manda are such farmers. They make villagers say that farmers are proud for nothing because we produce cash crops just as well as they, and we even feed them on beer. Yet they too are proud—buying bottled beer and eating only luxury foods. But when they use up the money, the ordinary villagers who used to drink and eat with them will laugh.

"If you find money from your cash crops, do not waste it like that, trying to appear a big man. Save it for the future. When you are really well off, that is when you can decide upon whether to become a commercial farmer or not. What you need in this world are two things, a good attitude toward work and money. When you have got these you can progress."

Money

People in Kefa village try hard to earn money. Some work in their vegetable gardens and some cultivate hybrid maize and cotton. Some brew beer and distill illicit liquor. Some do piecework, run businesses, or sell hats or baskets or medicine. Some simply beg from those who already have money. Once gained, the money is spent on clothes and other household possessions like paraffin, matches, and soap. Some save money for their new houses and doors and window frames. Some have their hearts set on livestock or on employing laborers to hoe their field during the rainy season and on having a tractor to carry their maize home at harvest time. There are the recurrent expenditures like beer and relish, and the unique needs at special times like Christmas or a funeral.

The needs and wants of the villagers are many, but there is not much money around to cover them. Most Kefa residents earn less than K. 100 a year, and the women earn much less than the men. Although the exact amount a person earns is not easy to find out, we tried. James Phiri disclosed that his earnings this year were quite good. He sold eleven bags of hybrid and earned K. 73.35 and from the vegetable garden he earned K. 80. Kabanda Nyuni, his brother, admitted: "I only sold vegetables and tomatoes from my garden. My earnings were one shirt and one short trouser for myself, a dress for my wife, and clothes for my two children. The rest I spent right away and I do not know quite how much it may have amounted to." But Evelinar, the wife, said "We earned K. 14 from the vegetables and K. 20 from brewing beer."

Simon Sakala related he had got money from his hybrid and from selling rape, tomatoes, and cabbage but that he spent every penny on his daughter Rothia's funeral after she had died from measles at the age of two. Timeke Daka said she had brewed beer twice and earned altogether K. 42.60. Square Banda reported a total earning of K. 7.50 from the sale of ten straw hats, but he said nothing of the medicine or the marijuana that he had also sold. But then marijuana and hashish are strictly prohibited in Zambia.

Mary Mwale said she earned more than K. 200 growing cotton and local maize and that she had also got K. 4 as a free gift from her husband in Lundazi. Rachel Lungu had worked as a beer hall waitress but had spent whatever she had earned and could no longer remember the amount.

The most successful earners in the village seemed to be the headman, Tilele Zulu, and Tilele's husband, Lemekani Mbao. The headman had earned almost K. 300 from his hybrid maize, Tilele had got K. 260.70 from her cotton, and Lemekani had earned K. 200 building houses and K. 20 helping Tilele to weed her cotton. As an annual income even K. 300 is not much for a family. But needs and wants notwithstanding, most families in Kefa and neighboring villages are basically self-reliant.

When we asked people how they would have spent K. 100 if they had it, the answers varied from person to person:

Mary Mwale would buy clothes and pay the children's schooling; Mtole Mbao and Lomanzi Tembo, both village elders (and women), would employ people to cultivate their fields; Tilolele Banda would buy household articles like soap, salt, and paraffin and use some for medicine and the grinding mill. The men, Positani Banda, James Phiri, Square Banda, and Tisalire Phiri would invest in fertilizers and employ workers to grow hybrid and other cash crops. Robert Manda, another much respected village elder and the owner of one of the largest herds in Kefa, would buy "luxury goods" (whatever he meant by that!).

Lefati Phiri with his deformed arm would have somebody cultivate for him but would also save some for "daily problems" and Kangachepa Sakala, who is old and ill, said resolutely: "If I had money, I would use it to eat, and use some to pay people to weed my field." Agnes Njobvu, who is also very old, said: "I would buy plenty of food for eating because I am too old. I am not fit for investing anything in the future." Lemekani Mbao and Mwada Simba wanted to invest in livestock, but Tilele Zulu, Lemekani's wife, said: "My dream for the future is to have enough money to open a grocery store here in the village. But my most immediate plan is to extend my fields and grow more cotton. Then, if God wills, after perhaps three or four years I shall have enough money for my shop."

And Micheck Phiri, Mwada Simba's husband, said: "If I had money I would go for beer right away because I am very thirsty!"

Many villagers try to save a little by putting some money aside whenever they earn something. The more professional savers follow the example of Tilele Zulu and Simon Sakala, who have opened an account with the mobile Post Office that comes every Wednesday to Dalala Stores, close to Kefa. Like Lemekani, some prefer to save by investing surplus in livestock.

"With livestock I can see my money, and if I am lucky after a few years my capital will be doubled. To invest in livestock is much better than to hide the cash in a clay pot in the floor or stick bills into the grass roof of your house. It is much better than to give your money to a relative for safekeeping. There are bad characters who do not hesitate to turn to charms and even witchcraft because they are jealous when their relatives prosper and even people who used to be the best of friends may turn against each other because of money."

Lemekani Mbao referred to the tragic story of how Laimen Phiri came to kill his best friend Dandaulani Mwale, the headman's son proper:

"Laimen Phiri and Dandaulani Mwale used to be the best of friends. Laimen was said to be 'the controller' of the friendship. One day Laimen sold a cow and throughout the rest of the day he spent money freely on food and beer for himself, Dandaulani, and others who joined them. By the end of the day he gave whatever money that was left to Danda for safe keeping. It is said that Dandaulani took K. 26 from the money in his care and spent it for his own purpose without consulting with the friend and asking if he could use it. When Laimen came to hear that his friend Danda was spending a lot of money, he suspected that it was his money that he was using and he went in search of his friend to confirm his suspicion. But Dandaulani feared him and hid in the bush. As Laimen could not find the friend he got increasingly angry and people heard him say that he would take tough measures if he found that his money was missing. He even called on Dandaulani's mother [who separated from headman Kefa years ago and lives with Danda, in Kaliyoyo village, not far from Kefa] and told her that unless she would tell him where her son was hiding he might lose his temper and kill him!

"Three days later Dandaulani was found dead, hanging from a small tree in the bush. The tree was so small that it was clear from the beginning that he could not have killed himself, and Laimen Phiri was immediately suspected. The police confirmed that Dandaulani had died from cracks in his skull and that his bones had been broken. But there were no eyewitnesses and there was no proof as to the culprit. As the police would do nothing, it was up the the villagers to prove their conviction that Laimen Phiri had cruelly murdered his best friend for K. 26.

"The signs were many. On the very same day that Danda was killed Laimen went to Luangwa Valley on a bus. People said that he traveled in order to confuse people as to his whereabouts on the fatal day. On the bus he met with an accident. A Landrover hit the bus at the very spot where Laimen was sitting and he was the only person on the bus who was hurt. The villagers saw this as a clear indication that the spirit of Dandaulani had caused the accident to happen as a revenge.

"We believe," Lemekani ended his narrative, "that if one does something bad, one's spirit becomes unlucky."

When Laimen was found he was taken before the village meeting and accused of having murdered Dandaulani Mwale, the headman's son. But when somebody suggested that they should beat him severely, Kefa absolutely refused. The village meeting decided that Laimen and his entire family should be expelled from Kefa village. This decision was then approved by the Chief to include the Chief's entire area, and the Phiri family were given three days to pack and be gone. Those who had to leave were Laimen and his wife, his brother, a sister, his father, and one of the father's two wives. One wife, who was a Kefa village woman, was given the option to go or to stay and decided to remain with her relatives in Kefa village.

Many people were glad to see the Phiri family go, and some had already started to think how they could extend their field into a Phiri field or move into a now vacant Phiri house. Jenifa Banda, who was almost ready to give birth and whose mother was Laimen's sister, was afraid that she would not see her mother for a very long time. But she did, because

Laimen's sister came back to Kefa village shortly thereafter to help her daughter with the new baby and the headman personally granted her the permission to do so.

After a month an eyewitness turned up in the murder case. Mr. Zulu had been part of it all and he could no longer bear to carry this evil secret. As the police now had evidence, Laimen was arrested after having hidden in the bush around Kefa village for some time, creating fear and apprehension. It was some youngmen from Kefa who found him and handed him over to the police, but they did not beat him.

It took one year before the case was brought to trial and it ended as it had begun, with money. Mr. Zulu had been paid (or so people said) to go to Malawi to settle there and he did not turn up for the court case. The Phiri family had hired a well-known lawyer from Lusaka to defend Laimen, and the lawyer called the many Kefa villagers to the witness stand one by one and tore their evidence to pieces. When Laimen was acquitted, Chief Chikuwe and headman Kefa could no longer uphold their expulsion of the Phiri's, as their power lies only in their right to enforce government decisions.

Money is nothing new in Kefa village. It has been part of people's lives since the British levied head tax, but it is becoming more and more central to village life. In olden times it was cattle, labor, food, and beer that marked the transitions in life, but these days it is money that is increasingly being used, for example, when people marry and divorce, or when they die.

"It seems that Kefa village residents depend on money quite a lot." Sylvestor wrote. "They participate in many happy activities when they have money. I have observed that Kefa women more than women elsewhere smoke, drink, and divorce their husbands because they have money. [We should remember Sylvester is from the patrilinial Ngoni people.] And men get married to more than one wife."

And Agnes Njobvu, who is one of the oldest inhabitants in the village, supports Sylvester: "These days boys and girls are after money and they do not want to keep each other as husbands and wives for life. This is the truth as we see it, we old women and men."

Notes

1. "Zambia has a national herd of some million and a half cattle. . . The principal indigenous breeds are the Tonga, Barotse and Angoni which are each largely restricted to their areas of recent origins, namely the Southern, Western and Eastern provinces respectively. The Angoni is a humped Zebu and some attempts have been made to improve the breed to take advantage of its hardiness and fecundity." (Lombard and Tweedie, 1972:44.)

2. Quantity rather than quality is the aim of the local cattle owners who probably see a maximum number of heads as a way to minimize risks. Hellen's description of the Tonga

and the Ngoni, who "split up their herds by sending them to kinsmen who tend them and can expect remuneration in the form of their offspring," is also a description of the Chewa. "Cattle change hands for a variety of reasons . . . they may be given in the form of *lobola* or bride wealth; they may be used in the settlement of legal action at the village court; and finally, they may be sold for money." (Hellen, 1968:185.)

3. "The traditional cattle-owners have come under widespread criticism for their alleged reluctance to sell their cattle . . . such blanket condemnation fails to consider the demand for draft oxen, the very low productivity of the herd, the logical reluctance towards selling breeding stock and the fact that it takes an ox five or six years to grow to maturity under traditional management. The low productivity of the traditional herd is a result of too few bulls, lack of control over breeding and grazing and the lack of hygiene. The result is a very low calf crop every year, combined with high mortality, particularly among calves. It is likely that a cow only has a 15 to 30 per cent chance of weaning a calf every year . . . Despite this low productivity it is clear that maintaining a cow in the traditional herd at zero cost with 15 to 30 per cent chance of weaning a calf each year is a more profitable and logical use of resources than selling her and investing in a savings bank. Further, it may be good manners for a large cattle-owner to retain stock to meet social obligations, which can be the only opportunity that some less privileged rural people have to consume meat." (Lombard and Tweedie, 1972:47–48.)

4. "Zambia's pig meat problem is very similar to that of her beef. About half her consumption is imported when it could easily be locally produced. A small commercial herd on the line-of-rail totalling 20,000 contributes virtually all the official marketed output, while a large traditional herd of some 70,000 'bush' pigs, found mainly in the Eastern Province, contributes very little except to its local economy . . . The 'bush' pig remains a problem. He is a small black hardy animal and feeds by scavenging. African swine fever is prevalent in the Eastern Province." (Lombard and Tweedie, 1972:50, 51.)

5. "The Bemba attitude to pigeons is characteristic. These birds are kept by one or two men in most villages and housed in elaborate pigeon houses built with considerable trouble and protected with magic rites. But they are hardly ever eaten because 'People want to keep many pigeons, so they are afraid to waste the seed' [i.e., reduce the stock]. They like to see the birds flying about the village. They are things kept as a sign of rank. They just flutter and flutter about. They show the rank of the owner of the pigeon house." (Richards, 1939:64.)

6. According to a survey carried out among 1850 heads of household by IDZ in 1973, 20 percent of all households in Chief Chikuwe's area earned money by brewing and selling beer.

7. "Both the Ngoni and the neighbouring Chewa tribe tell of poisoned beer and accusations in conjuction with beer parties. Today it is still the custom with non-bottled beer in most rural areas that the host always takes the initial drink to show that the beer is harmless." (Hedlund and Lundahl, 1983:65.)

8. "Briefly speaking, there is no specialization of labour in this area except on a basis of sex. Handicrafts—such as basket-making, iron-work, and pottery, are chiefly in the hands of a few individuals, who are reckoned to have special skills in this direction . . . None of these craftsmen or women are employed whole time. They merely take a day off now and then to ply their trade, whenever any one can be found to employ them." (Richards, 1939:382.) So it was among the Bembas in the 1930s and is among the Chewas in the 1980s.

9. We made a small survey of shops in a radius of 5 kilometers around Kefa village. About 5000 people live in the area. This is what we found: Chiparamba Turn-Off Store was comparatively well-stocked; Chingoma Bottle Store sold only bottled beer; and when in stock Zulu Grocery, Alesi Grocery (owned by a woman), Chisokoni Grocery, Mbewe Grocery, and Ziwazako Grocery were all closed down. Kefa store (Staff's) sold soap and biscuits and was said to be "opened or closed according to the cash situation of the owner." Daka's Store, Soft Grocery, Dalala Store, and Gia's were open.

10. "In all probability, the flow of remittances from urban areas is small. The survey undertaken by Marter and Honeybone in the mid-1970s indicates that the general pattern in Zambia, including Eastern Province, was that only a few households receive contributions from relatives in urban areas and that the amount of money is small. In fact remittances are often notable by their absence as in the situation, often encountered, where married women are left unsupported by husbands who have moved to urban areas." (Hedlund and Lundahl, 1985:53; quoting Marter and Honeybone, 1976: The Economic Resources of Rural Households and the Distribution of Agricultural Development, Rural Development Studies Bureau, University of Zambia, Lusaka.)

11. According to van Binsbergen (1981:162) some of the social and economic principles underlying the system of witchcraft are "insufficient ideological justification of high status; the fact that a person's advancement—based on a redistribution of commodities present within the village community, including people eligible to become spouses or slaves— would often be at the expense of his neighbour; and the propensity to intergenerational and inter-factional conflict as built into the structure of village society, along with the absence of effective judicial means to resolve such conflict."

CHAPTER 6   FAMILY LIFE

Mutu umodzi susenza denga
One Head Cannot Carry a Roof

amuna wanga	My husband
amuna wanga tizienda abili	Let us move together
chikondi cha nkhunda	And love each other
olande—londe—londe	Like doves, like doves

Dahlschen, 1970:14

As in so many other societies, neither the nuclear family nor the extended family in Kefa village present a typical structure.[1] At the time of our study, there were one-hundred-and-seventeen people over twenty in the village, seventy-three women and forty-six men. Of the fifty-six households, only about one in every two consisted of parents and children. More than one third of these were without adult men. A few households like those of Kefa Mwale and Zindikani Miti are polygamous. Square Banda, Kefa's sister Mtole Mbao, and several other villagers live all alone, while Mwasida Mwale and her husband Robert Manda live with their daughters, grand-children, an adopted relative, and a manservant.

In contrast to the town, where poverty usually means overcrowded housing conditions, poor households in the countryside have few members. Perhaps it is instead that few hands mean few skills, little food, and limited access to other resources. Also in contrast to town, a human being in a village is rarely a liability. In subsistance societies there are no inactive members except the severely ill and the disabled. Even children contribute from an early age to the family labor. When two young people look at each other and long for marriage, or when their marriage is decided upon by the elders, there is rejoicing. Even when a man and woman start living together without being formally wed, village reactions seem relaxed as long as genealogy represents no obstacle.[2] And when a child is born, in or out of wedlock, the new community member is welcomed by all, because a child, no matter what its parentage, is an investment in the future.

Children

When a woman becomes pregnant, she is supposed to tell her hus-band first and he will carry the news to his parents. Early one morning soon thereafter the parents come to instruct the mother-to-be how to behave as a wife and an expectant mother: "Stop behaving like a girl, remember you are a married woman. Change your ways. Improve your character!" And they give her gifts of cloth and ornaments to emphasize and celebrate her new status.

As at puberty and during the wedding ceremony, the elders instruct the new couple how to behave. The man is told to stop playing around with other women or his behavior will certainly lead to the death of the unborn child. The Chewa believe that difficult labor or death in childbirth is due to the infidelity of a husband, and occasionally of the woman herself, during her pregnancy. The woman must also avoid certain foods: The *foula* gourd will cause the baby to be born with legs first, eggs will render it powerless, and salt will give it asthma. If the mother sees a monkey the baby may look like one, a lazy mother will bear a lazy child, and so on. That is what people say, but whether they believe it is another matter.

During delivery, the mother sits on the floor, legs apart, supported and gently rubbed by her mother and other elder women, who are her *aphungu*—advisors. The husband stays with relatives and friends, anxiously waiting for the grandmother to announce the news. Once the baby has arrived, neighbors, relatives, and friends visit the newly born, carrying hot porridge and other good foods. Some of the food has special medicinal herbs cooked into it to take the mother's pain away and help her recover quickly. The mother is allowed to rest for one week or so if there is no pressing task to be done like planting, weeding, or harvesting. During this time female relatives and friends cook and draw water for the household.

So many dangers threaten the life of a new-born child. So many lives are lost through spontaneous abortions, premature births, stillbirths, and deaths shortly after birth. This precariousness of living has been duly recognized in the Kefa view that it is only when the parents resume sexual relations, about three or four months after the birth, that a child becomes a full-fledged human being. For this to happen the child must be "thrown on the bed" at the parents' first sexual encounter. The baby, mother, and father are all nude. Depending on the sex of the baby, the mother or the father hands the other the infant across a fire lit inside the hut and carries it around the flames in the direction of the life-giving and merciless sun. This is then repeated by the other parent. Only in this way can the baby become an *otentha*[3]—a "warm" human being—and only an *otentha* can be buried in the village graveyard. Children who die before this "rite de passage" are *nthayo*—cold—and are buried in special infants' burial ground. There is no particular funeral ceremony in connection with *nthayo* burials; men are not present and "the woman do not even cry." Thus, sexual intercourse is not only the origin but also a symbol of life as it is ritually connected with making the child a full member of the community. It may also be a way in which a man asserts his claim to full fatherhood to compensate for the fact that birth is entirely a woman's business.

The baby is put to the mother's breast almost immediately after birth, and for the next six months it is nearly always with the mother, who feeds it whenever it cries. As the song goes:

> lu-lu-lu
> lu-lu-lu
> Mwana akulila   When a baby is crying
> Linda ndi tulo   It sometimes wants sleep
> Lina ndi njala   It sometimes wants food
> lu-lu-tu[4]

After about six months the baby is given porridge in addition to breastmilk, and, if available, milk. Soon thereafter *nsima* is added from the mother's plate. There are no special foods or meal hours for children. How and when they are fed depend on the ambition, economic situation, and work burden of the mother, and possibly on what she has learned at the Under-Five Clinic at Chiparamba, which most young mothers in Kefa village visit to check on their pregnancy.

A new pregnancy is not welcome before the baby walks. To prevent the mother from conceiving too soon, the *aphungu* prepares a special medicine of roots and herbs for her. When she does become pregnant again, breast-feeding is discontinued. *Unjise* is the Nyanja word for the illness that can strike the last born when the mother becomes pregnant too soon. In Kefa village, as in all of Africa, kwashiorkor is often fatal. And that is the most likely reason why a second born is called *woponda mnzace pamutu*, he who treads on his fellow-child's head.

If the mother does not conceive, breast-feeding is often continued as a supplement for two or three years. This may lead to marital problems like the one that Agnes describes:

"Jackson Phiri has a wife from Taswela village and they have a small son called Josam. One day the parents were quarreling. The husband wanted the wife to stop breast-feeding the boy. But she said: 'How can I stop? The boy is still young.' Then the husband beat the wife and after some days she decided to stop breast-feeding the baby. From then on the husband was very happy and the quarreling in the house ended."

While adults are not supposed to need food in the morning, many mothers try to cook a light meal for their small children, provided they have the time and raw materials needed: porridge made from maize flour and water or milk, "slept over *nsima*" (from the night before), and "tea" (sugar and hot water) are typical breakfast foods. When a small child "cries from hunger," which we observed often, the mother, and occasionally somebody else, will give it groundnuts, a gourd, or a fruit, or cook *nsima*.[5] We also observed adult men eating the food meant for a child. A father may persuade his toddler to relinquish a pawpaw, a newly roasted maize cob, or a piece of meat. But he will also share his snack or beer with a child.

For a number of reasons—including schooling, desertion, divorce, and death—many village children grow up away from their biological parents. The schooling system takes many children away from home if they want to continue school after grade four. Lower primary school is within the reach of most villages, but upper primary school is not. When a married couple goes to town to look for a job, they often leave the children with rural relatives. Even parents who can afford to keep their family in town may out of pity for aged relatives send them their children for company and for help with their daily chores. The separation between biological parents and children is not a new phenomenon and communal responsibility and reciprocity have been developed accordingly. As a result an individual rarely has only one mother or father to rely on.[6]

Amai—mother—is a term that encompasses a person's biological mother, her sisters (including her female cousins), and the father's brothers' wives. *Atate*—father—covers the biological father, his 'brothers' (who are also his male cousins) and the mother's husbands. A young person will therefore have *ambuye*—grandparents—everywhere, not only among the older people in his or her own village. Sex does not necessarily control the use of *mai* (the *a* is added for respect) or *tate*; it is determined by whether a person belongs to the lineage of the mother or the father. Thus a father's sister is also the "father" or *tate*, usually called *tate wamkazi* or "female father." The mother's brothers, however, are not called "male mothers," but are referred to by the special term *atsibweni*; they play, as we shall learn, a very special place among the matrilineal Chewa.[7]

Not all *amai*, *atate*, and *ambuye* are equally important, but family members are there to help and support each other, even when the nature of the relationship is not entirely clear.[8] Sylvester tells us:

"When Mwada Simba's family talked about Sonile Ngoma, they said 'she is your sister,' but Mwada does not know how they are related. When I asked Sandikonda Daka [a village elder] he said: 'Mwada's mother and Sonile's mother were sisters. That is how they are related.'

"Mwada used to live in Lundazi [a small town 200 kilometers away], but when her husband died she decided to settle with her relative Sonile, in Kefa village. So it was here in Kefa village that she befriended and came to love very much her present husband, Micheck Phiri, who is fifteen years her junior.

"Sometime later, Mwada's house burned down. Sonile's grandson, Moses, who was only six years of age, was the cause of the accident. The fire ate all Mwada's possessions, like pots, plates, blankets, and dresses, and also Micheck's clothes and shoes. But Mwada did not complain. She said, 'This is my family and there is nothing I can do about it.'

"It was after the fire that Mwada and Micheck turned their friendship into a proper marriage. Sonile and her family were not happy to see Mwada, who was beyond bearing children, marry such a young man, but Mwada worked hard on her marriage so that Micheck should not lose courage. No bride price was paid because Mwada did not want Micheck to pay anything to Sonile when she did not even know how they were related. She also wanted to get to know Sonile and the husband, Andrick, better. When she did, she said they were too talkative, as they were ever gossiping about other people's affairs, including those of Mwada and Micheck.

"Henly and Lohan, Mwada's sons from Lundazi, used to go to Sonile for meals. But soon Sonile and Andrick wanted the children to quit eating from their pot. They said: 'You, Mwada's children, you are no good. You are just like your mother, too proud. She does not want to share her food with us, so you too should eat separately, and not come to our house whenever our *nsima* is on the fire.' When Mwada heard this she made the children stop visiting Sonile's house at mealtimes. From then on they had only their mother to depend on because they had no relatives in the village."

Growing Up

"The most convenient summary of the valuations that Chewa make regarding conduct is to be found in their concept of the 'good person,' *munthu wabwino*," Marwick wrote in 1952.[9] It still is. A good person is one who is sociable, hospitable, mild, self-controlled, respectful of his or her social superiors, and willing to do them favors. He or she is also potent and fertile. A woman, in addition, is subservient and hardworking. Children are expected to be nonviolent and to serve their elders willingly. Little girls are repeatedly admonished to look carefully after property, especially pots.

Aggressive behavior among adults and children is actively discouraged. The Chewa rarely beat their children. We only saw that Lifenso, nine years old, got a spanking because he stole sugar from a neighboring house, and that Evelinar Njobvu's six-year-old Moses got a thrashing twice because he pinched groundnuts and because he ate without having washed his hands, but on other occasions he did both without any repercussions. Children in Kefa village rarely cry.

Agnes wrote: "Children under five years of age are mostly looked upon as human seeds. All they can do are small jobs like collecting fire to light tobacco [homemade cigarettes], pass drinking water to adults, and help their mother by running to a neighbor to borrow things." Yet by the age of four Simon helps his mother cook relish, and Nyawa at five is a much used babysitter. Like most other age-mates both the children are active "food gatherers," visiting relatives and sharing in their meals.

More so than boys, girls are truly useful from a very early age. Often play and work intermingle as when a five-year-old carries a younger sibling around most of the day or goes to the water hole with her own pot. Play as well as work is encouraged by the elders: *Madimbi* is the game in which little boys and girls act as a married couple; the little girl, borrowing her mother's utensils, cooks food for her little husband. *Mashanga*, picking leftovers from the fields, is another cherished activity. Groundnut fields are scrutinized with particular care as the nuts are so delicious and can be eaten on the spot. Grownups, remembering how they enjoyed *mashanga* when they were young, do not worry if they do not harvest every nut.

Moving about in groups, mostly boys, who have fewer duties at home than the girls, explore the village surroundings, picking fruits and berries that adults no longer consider worthwhile and reporting the location of mushrooms, beehives, and mice.

Around the age of eight or nine most children go to Mtewe lower primary school, and many parents work hard to keep them there. A school child needs uniform, books, and pencils. Because there is no upper primary school within walking distance from the Kefa village, from grade five upward money must be found for transport and the daily upkeep of a school child, unless there are relatives in the area with whom he or she can live. To most parents school expenses are a real problem. To solve it so many mothers cultivate cash crop or brew beer, while others look for money wherever it can be found.

Tilele Zulu and Lemekani Mbao are facing the problem right now, as Esinaya is due to start in grade five. The best solution is to send her to Mazimoyo school where Tilele's mother lives. Lemekani asks Esinaya if she would want to go, and Esinaya says that if she were to live with her grandmother she could continue schooling and help the grandmother in the house as well.

Children discontinue their education for a variety of reasons. One is the lack of school places; for example, in Eastern Province there are 12,000 seventh grade graduates and only 2,000 secondary school places. But many never complete even the primary school.[10]

When Astes' father, Kwezekani Mbewe, died because of the fatal blow of the axe handle, Astes no longer knew who would pay her school expenses. Brighton explains:

"If she cannot go to school any more Astes says she will go home. By 'home' she means the home of her proper mother, who died several years ago. She will stay with relatives and if possible find a husband from there. Astes assists her mother [stepmother] and grandmother with the cultivation. She says that a mother should not do all the work as long as she herself is young and available. Astes is so decent and modest, to think that she is an orphan makes you want to cry." (Astes wants to leave Kefa village because her stepmother Tiku, having become a widow, will go back to her own village.)

In Micheck's family it was the twelve-year-old Tembani who was sent out to earn, but that certainly did not solve Micheck's problems. Tyford reports:

"Tembani and Henly are Micheck's stepsons. Tembani used to live in Lundazi with his father,but now he has come to Kefa village to stay with Mwada, his mother [mother's sister]. Headman Kefa employed Tembani to look after his cattle and Micheck was glad that the boy got a job because now he could help buy a school uniform for Henly. But Tembani, just like Henly, is only twelve years old and Micheck is supposed to dress both of them. A letter from Mwada's relatives in Lundazi asked why Micheck did not look for a job rather than depend on the young boy Tembani to buy a school uniform for his son Henly. Micheck believed that Andrick, Mwada's sister Sonile's husband, had caused the letter to be written and complained that Andrick was backbiting him. The two men fell to quarreling and near-ly attacked each other. Their wives, Mwada and Sonile, quarreled too, until Evelinar Njobvu made them all go the headman Kefa to ask him to resolve the case.

"At the village meeting Micheck was reproached for his behavior. He was told he had a bad character and was repeatedly creating problems for others. Hearing this, Micheck got very upset and shouted that Andrick was behind it all, practicing witchcraft against him. But the headman told him to be quiet and said: 'You, Micheck Phiri, married into our village, but you did not pay any money for your marriage and you have no children from here. Unless your behavior is improved there is nothing to prevent me from chasing you away.' Micheck then felt very sorry for himself but he prom-ised that he would definitely improve and look for work to pay Henly's school uniform himself."

Yanzulani and Mwaninyana have eight children and each one of them has been educated. Yanzulani is a builder with a house in Chipata as well as the one in Kefa. He neither smokes nor drinks and he has only one wife. Mwaninyana has a business of her own—selling fish and cooking oil, and occasionally beans and cakes. The well-to-do family cooperates with whoever asks for its help, but family members never go to other peo-ple's house to chat. They work hard and that is how they afford to educate all the children. Yet recently much bad luck has fallen upon them. The first-born used to have a good job, but now he is in prison because he stole money from his working place. The second-born, who easily passed his exams and went to study law at the University in Lusaka, was killed in a car accident. People in Kefa said: "The parents worked so hard for so long to educate their son, and the car killed him in no time."

Although parents want their children to be educated, they also fear it, and rightly so. The brightest among the students are invariably lost to the village, which has to make do without their intelligence and labor.[11] But education is more than a stepping stone to urban living. It also teaches young people new ambitions and provides them with new value systems. Rural living becomes associated with everything that a youngster wants to escape. The material and cultural achievements of generations of ancestors embodied in yesterday's village living has no place in today's curricula.

School curricula are in no way related to rural life and many of the young villagers do better out of school than inside. Faides Phiri is the mother of five sons. Without the help of her older boys she would not have been able to feed the younger children. Her first-born, George Zulu, is eighteen. He is employed as a laborer and he helps his mother with money for paraffin and clothes. Joseph, the second-born, who stopped school in the fourth grade, is more useful to his mother. It is he who hoes her field and helps feed the younger children. So, thanks to her sons, Faides, with no husband to rely on, is well off.

Young people are not all equally helpful.[12] Danga Banda, Square's "son," would only sell his green maize, giving none to his father. Alines, who is sixteen, refused flatly to help her father in the field, saying she had enough work in the house. Jessie Tonga had to pay her sons to weed for her, and even headman Kefa cannot persuade his sons Paskale and David to work for his wives.

When Square Banda and Paskale Mwale, who is sixteen, were talking as they sat by the fire in the evening, Square began to give the boy advice on such matters:

"You, Paskale, you have got a father, but your mother is not here [she divorced Kefa and went away]. Now you must look after your father's cattle because your father's property is your own."

And Paskale said that, yes, he would do so, but his problem was another one. "Our mothers do not want us. Especially our mother Lelia is no good and she encourages our other mothers [Kefa's wives] not to give us any food. When milk is brought to the house she takes it all for herself, and if we sell it, she wants all the money to be hers. So for four days now David and I have not eaten anything from our mothers. We have two good mothers, Regina and Nyamanda, but now Regina is away and Nyamanda is not well so she does not cook, and we do not get food anywhere."

Square answered: "I know your mother Lelia. She wants all your father's property to be hers. You should report this to your father, so that Mr. Kefa can deal with her and tell her to keep you properly.

But Paskale replied: "We have reported it to Mr. Kefa, but he does nothing about it."

Square Banda then said: "*Chabwino*—Okay, if it is like that I only have one advice. Try to beat your mother. She is proud and she does not like her husband's children. That is bad behavior on her part."

Lelia sees it differently. She refuses the boys food because they do not help her, or Kefa's other wives, either at home or in the field.

It is Sylvester's opinion that:

"The behavior of children is a reflection of the character, knowledge, and interests of the family head. If the head is not firm, the children will never learn to behave and participate in village affairs. *Kuongola mtengo mpoyamba*—a tree must be straightened when young. Only in households where the parents cooperate, and that is mostly in families where the wife obeys the rules of the husband and also where the husband depends on the views of the wife, children behave as their elders would wish. There are households where the women still seem in charge even though the man is present. In such households women defy the husband's house rules and the children become talented in cheeky behavior. And there are households where there are no men at all and where the mother only advises whoever is willing to cooperate with her. In such households there is no order. The mother forces no one and on occasions daughters even bring their boyfriends into the mother's house. When she tries to stop them from living with their lovers, the daughters do not obey because they are not afraid of her. They know they will not be beaten as they would have had there been a father in the house."

Sylvester belongs to the Ngoni people and is used to tougher child raising than that which the Chewa generally practice.

Until the age of three or four children usually sleep with their parents. At that age most youngsters move to a grandparent (any elderly relative) for sleeping and sometimes also they eat there. The girls remain here until they marry, while young boys of ten years or so may build themselves a house of their own where they sleep in a group, eating with their fathers or other male relatives.

Thefts, fights, and sexual intercourse are actively prohibited and adults will intervene if they observe such behavior. However, parental control to what young men do at nighttime is usually limited. Or as Ketelina Daka, Kefa's first wife, put it: "As boys grow up they may play or work during day, but at night they watch dances and do illegal things like drinking beer or liquor, playing cards for money, and having fun even up to three in the morning." Girls are under much tighter control, staying as they do with an elderly female relative.

Although boys and girls begin school in equal numbers, some parents insist on keeping their daughters at home once they reach puberty. Hence, they are to be taught in the village by the *aphungu*—the wise elderly women.

"Girls are fortunate," Agnes told us, "because at the maturity ceremony they learn how to behave in every way. This is not the case with the boys, who have no puberty ceremony."

The young girls are initiated in groups or individually, depending on the number in their age group. Zalenji Mwale, Kefa's daughter and possible heir to the headmanship, is a *phungu* as are Romanzi Tembo and Fatines. There are other *aphungu* in the village, women who are deeply respected for their skills and wisdom.[13]

At a girl's first menstruation[14] it is the grandmother who makes the message public. For four weeks the girl remains inside a grandmother's sleeping hut. She must neither cook nor touch the fire. She is only allowed out after dark to relieve herself. If need arises before that time she will use a pot.

During her seclusion, the young girl is frequently visited by the *aphungu*, the grandmother, and other mature girls and women. They all come to instruct the new woman-to-be and growing up to adulthood takes a lot of learning for a young girl. The instructions mostly take place at night and the women sing and dance to celebrate the attainment of yet another woman. The girl is taught how to cook well, and how to look after the relatives of her husband-to-be. The house and yard must be kept clean and tidy. Some of the instructions, mostly those concerning how to treat and how to please her husband-to-be, will be repeated on her wedding day.

To be a good housewife takes a lot of learning, and a lot of advice about what not to do. The medium for instruction is often the dance and the language pantomime. One such dance concerns the need to pound—well and often:

> Do not pound for your husband only and feign ill when his relatives come for a visit;
>
> Do not run about in the village begging for mealiemeal, pound your own;
>
> Do not postpone serving food when a visitor comes, share your *nsima*;
>
> Do not be lazy and pound so little that people who eat from you do not get satisfied;
>
> Do not hang around doing nothing until the moment you see your husband's brother—and do not flirt with him.

During the instructions the young girl is introduced to bush medicine including remedies that may help her avoid unwanted pregnancies. She is also fortified with concoctions that will protect her from asthma and ensure her fertility.

At the end of the four weeks, the girl emerges into the public again and she is celebrated with the *m'meto wanamwali*—the haircutting ceremony for initiates. The ceremony is a true festival. Female relatives, friends, and neighbors come from all over the area to cook, eat, dance, and advise the girl, or girls if there are several initiates. The best of drummers will be present and the girl receives gifts of money, but otherwise her role is a passive one. She sits quietly and with lowered head. Cutting off the hair is the apex of the ceremony, signifying, as shaving the head always does, that a new phase in life is starting.

Excision is fortunately not practiced among the Chewa. On the contrary, teachings in connection with initiation include how to enjoy sexual encounters and sexual intercourse. Even if intercourse is forbidden for the unmarried girl, young people come together from an early age and intimate relations are considered part of life for the young (and their elders). Most Chewa dances, and they are all danced by girls and women only, emphasize a body language that speaks of sexuality. Still, if a boy or man is caught having sexual intercourse with a young girl, the case is immediately taken before the headman, after the parents have been informed as to what has happened. If the girl is considered a virgin, the boy is automatically charged *chidumu*—damage money—whether the girl is pregnant or not.

Boys have no ceremony through which their adulthood is recognized, and it is only as a father of growing children that their status as men is firmly established. A generation ago this was different. Older people remember how they used to gather in a special meeting place, *mphala*, where the elders taught them how to make hoe handles, mats, cooking sticks, and baskets. While working together, the elders would advise the youngmen, jokingly, but meant seriously, so that they could inherit the understanding and the behavior of their elders.

> "I have noticed that some parents [fathers] seem to encourage their sons to participate in illicit activity," Sylvester wrote.[1] "They think this shows that the young men are spirited. They themselves did the same things when they were young. They tell the boys that men who never did such things when young are those who remain barren as they grow older."

Courting

People say that a boy should marry "when he is ripe enough to control the marriage." He must be able to control himself as well as his wife.

Once married a man can no longer depend on his mother's granaries; he must set up his own. To do so, he must clear a field of sufficient size to be able to feed himself and the wife (and of course also visitors). He must build a house. The wife-to-be may provide most of the labor both as regards cultivation and housebuilding, but the husband is the head of the household. He must persuade his family to contribute to the marriage payment, which is the gift the groom's family presents to that of the bride. Or he must raise the money or find the goods himself.

Today, marriage payments are on the increase, or seem that way because those who do not have access to cattle have to pay the equivalent in cash. And a cow is expensive for those who have none. This is one reason why boys and girls marry at a later age than did their parents. Besides, as the world changes, new options (of jobs, travels, schooling) make youngsters less eager to settle down and to live as the older generation does.

Marriage also offers new possibilities to young people. It confers status. It is a prerequisite to fully fledged parenthood, which is the only way to secure complete community membership and to provide for one's old age. Marriage also means freedom from parental meddling and to sexual intercourse. It releases productive potential, as young people usually work harder as heads of their own household than as dependents of their parents.

Marriage is also the confirmation of a long cultural tradition. Through it, men become "owners of women" and women's domestication is continued and completed.

"A girl should marry when she matures. Once fertile, there is no reason why she should waste more time in her mother's house. Some parents prefer a not-yet-matured girl as their son's wife. They think that it is good for a man to marry a young girl as she is easier to control. And they want a girl who has not yet had any sexual experience," Lemekani Mbao explains, contemplating the marriage prospect for his sixteen-year-old daughter Alines.

In the past marriages were arranged between the older members of the two families concerned. This practice continues for some villagers, and a proposal may take place in the following manner, Sylvester tells us:

"Uncle[15] of the boy: 'This year we have got a good harvest.'

"Uncle of the girl: 'Oh, sure. I have done well this year, see how the maize grows!'

"Uncle of the boy: 'That is because you have such hard-working daughters.'

"Uncle of the girl: 'Yes, that is so, but it is also so that girls do not work as well or as hard as boys.'

"Uncle of the boy: 'Yes, my nephew [*aphwa*] is very hard-working. He is a man whom you know, and he is already thinking of marriage. In fact, I was thinking of proposing him to your little mother [*amai ang'ongo* means lit. little mother; here niece]. I do not know, is she old enough for marriage?'

"Uncle of the girl: 'She is still young. Just look at her body, it is not fully grown.'

"Uncle of the boy: 'That is the best age for marrying. When she becomes mature, very soon a woman becomes stubborn and difficult to handle. That is why this time now is good for marrying . . .'

"And so they go on. When the elder relatives have reached agreement, they take their decision to their sisters. Then an old relative who knows both families will take the boy to the girl's family to introduce him. If relatives on both sides agree, it is difficult for the young couple-to-be to refuse."

Today, young men earn money cultivating cash crops and vegetables or doing piece work and are less inclined to let their relatives decide whom they should marry. The newly wed Jones Mwale explains:

"If your mind is set, you consult with your relatives and send your uncle, grandfather, or some wise friend of your father to visit the girl's family and confirm the seriousness of your intent. Members of the girl's family consult with each other and pass a reply to your family through the negotiator. A wife's mother is *mpongozi*[16]—mother-in-law—and a person to be greatly feared and highly respected, so that if your intention is marriage, you start immediately to be afraid of the mother of the girl and treat her with utmost respect."

The father-in-law to be is also treated with respect by the son-in-law, but not to the same degree as the mother-in-law. Respect is also paid by a woman to *her* in-laws, but as they usually live in different villages, the prescribed relationship between daughter-in-law and parent-in-law is less consequential. The usual pattern is that the boy comes and lives in the girl's village, at least for an initial period of time.

E yaye!	*E yaye!*
Ufu afuna ine	You who propose to me
Apereke makumi atatu	must give thirty pounds
Khumi limodzi ndakana	ten pounds is too little, I refuse
E yaye!	*E yaye!*
	Dahlschen, 1970:30

A generation ago the marriage payment was in the range of K. 10–15. Today a husband may be charged from K. 30 to K. 250 and the amount seems to keep increasing.[17] The actual amount depends on the wealth of the groom, the girl's family connections, her age, beauty, whether she has been married before, and so on.

There are different types of marriage payments, or bride price or bride wealth as it is also called. Some are mere tokens, others represent a considerable transfer of wealth. *Chamlomo* is a small gift in cash from the boy's family to the person negotiating the marriage, to show that the family is seriously contemplating marriage. *Chimalo* is the actual bride price. It is a transfer of money or goods from the man to the girl's family to make it easier for them to bear the loss of a family member, as she will no longer work in the mother's field and kitchen, but will work for the husband and his family. The bride's family decide the amount. It is said that it is not only the attraction of town life which makes young men leave the village but also the greed of village elders, who want too much money for their daughters.

Chimalo helps to stabilize a marriage. A woman's family may try hard to dissuade their daughter from divorce, for this will mean repaying money or cattle received as *chimalo*. Many families, however, are quite prepared to "release" their daughter, as Brighton put it, if she wants to discontinue her marriage. For this purpose they take care to invest cash payment in cattle, so that the *chimalo* will not be lost. *Chimalo* not only makes it troublesome to break up a marriage, but it also turns unmarried women into an asset that can be exchanged for bride wealth at some moment in the future.

Among the matrilineal Chewa a girl's guardian is her *atsibweni*—the mother's (eldest) brother. It is he who is supposed to give her away in marriage. But in the changing Kefa world increasingly dominated by money and men, matrilineal traditions are dying out. Elders, both men and women, lose their hegemony as men with money suit themselves rather than follow the advice of the elders. As a consequence, there is growing confusion as to the proper way of doing things. Sylvester tells us:

"Mr. Mbao is called by headman Kefa to discuss the virgin named Morin, who is getting married to Mubanga. Mubanga works for the Water Affairs and is a Tong by tribe. He fell in love with Morin when the Water Affairs Department was looking for water in Kefa village. Morin is the stepdaughter of Isac Phiri. Apparently Morin is not yet matured, but Mubanga wants to engage her for marriage right away, so that she will not get married to anybody else once she matures. He is charged K. 20 as bride wealth.

"Now Mr. Mbao and Mr. Kefa discuss who has the authority to charge bride price. The bride price has been charged by Isac. But as a rule the father should not charge his daughter's dowry; this should be charged by the brother of the mother. Mbao and Kefa come to the conclusion that it is Danga and Jackson [Square's "sons"] who should charge bride wealth because they are Morin's nearest relatives.

"Mr. Kefa says: 'As they are her brothers they are the right people to charge and make use of the bride wealth according to our Chewa customs.

For the money something valuable should be bought, like a cow or whatever makes a profit. Then if the marriage finishes, or our relative [i.e., Morin, who is also related to Kefa] makes an error, we can sell the cow and pay to release her from marriage.'"

The size of the bride wealth varies. Simon Sakala paid a cow for Jenifa Banda, and Jones Mwale, who married a few years later, was asked K. 190 for Bernadette Tembo. But, when Mwada Simba married the much younger Micheck Phiri, she told him not to pay anything at all; she had already married two husbands and did not want her remote relatives to take any money from her lover. Mabuto Ngoma paid only K. 1 for his wife. It was just a mere token gift, for the wife belongs to the Senga people among whom the bride wealth is no more than symbolic.

Lemekani Mbao is Ngoni through his father. The patrilineal Ngoni not only pay bride wealth but also *lobola*, an additional payment transferring the right to the children from the mother's lineage to the father's "so that the children of the marriage belong entirely to the husband," even after a divorce. Lemekani paid K. 3 and a cow for Tilele Zulu; the money was the bride wealth, and the cow the *lobola*. "Nowadays, many Chewas, too, want to pay *lobola* just like the Ngoni, so that the children from the marriage belong to them. In this way, people who can afford it take charge of their own family." Headman Kefa explains, "They do not want to depend on their uncle, whom they may not even know."[18]

Kefa's third wife, Regina Shawa, is also Ngoni. Kefa paid K. 1 and a cow for her. Regina says: "A girl must marry so that her parents can earn. Women marry because they need men. If they have men without being married it is not good. And the parent will not get any money." In actual fact, many girls "have men" without being married. But the pragmatic Chewa have applied their marriage payment system even to such uncontracted unions. *Chidumu*—damage—"is the name for the payment given to the girl's relatives apologizing for making their daughter pregnant without marrying her first," Brighton explains. "The word comes from *dumula*, which is to do something unexpectedly to someone, for the parents never expected their daughter to become pregnant."

The damage payment depends on the relatives of the girl and how much money they think they can get out of the man. If he is willing to marry the woman, it is added to the other marriage charges.

The code of honor says that if an unwed pregnant mother cites a particular man as the father, he should not deny it. Tyford tells us:

"Grace Daka, who was only seventeen, and Jumapili Banda met once in the garden for love, and Jumapili paid Grace K. 1 for serving him so. When Grace became pregnant and her parents asked her about it, she said:

'Jumapili Banda is the only man I met and I think he is the one who made me pregnant.' Then the parents called Jumapili, his family members, and their own relatives. When James Daka asked Jumapili before the meeting if what his daughter said was true—was it he who had made her pregnant? Jumapili answered: 'Yes, if she says so, that is all right with me.' James Daka said: 'I would like you to pay me K. 200 for Grace and the damage that you have caused us.' Jumapili replied that he would not mind paying but that James was asking too much. James agreed to reduce the amount: 'I will charge you K. 176, but nothing less than that. And this money I want by the end of August, because I shall need some cash just then.'

"Jumapili agreed to give Mr. Daka the money in cash, but added: 'What I meant is that I will pay *chimalo* [bride wealth] as well as *chidumu* [damage money] because I want the girl to be my wife and stay in my house. And I shall look after her while she is pregnant.'

"This Mr. Daka utterly refused: 'You cannot marry my daughter,' he told Jumapili. 'You have no money. How can you dress her? Look at yourself. Even here standing in front of us, your clothes are dirty. You are a poor man. I do *not* want you to marry my daughter.'

"Jumapili merely replied: '*Chabwino*—Okay—Mr.Daka, if you know that I have nothing to give to your daughter, there is nothing I can do. I leave her to you.'

"Grace said nothing, while other people present tried to persuade Mr. Daka to accept Mr. Banda's proposal to marry his daughter, but he refused. When she was seven months pregnant, Grace fell ill. It looked as if she was about to give birth and Grace was taken to Chiparamba Health Centre. Once there, she gave birth and died.

"After the funeral Grace's family brought a case against Jumapili Banda, accusing him of having killed their daughter. After hearing the witnesses, the Chief passed judgment. This is what he said: 'This misfortune struck you, not through any fault of Mr. Banda. It was Mr. Daka's mistake that Grace has died as a member of her father's household. Mr. Banda can not be blamed. He offered to pay for the girl, and he was ready to marry her. But Mr. Daka wanted more money than Mr. Banda could pay. It is because of your greed, Mr. Daka, that your daughter died while in your own house, and not in that of Mr. Banda. It is you, the parents of Grace who are at fault. This sad event has taken place because some parents do not think properly where their daughters are concerned. So, please, if you have a daughter that becomes pregnant, try to force the person who made her so to marry her. Do not charge too much or you may end up like Mr. Daka here who has lost his daughter and gained nothing.'"

For some, like Kamaswanda Njobvu, almost any amount of money seems too much. When Kamaswanda first came to Kefa village he brought a wife. But they quarreled, and she left him and went back to Petauke where they had come from. Shortly thereafter Kamaswanda became friendly with Rahaby Sakala and made her pregnant. When people saw

Rahaby sleeping openly in Kamaswanda's house they wondered, for no proposal had come for her. In February headman Kefa called a village meeting and said:

"I have called you friends together to help me. Kamaswanda Njobvu has made my sister's daughter pregnant and we, the owners of the woman, are not aware that any marriage has taken place between the two. And we have charged Kamaswanda *chidumo* of K. 30, but he has not paid anything." Then Kamaswanda stood up to explain what had happened: "When I came back here after doing my business of making baskets in Katete I hoped to pay. But contrary to my expectations, I never sold enough baskets and I still do not have the money." Then the counselor of the marriage, who was Micheck Phiri, reminded Kamaswanda that he had been charged "damage" in September and now it was February. Lemekani Mbao supported Micheck saying: "A long time ago I heard Mr. Kefa ask for *chidumo* and you, Kamaswanda Njobvu, promised you would pay him within one week. And now you promise that you will sell your baskets tomorrow."

Hearing this, Kamaswanda got annoyed. He said he had already given a basket worth K. 30 to Lelia (Kefa's fourth wife) and fish worth K. 1.40 to Agnes (another Kefa relative), and Kefa himself had used him to work in his field and had paid him only K. 2 for the hard work he had put in, and that was far too little. Kamaswanda concluded by refusing to pay "damage" at all. Furthermore, he said that Rahaby had aborted so many times and this she did so that her relatives could charge *chidumo* over and over again! She had slept with so many men why should he in particular pay anything. In fact, he owed nothing to anybody. He would not even pay back the loan of K. 10 that he had got from headman Kefa, or the K. 5 that he had taken from Lelia, or the 60 ngwee from Keteline (Kefa's first wife) that he had spent on buying Eliah Phiri's three-legged bed.

At this point headman Kefa made Kamaswanda sit down. They had heard enough. Time had come to pass judgment: Kamaswanda was told that he must pay K. 30 within four weeks, or he would be summoned before the Chief's court, where Kefa would ask the Chief to accept that he, headman Kefa Mwale, chase the troublesome basketmaker Kamaswanda away from his village!

Four weeks later Kamaswanda had still not paid. Sylvester, who reported the incident, told us: "In Kefa's opinion Kamaswanda is a troublemaker and a very uncooperative village resident. But Kefa is too kind. Because Kamaswanda has a girl from this village as his wife, the headman does not want to expel him."

Courting is not the prerogative of youth.[19] Men in particular marry throughout life, especially if, like headman Kefa, they have money. At seventy-three years of age Kefa took a new wife, Nyamanda, from the neighboring Kamanga village. Whatever the age of bride and groom, a properly contracted marriage always presupposes negotiations between families and marriage payments. Unless, of course, the marriage proposition is merely a conversational joke—such as Lemekani's offer to marry Nyokase when they were relaxing in Nyokase's field hut!

On such an occasion Nyokase said:

> "I have problems. I cannot get any soap, and I have no money to buy clothes or even to take the pounded maize to the mill. I think I must definitely find myself a husband again. Even if he is poor, he might help me at least a bit."
>
> And Lemekani answered: "If this is your problem, *chabwino*, okay, why don't you marry me. Let us go together to my house right away, and I shall be your husband."
>
> But Nyokase said: "I cannot go with you. You have no money to buy me soap or clothes. Besides, your wife is too talkative and she will certainly not be quiet if I came to your house. And I know not only her but you too. You love your wife too much. Yet you do not help her in the field. Just like me, Joseph's mother [Lemekani's wife] hoes alone. You men are useless—that is why I divorced in the first place. But I am glad you are here. You remind me that for a woman to get money the best thing is to work hard alone."

Such "joking marriages" usually take place between close relatives.

Square Banda, the cripple, has his "wives in jest" and one of them is Masulu, his cousin. The two of them were chatting one day when Masulu said: "Why don't you marry? You just move around giving people medicine, but you do not marry. Why not? You cook your food alone, where is your wife?"

But Square answered her: "How can I marry when I already have a wife, and that wife is you! If you did not know that you are my wife, on this very day I shall make love to you. We can go to your house right away and I shall convince you that you are my wife and that I need no other women to marry." They chatted on for a long time, for they were in a good mood.

"They chat and joke because they are related," says Brighton.

Marriage

Among the Chewa, for whom sexual relations are rarely confined to married life, a marriage is nothing absolutely new for bride and groom. What is new is the commitment and responsibility that marriage implies. These are clearly underlined in the marriage ceremony.

The bride plays a central role. She is seated higher that the others as a way of showing respect for her. To persuade her to eat with the others, she receives small money gifts and later more small money gifts to enter into her new husband's house. The couple also receives money and food gifts from the wedding guests. In addition to the general rejoicing and communal eating and drinking, the bride and groom are instructed in rituals and rules regarding reciprocal care and concern by their respective *nkhoswe*, who have been ritually appointed for that purpose.

The *nkhoswe* are wise elder friends or relatives who serve as marriage counselors. It is their responsibility to bring problems that affect a marriage to the attention of the senior guardians of the two families, or matrilineages. Problems must be solved whenever they arise and not allowed to poison the relationship between spouses, between families, and even between villages.[20]

It is the *nkhoswe* who instructs the couple as to the duties and pleasures of married life. To the bride these teachings are not new: She has already been instructed by the *aphungu*—the wise women in the village at her maturity ceremony. Now the instructions are repeated, but the groom hears them for the first time. Before intercourse, they are told, bride and groom must shave the pubic hairs of the partner. A razor blade is used and the hair is placed in a specially made small mud pot and hidden. Then the couple washes in hot water. The *nkhoswe* reminds the bride and groom that during intercourse "both the boy and the girl must dance on the bed, and not only the boy," as Zenaida Mwale, Kefa's daughter and *phungu* explained us. Chewa women are well prepared to be active partners, given the rhythmic movements of the pelvis that girls down to the age of ten excel in during the frequently held dances in Kefa village.

When they have completed intercourse, the wife wipes her husband's penis using a special handkerchief. Henceforth this is her duty after every sexual encounter as long as they remain together as husband and wife. The teachings of the *nkhoswe* emphasize the need to love, care, and cherish each other. Fidelity is not demanded, except during pregnancy when infidelity by either spouse is believed to lead to a premature or still-born child. At other times it is accepted that human nature is such that a man and a woman may long for each other, irrespective of their marital status, and that no harm is done if they come together as long as discretion is used. If not, divorce may be the result. It is also accepted that men are more sexually active than women and that a women may be doing the man "a favor" that deserves some reward, if the man is not already "the owner of the woman," that is, her husband.

A wife has many responsibilities, and some of them are highlighted in a Zambian song:

> Listen to my advice, my child
> The marriage you are going to enter
> Requires that you respect your husband's family
> Hatred is very bad

It is also bad to gossip about your husband's family
When I die, you will remember me and my advice
Tidiness is very important
Keep your husband's clothes clean
Dishes and household untensils should be clean also
Do not forget to sweep your home
These are the responsibilities of a married woman[21]

It is the wife's job to cultivate, gather, process, prepare, cook, and share food. Food preparation is the most time consuming of all women's work. But women also draw water and collect firewood, serve their husbands and provide for them sexually, and bear and nurture children. In addition, women are supposed always to be cooperative and obedient.

"The wife is the servant of the man and when he wants something she must do it right away," Regina Shawa, Kefa's third wife, explains. "For example, if the wife is busy pounding and the husband comes home hungry and wants to eat, and she says, 'Wait until I have finished pounding,' she is wrong and the husband is right in beating her. Being the wife, the woman should always serve the husband first."

The husband is the undisputed head of the family; most women, although certainly not all, leave every important decision to the man. In fact, decision making is one of the husband's main responsibilities. A husband must also help the wife to cultivate food crops, provide money to buy clothes and other household goods, and finance the children's schooling. He must also beget children. And he should respect his wife, and even more so, her relatives.

"Men are stronger than women and that is why they do all the important work. Women have stronger necks than men and that is why they must carry things on the head," Sandikonda said, explaining the division of labor within the family. It may be that in olden days when young Chewa men were busy hunting and defending their villages, the division of labor between the sexes was more balanced than today, when most jobs are in fact women's jobs, both in the home and in the field. Men today therefore have more time to relax and chat with other men, drink beer, and move around. They also have more time to undertake new economic activities, grow cash crops, and do odd jobs. This freedom gives them much better access to information and to money, two very important resources in controlling the family as well as the community.

But women too have means to secure their position in the community and even take charge of the household. Women usually have a wider network of friends than do their husbands, people with whom they cooperate and who will support them in times of need. "Women are too good to each other," Brighton comments.

Since the wife is usually the main "breadwinner," some men, like Lemekani Mbao, say "In this house I am mostly busy with my own personal affairs, and I am mostly out of the house. For that reason I let my wife do as she wants, because when I am not here she should have as few problems as possible." Few men may relinquish their male prerogatives as easily as Lemekani.

Kwerekani Phiri, who has a permanent job outside Kefa village, one day called his two wives, Jessie Tonga and Tisauke Phiri, and stated: "Now that I am working far away John Scout Phiri will be the head of the family and you must obey him in all matters." John Scout is Kwerekani's son.

Some women follow the example of Mwada Simba, who said: "I feed my husband with knowledge and let him think he is the one to make the important decisions in our house." Being the older spouse, Mwada has an advantage usually monopolized by men—that of experience. She continues: "Because I am older than Mr. Phiri, I have seen and heard more things in life than he, so I decide many things myself."

"A wife who opposes the husband deserves to be beaten, no matter whether she is right or not. But a good husband should not beat hard, or often." Regina, who comes from the neighboring Ngoni people, thinks that Chewa men are much better than the Ngoni: "When a Ngoni man beats you, he does it hard." But when headman Kefa hit her with a stick because she and Lelia (third and fourth wives of Kefa) were quarreling about a hen that had disappeared, she took the stick he had used and hid it, to show it to her brother and to complain about the husband's bad behavior. It was the first time in their ten years of marriage that Kefa had beaten her.

Infidelity and jealousy are the most common causes for wife beating. Kambula Banda has two wives and a younger brother. One evening, when Kambula was with his second wife, his brother visited the first wife, chatting softly with her until everybody was sleeping and the village was very quiet. When the wife also got tired and retired to her hut, young Banda followed, removed his clothes, and slept next to her. Kambula, the owner of the woman, had suspected that something was going on, however. During the night he entered the wife's hut and found the brother stripped of all his clothes sleeping next to his wife. He then beat his wife badly, as he was very upset to see her next to his brother. He also told the brother to leave the village and settle somewhere else. And the villagers agreed with him, saying that they suspected that the affair between the brother and the wife had been going on for some time.

Alcohol makes men violent all over the world, but in Kefa village the women occasionally fight back. Brighton tells this story:

> "Micheck had been beating the wife Mwada all night and was still beating her. The fight had started when Micheck insulted Mwada's parents, saying

that they had not taught their daughter proper manners as she did not know how to behave toward her husband. Mwada had insulted the husband by saying that all the possessions in their house were hers and that he was a good-for-nothing. Then she had packed her *chitenge*—piece of cloth—and said she would go away to Chipata. She hugged her son Henly, telling him not to worry, as she was not dead yet, that she had never really married the present husband [Micheck had not paid any bride wealth], and that they were just living together. And Micheck shouted that anyway she was much too old to be his wife.

"A long line of humiliating arguments followed, but when once more Micheck wanted to beat Mwada, the wife took a bamboo cane and hit him back three times." Brighton, who had been observing the couple, separated the two and called their *nkhoswe* so that their problem could be solved.

"On the next day in spite of the quarrels and fights of yesterday, Mwada and Micheck resumed their love. Micheck explained to the wife that he had beaten and insulted her because he was jealous of his best friend, who was earning money while he himself did not have even one ngwee. In order to show their love, they hugged each other unnecessarily" [in public]. Brighton finished his story, adding: "Micheck explained his behavior by saying that the wife is envious of him because she is old while he is still young." When Brighton advised him to become a polygamist, he said he could never manage two wives. " 'For me one is more than enough,' said Micheck Phiri.

"Everybody feels very sorry for the husband Micheck, because in the village it is only through the wife that he is respected. Otherwise, he only drinks and everybody thinks he is crazy."

Many men agree that one wife is enough, but not Kefa Mwale, Kwerekani Phiri, Zindikani Miti, and a few other villagers. It is also a matter of money. For a man it is expensive to marry; for a woman it is hard to manage without access, however limited, to a man and his earnings. If a husband decides to take another wife, there is little a woman can do, even if she does not like the situation, except to divorce the man. We shall learn more about this below.

Kwerekani Phiri has three wives. He can afford them because he is permanently employed by the Public Works Department. He never helps the wives in the field, but gives them money so that they can buy salt, soap, and paraffin, and take the maize to the mill for grinding. All the same, Kwerekani's wives are not pleased with their husband. When he comes to Kefa village, and he only comes during weekends, he spends most of his time at the beer houses. Tisauke, the hardworking cultivator set on earning independently, has been considering divorce, but says: "I am reluctant to divorce Mr. Phiri because I do not want my children to remain without a father. Besides I have already divorced three husbands and one cannot go on divorcing husbands all the time."

In a polygamous household, each wife has her hut and the husband moves from one to the other. Each wife cooks for him on an agreed number of days and during this time he sleeps in her house. When a man marries a new wife he may want to spend more time with her than the others, but he can do so only if the other wives agree. If they do not, they can take the matter before their relatives and the husband may be forced to pay his slighted wives a compensation because he has failed to observe his duties as a husband.

Whatever a polygamous husband brings into one wife's house, he must bring for all other wives as well; thus each gets the same amount of meat, money, or other things. When Kamaswanda Njobvu one day returned from Chipata with two dresses for his second wife Rahaby, and only one for the first, people said: "The basketmaker is always asking for trouble. How can he be so stupid as to buy two dresses for one wife and only one for the other? He should have bought the same number for both. Otherwise, how can there ever be peace in his house?"

In a society where the man is often the undisputed head of the home and in control of most of its resources, a conflict of interest exists among co-wives. Each wants a maximum share of the man, and of his resources, for herself and her children, and many women are prepared to compete for it. But not everybody. Gia, the rich shop owner in the area, is also the "owner" of three wives, and the household is well known for the fact that Gia's three wives cooperate in every way, cooking and eating together. Most women are not happy to be one of several wives, though co-wives may mean less work as each one cooks for the husband at intervals. When they do accept polygamy, it is that their choice is to be one of several wives, or no wife at all. There are too few men around and women are at a disadvantage when it comes to choosing marital status. Of the thirty unmarried adults in the village, twenty-four were women and six were men.[22]

The shortage of men and the increasing demand for marriage payment, in addition to the problems of cooperation affecting marriages everywhere, make marriages among the Chewa unstable and often of limited duration. But, whenever marital problems reach a certain magnitude, relatives and neighbors, led by the marriage counselors, come together to help the spouses sort out their differences and come to terms, if possible. Both husband and wife can call attention to the fact that they are not happy in their marriage. The first attempt to solve the problem will be made by the *nkhoswe*, after which the grandparents and uncles will do their best. If they fail, other members of the family, the headman and the villagers and ultimately the Chief will be involved. But family members and village residents will try hard to solve the problem to the satisfaction of those involved before it ever reaches the Chief's court.

Micheck Phiri is the *nkhoswe* of Tisenkenji Phiri. One morning he called Sandikonda Daka, Mwanishupa Phiri, Hundred Banda, Sonile Ngoma, Kamaswanda Njobvu, and Mwada Simba, and Tisekenji Phiri and the husband Abiro Banda to solve a problem. When they all had squatted in front of his house, Micheck opened the meeting: "Thank you so much for gathering here. I want to draw your attention to the matter that Tisekenji Phiri reported to me yesterday regarding some problems that stir the peace of her house. The matter is this; that Mr. Banda here insulted her and will not respect her parents. Now we want you to tell us, Abiro Banda, if you were drunk yesterday when you did it, or what the problem is. But first Tisekenji must make a statement so that we all know the nature of the complaint.

Tisekenji Phiri said: "My husband cursed me yesterday, and also the day before yesterday. That is why I have asked advice. Now I want him to tell me the reason for behaving like that towards me, his wife."

Abiro had this to say: "I did curse my wife yesterday because she is not willing to do the jobs expected of her. Yesterday I bought scones, but she refused to make tea for me. The day before yesterday I also bought scones and she refused to help me. I got annoyed because of her bad behavior and I cursed her."

The people sensed that something was terribly wrong. Not making tea is such a small problem that the real problem must be of such seriousness that it cannot easily be said aloud. It would be utterly disrespectful of a son-in-law to talk openly about more private things in his marriage in front of the mother-in-law. So the mother-in-law (actually the mother-in-law's sister) was asked to leave so the other relatives could sit together and help the young couple to come to terms.

Abiro himself explained: "This is the problem as I see it. I curse my wife because for more than one month and some days now, she refuses to sleep with me. So now I sleep alone and she sleeps alone. How can this be a marriage?"

Micheck asked Tisekenji if what the husband said was true and she said: "Yes, it is true. I refuse to sleep with him because I am pregnant!"

Sandikonda Daka responded: "Even if you are pregnant you must do your husband the favor and sleep with him. You cannot want to punish the man in your house so hard by refusing to be with him, so that he must sleep alone. And by telling your mother about these problems you have also done a serious mistake. These are household problems that can be solved only by your *nkhoswe* or by the relatives that negotiated your marriage."

Tisekenji Phiri did not agree with Sandikonda. She refused to change her behavior and the discussions were about to end in a deadlock (which meetings do if unanimity is not reached). It was only when the headman was about to be called so that the problems could be discussed in front of the entire village that Tisekenji realized her mistake and agreed to change her ways.

Separation

In the course of their lives most Kefa villagers marry twice or even three, four, or five times. Spouses die and divorce, and whoever loses a partner looks for a new one. "One head cannot carry a roof," goes the Kefa saying. It is difficult to be single, perhaps more so for women, many of whom remain alone for a long time. Men, having a much greater choice, tend to remarry quickly. In Kefa one of every three women is unmarried, while all of the men are married except Square Banda and Lefati Phiri, both disabled, and Simon Tonga, who feeds himself on beer.

Not all women mind living without a husband. Timeke Daka says that she prefers it.

"I was widowed once and divorced twice, but only my first husband was any good. These days people are lovers only of money and beer. Times are changing and men no longer look after their wives properly. Now, if a woman wants to be well off, it is better for her to look after herself and depend on nobody. Look at me. This year I will start growing cotton, so that I can find enough money for myself. Here in Zambia, if you work hard, you can find money. But a lazy person finds nothing except problems all his life."

Women are supposed not to mix with men to whom they are not related, or to do so only moderately.

"If women mix with men, other people will say they are after the man and that is no good. And women hate other women who talk softly to their husbands. So when a man and a woman meet in the bush, and that is what they do when they want to love each other, or the woman needs the man's money, they take care so that nobody sees them. They do not want to trouble their friends," Regina Shawa explained to us.

A wife who is suspected of adultery is in trouble. Kefa says he has divorced three wives for that reason and many other men have done the same. He also confides that many children in the village are not biologically related to their fathers because their mothers have been with other men.

Kefa himself has had a versatile marriage career. Simon Sakala, the nephew, describes it:

"Kefa Mwale is a man with many marriages and many children. First he was married to a Bemba woman, and he produced the son Manhaliya and two daughters. He then went away and left the children with the wife.

"The second marriage was at Lundazi where he had one son whom we don't know by name, because Kefa left the wife when she was pregnant. His third marriage took place in Nkhundu village in Chiparamba, where he had two children who were daughters. The fourth marriage, to Ketelina Daka, produced one daughter, Zalenji Mwale, who lives in Kefa village and is the mother of Gilbert Zulu.

"The fifth marriage, to Jeneti Lungu, produced the daughter Ntahmbo Mwale. In the sixth marriage he had five children and they are Tumeyo, Pasikali, Yavulira, Falawo, and Christina. In the seventh he had the son who was murdered, Dandaulani, and the wife gave Kefa *nsuzulo*, the token money for divorce, and left him.[23]

"These are Kefa's real marriages and the children he produced from them. But he has had other marriages too, from which he did not have any children, like those with his third and fourth present wives Regina Shawa and Lelia Mbewe. And he has had many friendships. To count all the children that were the result of these friendship pregnancies should make the number of Kefa's children come to about thirty-five."

To have ten or more marriages and thirty-five children is not usual, but it is highly respected. But as of late Kefa is in trouble with two of his wives, for neither Lelia Mbewe nor Regina Shawa is pleased with him. Brighton reports:

"Lelia Mbewe is the fourth wife of Kefa the headman. She is a bit old but brown [i.e., of fair complexion, which is considered much more attractive than darker skin] and beautiful. Kefa loved her very much. But suddenly he married a fifth wife from Kamanga village. When Nyamanda came, Lelia was no longer Kefa's favorite. And Lelia complained aloud that when Kefa married her he had told her he would not marry another wife.

"Now Kefa says that he had always planned to have five wives. Since she heard this, Lelia has not weeded in her field. She says that she will go to Lusaka and stay with her [elder sister's] daughter, but the headman refuses, thinking that if she goes she will never return to Kefa village. Lelia still has some maize from last year and that is what she is eating now. When the maize is finished she says she will just starve, or she will go to her brother, who as a messenger to Chief Chikuwe receives a regular income. He will take care of her if she divorces the husband.

"Regina, the third wife, is also thinking of separating from Kefa Mwale. Lelia and she fought about a hen and headman Kefa joined in the fight and beat her with a stick without even asking why his wives were fighting or who was right. Now Regina is waiting for her brother to come and see her. When he does, she will show him the stick Kefa used on her and ask him for a divorce. 'It is the first time the father of Paskale [that is, headman Kefa] beat me,' she says, 'but it is no good. I contribute to Mr. Kefa's income by weeding in his hybrid field, but I never get anything back.' "

Micheck Phiri, ever working for Kefa, has his own reasons to be displeased. A few days back his wife, Mwada Simba, was on the way to buy a mortar from Chitonga village when Kefa Mwale stopped her to ask where she was going and with whom. Mwada said she was going with her son Henry because her husband was drunk and unable to escort her. When she returned home, Micheck started to quarrel with her. Because he had heard the headman asking where she was going and with whom, he concluded that Kefa wanted to meet her secretly.

Suspicions about adultery are more easily aroused that quelled. But before a marriage is allowed to break up, the problem that threatens to destroy it is discussed at the village meeting, where, invariably, the village residents encourage spouses to show generosity and forbearance. The case brought to the villagers by Lucas Banda is typical:

> Lucas Banda comes from Malawi, but lives in Kefa village because he married Kefa's granddaughter Agnes Phiri. Banda is the father of one child by Agnes, and Agnes is the mother of two children. One night Lucas found Agnes, the wife, chatting alone with Wickson Mwale, Kefa's youngest brother. They were talking very secretly and Lucas suspected that his wife had fallen in love with Wickson.
>
> The following morning Lucas reported the case to the headman. In the evening the villagers were summoned to a meeting to discuss the matter. The *induna* Penelani Khosa introduced Lucas Banda and his problem. Lucas wanted to know what sort of discussion had taken place the previous evening between Wickson Mwale and Agnes Phiri, and why the two had been sitting alone, chatting so quietly that nobody could hear what was being said.
>
> Wickson Mwale answered: "This is my granddaughter and I can share many stories with her, and she with me, her *ambuye*—grandfather. Last night she asked me to give her money so that she could buy biscuits for Christmas." Banda refused to accept the answer and said to his wife: "When I saw that you were having a secret conversation, I hid myself and I heard you say: 'We cannot do it now, because my child is still very young, and if we were to do it, you must pay me K. 10 for serving you in this way.' When I heard those words I knew that something might happen, and I thought I had better show myself before it is too late. Now I want to know just what sort of trade it is between you and Wickson Mwale that cost K. 10 and cannot be done just now because your child is still far from walking by himself."
>
> Neither Agnes nor Wickson could give any proper answer to the question. But Penelani Khosa said: "This is nothing to make judgment about." "They were just joking and chatting. Do not forget that Wickson is the *ambuye*—the grandfather, and this is the way a grandfather will talk to his little wife. So you can just go back to your house and be happy again."
>
> But Lucas Banda is not happy. He plans to take the case to Chief Chikuwe and to ask for a divorce from his wife there, because he is convinced that his wife has been with Wickson not only once but many times.

When every attempt fails to bridge gaps and bring together spouses who seem ready to part, the spouse wanting the divorce will give the other *nsuzulo,* the token of divorce. Any small thing, but mostly a small coin like a 5 ngwee piece, can be used. With it goes an explanation as to why the giver of the *nsuzulo* wants to end the marriage. The recipient of the *nsuzulo* takes it to his or her family and once more negotiations are opened up between the two families. This time the issue is how to settle the marriage payment, and, if there are children and no *lobola* has been paid, what to do with them.

How marriage payments are refunded depends in part on who gives *nsuzulo.* If the husband wants divorce he may have to pay extra. If it is the wife who takes the initiative, her relatives must repay the *chimalo*—bride wealth. Sometimes the relatives have already spent the marriage payment or may not want to give it up; sometimes, they support the divorce: Lately, the father of Tisalire Banda comes every day to her house telling her to divorce Simon Sakala, her husband. Mr. Banda has also complained to Simon's mother's brother who is Mr. Lemekani Mbao that if Simon cannot keep his daughter better, she should not stay in his house but come home. And this happens even though Simon has paid K. 120 as *chimalo* and a cow as *lobola,* so that the children of the marriage shall belong to him.

> Gilbert Zulu is planning to divorce his wife Tilolele Banda. He has given her *nsuzulo,* because: "She has proved incapable of maintaining cooperation with me." For this same reason he sent her away from Ndola, where they were living, to her own home in Mcache village near Kefa. When Gilbert later returned to Kefa village to see his grandfather Kefa Mwale and to build himself a new house, a village meeting was called as a means of saving the marriage. Tilolele's relatives were told to be present. At the meeting Gilbert listed his complaints. They included that Tilolele refused to look after Gilbert's two-year-old nephew (Tilolele had four children herself all under the age of six); that she took Gilbert's money and sent it to her parents in Mcache village, that she complained about her husband's character to her parents; and that she had failed to get a job though Gilbert had financed a typing course for her and thus had wasted his money for nothing. The meeting reproached Tilolele for her bad behavior and for failing to obey the husband, and she was prepared to improve. But Gilbert had made up his mind. He took the case to the local court where divorce was granted. It was decided that the first-born should go with the father and the other children would remain with the mother in her home. It is said that Gilbert has fallen in love with a girl in Ndola who is in her twelfth school year (Tilolele had been to school for only four years), and that he wants to marry his new love.

Not everybody divorces with the consent of the family members or the village council. Mtole Mbao, Kefa's sister, who is about fifty years old, says that when Simon Tonga and she divorced there were no negotiations, but in their case there had been no proper marriage and no transfer of money or kind as marriage payment. Enelesi Mawerera, who married a Catholic priest (possible in the village life of Kefa), was forced to divorce "because the church people said she was too young." Her relatives had to give back the cow they had got as bride wealth, but there were no negotiations. Misosia Banda was left behind when her husband went to Lusaka and she never heard from him again. After some years the relatives of the husband gave her *nsuzulo* so that she could be free to marry again.

Most marriages take place between families from different villages. Usually, but not always, the wife goes to live in the husband's village. If later on she leaves, because of death or divorce, she is likely to go empty-handed except for the clothes she wears and a few kitchen utensils. She will probably retain full responsibility for children under five years of age. How well she manages as a single woman depends on the help and support she gets from fathers, brothers,and uncles. She will need male help to build a new house for herself and to clear a new garden.

But in her overall capacity as wife, sister, or daughter, a woman is an asset. She cultivates food crops, she takes care of the house, she fetches and cooks food. She brings marriage payments and children into the family. And as we shall see in the next chapter, many women have special skills when it comes to treating illnesses and understanding the occult.

Notes

1. At the time of the study half of the 56 households in Kefa consisted of husband and one wife. Seven households (13%) were polygamous and 21 households (38%) were headed by single persons of whom 17 were women.

2. The anthropological descriptions provided by Bruwer (1955) still characterize genealogy and social structure among the Chewa in Eastern Province, Zambia. They are quoted extensively in this chapter to link up with anthropology as well as with the colonial area.

   "The local matrilineages composing the village population are members of exogamous matrisibs (*mafuko*) scattered throughout the tribal area. The matrisib is to a certain extent conceptualized as a maximal matrilineage, reckoning descent from a common ancestress. The rule of exogamy is strictly binding on all members of the same matrisib, but specific pairs of matrisibs show a preference for intermarriage. In practice this concept is embodied in the principle of conjugal relations between two local matrilineages belonging to different matrisibs and does in fact form the basis of preferential or cross-cousin marriages. "Chewa marriage is in its initial stages predominantly uxori-local and husbands move to the abode of their wives. There are however village internal as well as village external marriages." (Bruwer, 1955:115.)

3. *Otentha*: "To warm oneself at the fire or in the sun" (Scott, 1929:435). In this connection the warmth is created or conveyed both through the fire and through intercourse.

   "Cewa believe that difficult labor or death in childbirth is due to the infidelity of the husband (occasionally the woman herself) during the woman's pregnancy. This is regarded as a form of *mdulo* a condition believed to result from failure to observe taboos relating to ritual purity." (Marwick, 1952:223.)

"Stillborn children are called *nthayo* or *nsenye* and not looked upon as human beings. Burial is done secretly by senior women and no public funeral held." (Bruwer, 1948:186.)

4. Dahlschen, 1970:74.

5. Very similar meal patterns to those of the Chewa of 1980 were reported from the Bemba in 1935: "The concentration on a single meal is a habit to which the children are accustomed gradually. Bemba infants are suckled whenever they wish, and in early childhood they eat all day long if possible. Natives recognize that small children cannot go so long without food as their elders and cook them extras when they can. Women who stay at home in the village all morning roast ground-nuts for the little children, or bake them sweet potatoes in season, while all the young people forage for what they can get from various relatives, or look for fruits in the bush. Mothers going to work may be seen carrying smoldering embers on a bark holder, ready to make small fires to roast maize cobs if they happen to be ripe in the gardens. But when food is short the children have to go without and expect to do so, and as they reach adolescence they begin to adopt the tribal belief that it is childish and undignified to be eating at all hours of the day." (Richards, 1939:73.)

6. There were 101 children under 20 in the village. The average household had a little less than 2 children. The average adult person had 2.8 children alive, while women over forty told us they had 3.5 living children (on average) and men over forty 3.3 living children. Many of the children presently in the village were grandchildren of the heads of their household; the children's parents were living in Chipata, Lusaka, or Ndola.

7. "Although the biological mother and father are recognized and acknowledged, each individual has within the system of extended kinship a group of fathers, and a group of mothers. The mother is called *Mai*, Mama, the father *Tate*, *Tata*, or *Bambo*. The honorific plural with the prefix *a-* will always be used when addressing. It follows that each person will have a group of 'mothers' and a group of 'fathers.' In other words, a group of people will be called either *amai* or *atate*, whether a person belongs to the lineage of the mother or that of the father. Thus the sister of one's father also becomes your 'father,' usually called 'female father' (*tate wamkazi*). The brother-sister group on your father's side will therefore all be called 'father' or 'female father.' Your mother's sisters will be called mother, but your mother's brothers do not become male-mothers; they are called by the special term *atsibweni*.

"Grandparents, both male and female, are called *ambuye*. No sex differentiation is made, but *wamkazi* (female) or *wamwamuna* (male) may be added for convenience. In this generation the classificatory system becomes apparent. All the brothers and sisters of your grandmother and grandfather in both lineages, will be your *ambuye*. These *ambuye* call their grandchildren *adzukulu*. During the period between weaning and entrance into the sleeping hut of unmarried boys and girls, children are mostly with their *ambuye*. Here they receive a great deal of fostering and education, and as reward theirs is the sole responsibility to provide their grandchildren with a proper burial . . . Joking conversations between grandparents and grandchildren are often heard, and unsophisticated behavior between these two age-groups becomes a pattern of playful goodwill." (Bruwer, 1948:186.)

8. "Being the result of a closely articulated mechanism, social behaviour within the Chewa community seems a tangled complexity. When once the scope of extended kinship has been mastered however, what seemed irregular and illogical, clearly becomes the logical outcome of traditional thought. The classificatory system by which kinship is molded into a well defined entity proves in many ways to be much deeper and more realistic than our own." (Bruwer, 1948:185.)

9. In view of what Marwick writes about Chewa behavioral ideals little has changed, in the last forty years. According to Marwick: "The ideal man is well known (*womveka*), the centre of many friends and relatives. He is sexually potent and fertile. He takes care of (*sunga*) his matrikin: this may mean buying clothes for his female dependents and paying taxes and adultery compensation awards on behalf of his male ones. He manages

somehow to buy clothes for his wife and, if he is a polygamist, distributes his attentions and favours with meticulous fairness among his wives. The ideal woman, in addition to having the common-gender traits of being hospitable, mild, and self-controlled, is obedient and sexually faithful to her husband (he need not be faithful to her unless she is pregnant). In addition she is a good cook and slow in her bodily movements. The most important traits of the ideal child are: willingness to be sent on errands; non-violent; and, in case of little girls, being careful of property, especially pots."

"In everyday life Cewa constantly sustain these models of behavior. They reprimand children who refuse to go on errands or who break pots, and they quickly separate those who fight 'lest their parents should join in.' They gossip about adults who are mean, neglectful of their duties towards their relatives and wives, and those who are impotent or barren. And they take before the court those who show any tendencies towards violent behavior (ndeu). Anyone who loses his temper (psya ntima lit. burns in his heart) puts himself in the wrong—even in situations where Europeans would regard 'righteous indignation' as normal and commendable."

"The connection between some of these conduct valuations and the social structure is obvious. They have the function of minimizing tension that is likely to arise in certain social relations, e.g., that between co-wives of a polygamist or between unrelated village neighbours. The requirement that a man should respect his elders and do favours for them and that he should care for his matrikin clearly have the effect of uniting the Chewa basic social group, the matrilineage. Being conservative forces, conduct valuations tend to sustain the indigenous social structure and to defend it against the onslaught of European individualistic values." (Marwick, 1952:134.)

10. In 1977-78 there were 11,500 7th grade leavers and only 1,880 secondary school places in Eastern Province, i.e. 84 percent of the students would have to leave school. As 1,280 places were for boys and only 600 for girls, the girls had an even smaller chance than boys to continue their education. Even students in the 4th grade had to struggle for a place in the 5th grade as there were only 2,036 places available for 3,364 children. Kefa village children were not the only ones who failed to advance in the educational system.

11. "It does not seem to be the case that the migrants support their rural relatives once they have moved to town." (Hedlund and Lundahl, 1983:53.)

12. Audrey Richards (1939:215) observed that among the Bembas two generations ago "an elderly relative often shrugs his shoulders at a child's decision to do or not to do something it is asked, and says (ni mwine) 'he is the owner of the affair,' i.e. the child must decide."

13. "Phungu: A judge or counselor, one who hears and decides cases; Phunguwankazi alindirira anamwali aakazi, a female superintendent of the girls in the ceremonies of initiation; plu. aphungu. . ." (Scott, 1929:483.)

14. As in most other cultures, menstruation is not talked about among the Chewa, at least not directly. Instead, the term kusamba, to wash, is used. If a woman says "I did not wash this month,' the meaning is clear; she did not menstruate.

15. Audrey Richards' detailed study of the matrilineal Bemba people of Northern Province in Zambia (1939) provides many parallels to Chewa society in the 1970s and 1980s:

"Huts are circular or square in shape, with broad verandas in the case of men of substance. A man and his wife sleep in each hut,but any child over two or three is sent to sleep with its grandparents. . . Young girls usually sleep in the hut of a young married woman whose husband is temporarily away or with a widowed woman. They often change their sleeping-place each night. Boys build houses for themselves in twos or threes. . . ' (Richards, 1939:120.)

"The oldest living male member of the matrilineage is indeed the guardian or nkhoswe of the entire matrilineage. In practice however his functional duties are very often delegated to the senior male member of the next junior generation, in other words to the first-born son of his elder sister, the bele lalikulu (major breast). This man then, who is the mother's brother or atsibweni, becomes in practice the functioning guardian over his sisters and their children. In minor matters the atsibweni may again delegate this authority to his sister's son (his muphwa) as far as his sister's daughters are concerned.

Although authority therefore rests with the male members of the senior generation within the matrilineage, it is frequently the brother who acts on behalf of his sisters and their children in matters of practical interest."

"The children of those called *atsibweni* (mother's brother) and *atate akazi* (female father) are indicated as *asuani* or cross-cousins, a term emphasizing seminal bonds. The term *asuani* does however not only stress the seminal bond, but is a direct indication of potential spouses according to the system of preferential cross-cousin mating, thus denoting the continual integration of two matrilineages in the conjugal sense." (Bruwer, 1955:118, 117.)

16. According to Bruwer (1948:187) *ngozi* is the Nyanja word for "accident," "mishap," "something of ill omen." "One's *mpongozi*—mother-in-law—is avoided as far as possible." Bruwer also notes that the wife's father, *mnjira, mkwe lume,* or *atatawala* is treated with respect by the son-in-law, but the respect is much less severe than that between son-in-law and mother-in-law. The avoiding relationship also exists between daughter-in-law and parents-in-law, but is less obvious as they often live in different villages.

17. Writing in the beginning of 1950s on the basis of "a missionary sojourn of some sixteen years in the country of Undi," (the Cewa paramount chief), Bruwer points to how (1955:115): "Cewa marriage is characterized by the absence of valuable possessions passing from the wife-receiving to the wife-providing matrilineage. Tokens of good will are mutually given but have but little legal significance. The *cimalo* or *ciwongo* token which used to be a fowl or goat, has lately received legal status and now-a-days money is generally given by the husband. But the significance of *cimalo* within the traditional code was much more of a ritual than a legal nature although the two concepts cannot always be easily distinguished in Chewa society. The marriage negotiations do however include a probation period of labour service rendered by the son-in-law to his parents-in-law."
It seems that marriage payments have changed during the past 30 years, and that as the tendency to give *lobola* expands, they may change even more in the future.

18. "Direct European teaching and the introduction of a money currency have strengthened the father's authority over his children as against those of the mother's brother. The former pays tax for the household, buys the children's clothes, and pays the school fees. But on the other hand marriage is less stable under modern conditions, partly owing to the break down of marriage morality and partly to the absence of so many men at the mines. In these circumstances, those few men who remain in the villages are bound to look after their sisters' children as well as their own in the last resort." (Richards, 1939:116.)

"The payments of the Chewa people of the Chikuwe area associated with uxorilocal marriage (gradually developing into virilocal or neolocal residence) only give a man limited rights over the children born, who are members of their mother's matrilineage. Marriage payments and the later payment of *lobola* among Ngoni of Sayiri, on the other hand, with their virilocal marriage, transfer the woman's childbearing capacity and, subsequently, her children to the husband and his kin. In both cases, the marriage payments represent a considerable outlay which is absolutely necessary from the social point of view. Migration and wage employment help secure the resources needed to fulfill this obligation." (Hedlund and Lundahl, 1983:47.)

19. "A middle-aged widower and widow were discussing the possibilities of marriage prosaically together. The would-be bridegroom said, 'Are you the kind of woman who always has hot water ready for her husband in the morning, and never grumbles when he asks for more?' The prospective bride answered, 'Yes, that is what I do. But are you the kind of man who gives his wife a new cloth occasionally and doesn't spend his money all on himself?'" (Richards, 1939:103.)

20. "Marriage is to a great extent a factor of mutual interest between two matrilineage groups and preliminary negotiations are carried out between the *ankhoswe* or guardians of the two interested lineages. Generally it is the *mkokowogona* (the senior responsible relative within the matrilineage) who opens up negotiations with the *mkokowogona* of the potential bride. Thus grandparents on the mother's side act on behalf of their grandchildren. When the preliminary negotiations on the *mkokowogona* level have been carried out with

success, it is usually the brothers of both bride and bridegroom who act as further go-betweens until the negotiations reach the final stage.

"During the final stages when the marriage ceremony is completed the two respective *ankhoswe* who will be responsible for the specific marriage unit, are ritually appointed. This is done during communal beer-drinking, when members of two matrilineages concerned meet together . . . In this way the marriage unit is placed under the continual guardianship of two *ankhoswe*, one representing the matrilineage of the husband, and one representing the matrilineage of the wife and her children. The duties of these *ankhoswe* are manifold.

"Apart from ordinary domestic matters and problems which may need the attention of the two *ankhoswe*, they have functioning duties in regard to certain ritual ceremonies pertaining to the marriage couple and their children. The more important of these ceremonies are those concerning the first conception (*cisamba*), the birth of the child (*kubadwa kwamwana*), the initiation of the child into society shortly after birth (*kusambitsa mwana*), the initiation of children into adult society (*cinamwali*), and ceremonies pertaining to illness and death." (Bruwer, 1955:121.)

21. Dahlschen, 1970:14.

22. There were 117 people over 20 in the village in June 1977; 61 percent were women and 39 percent men. Most of the men had not been married before because they were still young, while almost all the women were divorced or widowed. Among the men over 40 there were 1.4 divorces per man; among the women over 40, 0.8. The average number of marriages by men over 40 was 2.2; among older women 2. But only formally contracted (i.e., with marriage payments) marriages were counted.

23. "*Sudzula, ku*, to finish and let go; to set a person free from work, etc. . . . to divorce a wife." (Scott, 1929:513.)

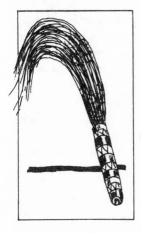

Kwa eni kulibe mkuwe
In Other Homes There is no Weeping

Many people sell medicine to their fellow friends. Once the money has been handed over, we never get it back, even if the medicine does not cooperate to make the sick person well. Instead, the doctor keeps adding rules and medicines, hoping that in the end his wisdom will procure favorable treatment for the patient.

A villager's view

Illnesses

"I have counted people who died and those still alive since the survey started, and we are missing sixteen persons. All of them died from their own diseases. Coughing, diarrhea, stomach pains, anemia, not going to the toilet, measles, swelling all over the body, vomiting, tuberculosis and rheumatism are the diseases from which Kefa village residents suffer and die," Brighton reported.

Disease is very much part of everyday life.[1] Not only do many people suffer from the ailments Brighton listed, there are also the permanently ill and handicapped: Mwazida Mwale with asthma, Simon Kamanga with an ulcer; Sandikonda with a constantly painful leg; Square, Lefati and Alesi, who are crippled; Chitanimoyo, who is mad; and Evelinar, who is occasionally possessed by spirits. And there are others. Sooner or later every child has diarrhea, coughs, infected wounds, running eyes and ears, swollen limbs and stomachs, fever, and measles—a consistent killer. Every household has lost a loved one—a child, spouse, or parent—prematurely. Every week death messages summon relatives and friends to a funeral. Life in the village can never be taken for granted.

Fortunately, many medicines and remedies are part of the common stock of knowledge.[2] Nature herself is the drugstore with healing herbs, mushrooms, and roots available for those who know how to gather them and how to use them. When soaked in water, *mtowa* and *mlozi* roots cure stomach pains, and *msoro* roots help against coughing. Fresh tomato leaves, externally applied, give instant relief from a wasp sting. *Kankhande* leaves, picked with closed eyes and burned to ashes, cure sore throats when mixed with ordinary food. Sweet-potato leaves cooked into a soup ease the common cold. Ochra leaves enable people without teeth to swallow food and, applied externally, cure ear infections. Pork is good for those with *nkhunya*, or falling sickness (epilepsy). Warthog horns around a child's neck ward off danger and disease. Unfertilized eggs can be used for several purposes, and *chimwemwe* roots "applied on the body make men lucky with ladies and ladies lucky with men they want to be liked by."

Some people have skill in curing particular illnesses. Robert Manda is a specialist for the falling sickness. When Masau, who was three, first had an attack, the mother went to Robert. She paid K. 3 and the medicine, *mankhwala*, worked well. When six months later Masau had another attack, the mother went to Robert again. This time she got the medicine free of charge.

When Ezidon's face was swollen with a toothache it was Micheck who told him what to do and who took him to the bush to look for the right medicine. And when Sylvester had a toothache it was Square Banda who cured him.

Fatnes Manda is another specialist. From her mother she learned how to cure epilepsy and pains in the abdomen caused by sexual intercourse. She uses roots and leaves, which she boils together and applies in a particular way. Just how, she cannot tell or perhaps will not.

Square Banda is the best known professional healer in Kefa village. "The best and most trusted African doctor, the first in medicine," is the testimony given by one of his patients.

"Plenty of people come and ask my help and I definitely heal them. I cure different diseases like the failure to get children both in men and women, insanity, rheumatism, venereal diseases, people who have been bewitched, epilepsy, and many other illnesses. To do so I use herbs, roots, and mushrooms, and my special knowledge is amulets that are very effective for winning love or money when gambling, and for finding employment," Square says.

Several times a week, Square is visited by patients. Some seek advice, some want medicine, some report on how they are getting on. Some come to thank him for having cured them, and some to pay as cures prove effective. Prices vary according to the patient's financial standing. When Kambula got medicine worth K. 6.50 he paid only K. 2 because that was all the money he had.

Sometimes Square gives his advice for free. When Livines needed a hoe to dig medicine for her husband, who had an upset stomach, she visited Square Banda. He gave her his hoe and also advised her on the location of the best roots.

Occasionally, aided by his two sticks, Square hobbles along, paying a home visit to one of his patients. He invariably carries his small bag of herbs, roots, amulets, and other remedies. Sylvester made this report:

"Tamala Phiri is one of Square's regular patients. She suffers from spirits, and also other ailments. On his way to her house in Kamanga village, Square makes frequent breaks to gather herbs. Medicines, he says, are picked in different ways. Some can be dug only when one is naked. Some must be picked while one is seated, some while one kneels. It all depends upon the disease. It is important to do things the right way; otherwise, the medicine loses its powers.[3]

"At Tamala's house Square instructs the patient as to how to use the medicine: 'Pound the leaves in a mortar, put them in a cup of water and mix, and then drink. And, please, Mrs. Phiri, this is important, take one cup in the morning, one in the afternoon, and one at night before you go to sleep.'

"Tamala Phiri's son is suffering from a swollen stomach. The mother has done all she can to get him well. She went to the clinic at Chiparamba and she consulted Mr. Kamanga who is also a traditional healer. Now she wants Mr. Banda's advice. He has treated the boy before and he was well for some time, but now he is ill again.

"Square said that he would try again: 'Today I shall give the boy a new medicine, which I think will cure him. The medicine is to be used when you bathe him. Boil it in water and wash the boy with a cloth dipped in it. I shall also give you something he can drink and a third medicine to boil into his milk porridge. All the medicines must be used three times a day, morning, afternoon and evening.' When Tamala asked how long the cure would take, Square answered, 'One week.'

" 'All people feel better after taking his medicine and people trust him,' Tamala told us afterward."

A local doctor's wisdom is often remarkable.[4]

Baluwa Khosa has been Mr. Banda's patient for fifteen years. When he was a youngman Baluwa was a well-known fighter, but one day he was thoroughly beaten up by another youngman. After the fight, Baluwa never felt quite right and he decided to see a doctor to get medicines and charms so that he would be well. He consulted Square Banda, who told him: "Okay, if you will pay me cash for this medicine, I shall cure you, but you must never fail to follow the advice I give you. Use this powder with *nsima* for two weeks. After that period, do not ever eat *nsima* again. You can eat maize in any form, but not *nsima*. If you do so you will lose all your health and will never get well again. By this medicine, taken in the right way, you will gain enormous strength. The strength will be enough to kill anybody. If you fight with anybody, the very first blow you give will be the end for them. So, in order to prevent many deaths, be quiet, do not fight, do not provoke people, do not ever quarrel with anyone, unless they come to your house at night with the intension to harm you."

This was the advice Square gave, and Baluwa followed the instructions. He never eats *nsima*, thinking that if he does he will go mad and become utterly powerless. And he never fights, because if he does he will surely kill somebody. So he keeps away from all quarrels. In this way Square Banda, the first in medicine, has helped him stay healthy (and out of trouble) for fifteen years.[5]

Ordinary foods like green leaves, gourds, different meat, eggs, and even *nsima* are used as ingredients in medicine under the guidance of traditional healers who mix their secret medicines with the food. The healer tells the suffering person how to take the medicine and when he or she is cured, never to eat that particular food again. Sylvester writes:

> "People believe that medicine works like a switch. You eat the same food again and you will succumb to the same illness which that particular food (mixed with medicine) helped to cure. Such food restrictions have no time limit. Once the treatment is given, you grow to whatever age and still do not eat the food. But when somebody says 'I have started eating this or that food again,' it could be that the treatment did not work and was recommended by a false doctor who wanted to cheat that person."

"In some tribes women do not eat certain foods, probably because the tribe never used to find that food.[6] But men eat anything except too much salt, which is said to make a man lose his strength and sexual powers. But individual men may refuse to take particular food because that food has been part of a cure, or because they do not like it."

Some food taboos exist, but they are not necessarily accepted by all. Still, most children do not eat eggs and grasshoppers because they are said to get *nkhunyu* or the falling sickness if they do. And barren women should not eat ochra leaves, pork or wild animals.

Today, such beliefs are diminishing. "People are starting to think differently because they learn about nutrition at the health clinic," Sylvester ends his report.

Some people pursue cures different from those used by everybody else: When Sandikonda Daka had a wound on his leg which never seemed to heal he poured a cotton pesticide in it (Rogor) which he bought from the cotton grower Tilele Zulu for 2 ngwee. Then he tied an old rag around his leg and washed his hands. Seeing our consternation, he said: "I always use this medicine and I am very satisfied with it, so whenever you have a wound like mine, try to get some medicine of cotton for it."

Sandikonda does not think much of Western medicine in general, and certainly not in regard to curing what he considers to be typical African illnesses:

> One day, when Sandikonda and Deliuze were talking Sandikonda said: "The family of Alesi Banda is no good. She was born with deformed legs.

Instead of treating her traditionally the parents took her to the hospital. As a result she still does not walk properly. She cannot carry heavy things like water and wood or she will fall. Yet she is a grown woman. How can she marry? The family were wrong in taking her for treatment to the hospital. Look at Chaluka Banda. That boy too was born lame, but the father refused to take him to the hospital. He used our own African medicine and now the boy is a man and he walks about. He is married and has his own children. If the family of Alesi had decided to look for African medicine for their daughter, she would have walked better now. So if you ever face the same problem, Deliuze, please try to look for our own medicine, because at the clinic there is no proper medicine for these problems."

Deliuze responded: "You are right. African medicine is very good, but nowadays everybody keeps running to the hospital. They do not use our own medicine, yet our medicine is very strong."

Most villagers make use of traditional as well as Western medicine. If the one does not produce results they switch to the other. Headman Kefa is one of them. When his hand was badly swollen, he first used traditional herbs and roots. Because he did not get better, he went to the rural health clinic. In spite of the pills that he was given his other hand started swelling as well, and he became convinced that he had been bewitched. As it is generally accepted that Western medicine has no power over witchcraft, Kefa resorted to traditional medicine, including blood letting. It was Regina, his third wife, who administered the old razor blade and cut both Kefa's arms from under the elbow to the back of the headman's hands.

Mwazi wabwino uti pyu, koma ukati bi waipy—healthy blood is scarlet, but the dark blood is bad—is a medical word of wisdom, and the blood that first came out was definitely darker than the rest. The positive effects of the blood letting were certainly not immediate. As the trouble continued Kefa went again to the clinic and to the hospital in Chipata, and he also took advice and medicine from traditional healers. And the villagers worried, as did Kefa's newest wife, Nyamanda, whom he had just married.

One day Nyamanda brewed beer and Kwerekani Phiri, Kefa's old friend, came to drink.

Nyamanda mused: "Why does Mr. Kefa keep falling ill? What I haved noticed is that whenever I make beer his hands start to swell. Now, I am wondering if I must stop brewing, because perhaps there is some connection between me making beer and his hands getting swollen."

Kwerekani answers: "No, it is no good that you stop brewing. In my opinion Mr. Kefa falls ill when it is his day for falling ill." But Nyamanda was not satisfied and insisted that she must find out why Kefa was ill and what was the cause.

Then Kwerekani said: "I am very sorry too that our headman suffers like this. Everybody here is worried about him. But it is my theory that he is ill like this because his son, Dandaulani, died a complicated death. It is when Kefa thinks about this, remembering his son and missing him, that he falls ill."

Many a local health problem stems from impure drinking water, and this is well known by educated youngmen like Brighton:

"Our water is so dirty and full of small animals. That is why we are getting sick and our stomach problems never end. Some time back we begged the government to help us with this matter. After some time they came and surveyed the area and told us we would have a water project. Then the Water Affairs Department made a bore hole, but still we have no water. Now the years are passing and we continue to die because the water we draw is no good. The government keeps telling us that we shall get water taps in the village, but all we see is that the work that is supposed to take one week takes a month, if it finishes at all. Now people fear that nothing will ever come out of it. And our problems increase because, while we wait, nobody wants to clean up the well, which our women use every day, and so our problem goes on and on."

Once each year or so health assistants from the nearby rural clinic visit the village to tell people how they must help themselves to stay healthy. They talk about mosquitoes, tsetse flies, and dirty water, and the villagers are warned to cook pig meat well and not to walk in stagnant water. But when the villagers ask why the children and the old people in the village, and others, too, keep dying, since it is neither from malaria nor from eating pork, the health assistants only tell them that whoever is ill must come to the health center.[7]

It is government policy that no one shall live further than ten kilometers away from a rural health center, and Kefa is just within that radius of the rural clinic. While young parents may carry their small children to the clinic, as James did with Rothia, who was only two when she died from measles, to take adult and old people there presupposes money as well as organization—if the patient trusts the clinic sufficiently to seek Western medical treatment. One reason for the poor reputation of rural health centers and hospitals is that most villagers try traditional medicine first, so that only the more serious cases may end up in the clinic and hospital. When they come, it is often too late. It is also a fact that health centers and hospitals cannot maintain the health of the villagers. They can only cure their diseases, and they cannot always do this.

Not only does suffering inflict hardship on people and bereave them of their loved ones, it also cements village solidarity and concern. When somebody is ill, the news spreads quickly and friends and particularly relatives soon start arriving to show their love and care. Tilele Zulu went all the way to Lusaka (600 kilometers away) and later on continued to Kitwe (another 400 kilometers) when she heard that two of her grandchildren there were ill. Before she went, she collected medicine from the bush which she prepared at home. She also pounded aspro and chlorochin tablets in her small mortar and baked it into some food that she had packed in her bag before she set off. To finance the trip Lemekani, the husband, had borrowed K. 10 from his brother the headman. Lemekani said Telele should go because she was the person who knew more about medicine. He himself would stay at home to harvest the maize.

When Micheck was ill with malaria a lot of people came to see him. Among them were three brothers (relatives) from Luangwa Valley (350 kilometers) away. They had heard the news of Micheck's illness from a neighbor who had met with a relative of Micheck's wife. The ailing Micheck asked his brothers to help his wife carry roof poles for their new house. When the job was done the youngmen were thanked with food before they went on to see another ill relative in Chipata.

It is not only adult people who receive visitors when they are ill. Even though nobody could have known that he was to die within only one week, many people from inside the village and elsewhere came to inquire about Ifenso, who was only eight years old.

Visitors can cause problems because they expect to be fed, but they may also help the household with jobs needing to be carried out. Most helpful are relatives who live inside the village. Women often cook extra food if a relative is ill and prevented from feeding her family adequately, and they regularly draw water for each other. When Tisauke Phiri was hospitalized at Mwami hospital about 150 kilometers away from Kefa, her friend Mwanishupa Phiri packed a basket with mealiemeal, *ntwilo,* and dried beans and left the village before the sun rose one morning to return only the next day. As Brighton put it: "She helps her friend in every way though the two are not related."

Not every illness is taken at face value. Poor Andrick Banda is said to be fond of getting ill when there is hard work to be done. Sylvester reports:

> "This year Andrick has been ill ever since the weeding started so he never helps the wife. Buth the wife works for him and cooks for him. People say that Andrick Banda is too lazy to work in the field. They say that each year about this time Andrick falls ill. He stays in the village doing nothing, yet when there is beer around he will drink until he is drunk. And most people think this is just crazy! How can anyone become ill only at weeding time. But when Andrick died, those who had thought he was just being lazy must have sat down and regretted their thoughts."

Any man is fortunate to have a wife, but more so if he is ill or unable to work. It is for that reason that Lemekani Mbao and Tilele Zulu worked hard to find a wife for their strongly handicapped son, Joseph. Joseph can move only when somebody pushes his wheelchair. The chair he got at the center for the handicapped in Kitwe town on the Copper Belt, where Joseph stayed for some time with his brother. It was Joseph who suggested to his parents that he wanted to marry. Robert Manda and Simon Sakala negotiated the marriage. Lemekani paid K. 34 as bridewealth to the girl's family and it was decided that the wedding cermony would be conducted by a Roman Catholic priest.

The girl comes from the nearby Kamanga village. She too is handicapped, but not like Joseph, who is completely lame. The girl can walk, with some difficulty. What is important is that she can pound and cook, even if she cannot carry the maize to the mill or draw water. She can even hoe, but not well. The young couple will live with Lemekani and Telele, who will help them with food and cash. People say that because Joseph is very lame he will never be able to work and will always be in need of help of others. That is why it is good for him to have a wife.

Square Banda is all alone in this world. He has no wife to do any jobs for him. Sometimes he gets exceedingly depressed and says: "God should help me. I have [extended] sons but they are of no use to me. Danga and Jackson are my relatives but I never feel it. Even other people wonder about their behavior and why they never help me." When pondering his problems, Square often sings sad songs to himself. Or he may find comfort in *kacasu* or *marijuana*—if he has any. No wonder spirits occasionally enter his soul and make his crippled body jerk and open his mind to new knowledge of amulets and herbs—and spirits.

Spirits

Though very much part of everyday life, spirits are truly extraordinary. When they descend upon a human being, materializing into what may seem like a continual agony, village attention is absorbed onto the person obsessed. Then, in the focus of fellowship, the possessed is free to act out his or her inner desires, giving full vent to personality traits that strive for recognition, without fear of reproach.

Spirit possession may take the form of a quiet trance or a violent seizure. Onlooker response is never despair, only concern. It is an age-old ritual and long-time members of the community know what to do. Yet, for the time being, the possessed person is a nonmember of the village. And no one can foretell the length of time or the consequences. Fortunately, remedies and rituals exist, and there are specialists to administer them. The close linkage that exists between the everyday world and that of the ancestors, between the so-called normal and the paranormal, the natural and the supernatural, the conscious and the subconscious, makes African culture very different from that of the West. In spirit possession this cultural dualism seems to flow together into one enigmatic and deeply significant manifestation.[8]

Vast Manda and Square Banda are Kefa residents who have been in close contact with the spirits for many years and have developed a new understanding about interconnection of things. Both serve as healers for their fellow villagers. Both are single, with no children of their own.

Vast explains:

"I was first possessed by spirits more than fifteen years ago and since then I have learned so many things and become wiser in my way of thinking than ever before—not only because I have grown older, but also because the *mizimu*—the spirits—have advised me.[9]

"When the time comes for the spirit to enter me, I feel dizzy. I get cold in the back and in the chest, and my legs and head are aching. Then the spirits appear and identify themselves. There is no need for me to consult a traditional healer, because I know them. If I should say what a spirit is like, I must say it has a white body. [At this point Sylvester hypothesized that it was an angel.] The spirits make me aware of things I did not know before. I gain new knowledge and come to understand every good and bad thing, what is about to happen in the village, in my family and to myself. When Kefa village was about to be selected as model village, I dreamed of houses being built. But this does not mean that I can dream of a car if I am in need of transport."

There are two main types of spirits, the *mizimu* and the *viwanda* (sing., *mzimu, chiwanda*). Even the *mizimu* and the *viwanda* are similar in many ways. They cause similar illnesses in people they possess, and they make people behave very much in the same way. None of them has a physical body, or if it does nobody knows its shape. But it has a soul, and to speak and dance it has to enter a human body.

Vast Manda is what she calls "a *mizimu* spirit member." She explains:

"The *mizimu* spirits speak of God, but the *viwanda* only dance. The *mizimu* are the book spirits [Bible spirits] or church spirits, because they always respond to the words of the Bible. They heal people, and they advise on what medicines to use to cure a person who is possessed by the *viwanda*, but the *mizimu* themselves cannot be persuaded to leave a person because of charms or medicines.

"The *mizimu* spirits come to women who are barren and advise them on how to conceive, and thereafter they become pregnant. But this does not necessarily mean that when a barren woman gets possessed she will get pregnant, because her spirit may have been of the wrong type.

"I have seen many people possessed by the church spirits. Because they have not paid proper attention to their spirit, it has come back time and again, sometimes after several years of absence, and made that person deadly ill. The spirits do this to force people to pay them proper attention. That is why the church spirit members meet in each others' houses where we dance and read from the bible. The *mizimu* leaders among us know who has inactive spirits and they will work to make the spirits come forward. The owner of the house where we meet will prepare food for the members, and the members in turn contribute cash so that the owner recovers his or her expenses. At such meetings food is served on white plate and cups[10] because the spirits want it that way, but when the spirits leave, the person who has been possessed will eat and drink from ordinary colored food containers. White vessels are reserved for the *mizimu* only."

Square Banda first met with the spirits when he was recovering from the illness that made him into a severely handicapped cripple.

"I was just a boy at the time. The spirits stayed with me for a long time and told me so many things about people, medicines, and dreams. It was through the spirits that I became *ng'anga*—a traditional healer and diviner.

"To be possessed by spirits is like falling ill. It does not cause acute pain, like a wound or an ailment that torments you, but you suffer, yes, you suffer. The body aches all over and then you feel that the spirits fill your body and soul and you see things you never saw before.

"The spirits feed on blood, and while you are possessed you become very thin. The spirits advise you on how to diagnose and cure diseases. When somebody asks me for my medical assistance, I often know already many things about them without being told. It is in this way that I can identify witches. And if I want to make use of witchcraft my spirits will advise how."

Square's spirits are of the *viwanda* type.[11] They force him to dance and give him new knowledge, but contrary to the *mizimu* they also teach the possessed how to harm others.

Each tribe has its particular *viwanda*. The Chewa people have the *zcewa* spirits, the Ngoni the *awiza* and the *mphanda*. There are many others, but they do not mix. Square, a member of the Chewa spirits, explains that the *zcewa* do not allow him to participate at *awiza* spirit meetings. "I could have assisted people who are possessed by *awiza*, like Evelinar Njobvu, but that is against the rules. The rules say that I have no right to work with both spirits when I am a *zcewa* spirit doctor."

The *viwanda* usually enter a person at night when he or she is dreaming. For instance, if one dreams of snakes and particularly black snakes, or of lions or cattle, dogs, mushrooms, or baskets, the *viwanda* may enter that person and stay with him or her as long as it takes to find an adequate cure, which will be some medicine or dancing. Although men are said to be more affected by *viwanda* than woman, and adults more than children, even a five-year-old can be possessed, particularly if elder family members are affected by spirits. Professionals like Square Banda do not accept any possession at face value: "I have noticed that there are people who dress in their dancing clothes even before the *chiwanda* forces them to dance. But proper spirit possessions result in people dancing whether or not they want to and are ready for it. Some people pretend that the spirits have entered them because they think that if others believe that they are possessed by the [*mizimu*] book spirits, this will protect them from being bewitched."

In many ways spirits are distinctly human.[12] Some give wisdom and fervor, while others are petty and demanding, ready to hurt and even to destroy, threatening in demeanor and difficult to understand. Evelinar Njobvu's spirits seemed to fit into the latter category. They came to her in the middle of the weeding season, four months after her miscarriage and just as she discovered that she was pregnant again. Sylvester followed up on the story, which started on 9 December:

"The *wiza* spirit entered Evelinar Njobvu today. They wanted mealiemeal and the husband's brother's baby. They only got the mealiemeal. After eating, the spirit demanded that every young woman in the village come and sing. And many women came and sang. Afterward the spirit said: 'In this village there is a woman who does not believe that we [the spirits] have come. She says that this woman we have possessed is lazy and that she only pretends that we are real. But she will see. On Saturday this woman we have entered will not work. On a Sunday we shall return, and unless we find a white dress and white cloth, we shall take this woman whose body we use into the forest and do something terrible to her. And this will convince the woman who does not believe in us that we spirits are real.'

"As the spirits were speaking, Dorothy [Evelinar's sister-in-law] understood that they were referring to her and she tried to slip away and hide with her baby. But the spirits soon found her, and she had to beg them to forgive her and to understand her agony. It was *her* baby they had asked for. The *wiza* said that they would understand, but they warned her. Then the spirits left and Evelinar Njobvu just sat quietly, as if half asleep.[13] All this happened on Friday and the villagers talked about it and worried.

"December 10," wrote Sylvester. "The spirits meant their words. All day Evelinar has not been weeding nor cooking. She is just crying.

"December 11: Evelinar is normal today, but when she heard what day it is, she was surprised, saying that the days were running too fast for her. When she was told that she had got spirits, she denied it. It is believed that when the spirits come, she does not know anything about it. Dorothy felt that it is a pity they do not know on what Sunday the spirits will return, because when they do, they will surely take Evelinar into the bush to their fellow spirits and eat her. It is only by dancing that the spirits can be persuaded to go away, but as Evelinar does not know about the spirits, she refuses even to dance. Now the husband, Kabanda, plans to take her back to her parents. She is pregnant and it is believed that the spirits will make her miscarry again. But the village residents say that if he sends the wife back to her parents, he will have to escort her, and he cannot find money for transport even for the wife."

Spirit possessions usually mean capital outlays. There are the drummer and the *ng'anga*, the traditional healer who prescribes medicines and interprets the wishes of the spirits, and there are the demands of the spirits themselves who ask for white cloth, white pots and plates, a white hen, and mealiemeal. Those who do not have the needed cash will ask relatives for help or plead with the healer and even the spirits themselves to reduce their demands.

Though spirit possessions disrupt everyday affairs, they do not disturb the pattern of village life. Spirits are part of life and the people who are possessed serve as links between two worlds. Sometimes a spirit is identified as a deceased blood relative who has had some cause not to let go of this world. As elders, spirits are revered and given the respect due to their status group, but they are never worshipped.[14] Because they confer benefits as well as ills on the people they possess, villagers are ambivalent toward their appearance.

Witchcraft

Witchcraft is a living force in rural Zambia. It is the personification of evil and a ready cause for all the suffering in this world that cannot be otherwise explained, whether it affects people, animals, or crops. But it is much more. It is a source of power not only to those who are active practitioners, but also to those who claim to be able to neutralize the witch singlehandedly or who join together with others to make him or her harmless. Because it is a craft practiced secretly by the solitary individual under the cloak of night, frequently suspected, but rarely talked openly about for fear of reprisal, fed by rumors and fears, frequently hinted at bur rarely ascertained, it is a force exceedingly difficult to understand and to combat.

The fact that the modern world denies the existence of witchcraft does not simplify anything. The Witchcraft Ordinance of 1914, amended in 1948, 1952, 1963, and 1964, now Chapter 30 in Laws of the Republic of Zambia, makes a witchcraft accusation, and not the practice, the main offence.

Ziyelesa Ngoma and a group of friends were sitting around the fire. The wind blew softly. It was getting late, and, apart from the soft murmuring of the wind and the fire and the quiet voices talking about this or that, silence was everywhere. Ziyelesa wanted to talk about a problem that puzzled him ever more—*mifiti* [witchpeople].[15] And he said: "Why is it that a witch's footprints are not visible? How can the witchfire fly in the air with the witchman? Why doesn't the *fisi* [hyena, a well-known associate of the witch] get burned by the witchfire when the witch rides at night? Why do the witches feast upon the dead? Why do the all power-ful witchpeople move about only at night?" But nobody answered. Not wanting to contribute to the conversation with their real opinions, the men only smiled, remembering the saying of the ancestors: *Osasimba masoka—* "do not talk about misfortune!" They were thinking that whoever answers well may be considered a witch himself.

Finally Zuwaila bridged the quiet by telling a story:

"When night was falling a youngman who had been wondering about those who move around at night [i.e., the *mifiti*] sat down to relax in his porch. Suddenly he was overcome by a dizzy spell. As if dreaming, he felt somebody took him for a walk. He could not see who it was, whether a human being, some animal, or something else. But he was led on, power-lessly, to the graveyard. There, in the flickering lights of no lamp he saw strange sights and found the answer to many wonders. But what he saw and heard was such that he could not speak of it. He had no words. When he woke up from his spell, he found himself back in the porch. At the moment he thought he had been dreaming he suddenly realized that his clothes were all torn and dirty."

Zuwaila ended his story. And nobody said more about witches that night.

Brighton reported:

"A witch is someone who does things with charms with the intention to harm others. Witchwomen are said to be tougher in the craft than men. Witchpeople are said to be scared of dogs, though they charm even animals to use them or parts of living things with blood, to carry out *tuyobela*—their somber art. For example, a witch may take a frog and by magic conjure it into someone's body whereby that person will surely die. In the past, witches were thought to stay near graves, but not anymore. To visit graveyards is part of their business, but these days people know that witchcraft is per-formed inside the house, and brought out to work at night.

"Such stories are told about witchcraft. They force people to believe what they cannot understand. Fear and hatred make the witch habit continue to exist. And fear of witchcraft prevents people from cooperating and trusting each other. Some shun their relatives, preferring to work with friends rather than their own kin. They think their own family members may bewitch them and take their possessions. More than anything else, envy and jealousy are sentiments that poison human relationships and make people think of witch-craft."

Any sudden tragedy may be ascribed to witchcraft. When headman Kefa returned from a funeral at Mphindila village he told those who gathered to hear the news, how the man who died had been ill only one day, and how on the second day he had died. "Mr. Banda had a very good brick house and he had cattle and goats and pigs. It is clear that he died because others wanted his property," he concluded, implying that they had made use of witchcraft to satisfy their greed.

Kefa Mwale is also exposed to other people's envy, and this makes him feel very vulnerable.

"When a headman is outstanding in doing good for his village, like me, other people think you are a witch. They think you make use of medicine [magic] to achieve success, and they in turn will make use of witchcraft to bewitch or test you. As a result, if you do not have charms to protect yourself, and I do not, you may die. Many people are envious of my village and say plenty of bad things to destroy the cooperation that rules here. They want me to become as lazy as they are. As you know I used to be a carpenter, but with my swollen hands I can no longer work. But I have taught my skills to my village children, who now work with their hands according to how I taught them. I tell you, I am really hated for my good thinking. Many other headmen have tried to dirty my name, but they have failed because the honorable Chief knows my good works."

Witchcraft is used not only to harm and hurt, but also to grow rich and powerful. Tilele Zulu explained: "Many want to use witchcraft to enrich themselves. That is why witchcraft is practiced more among poor people [Tilele's hypothesis]. They want to get rich quickly. For that reason many people fear to show their wealth. If they own a vehicle or a business, family memebers and even others who are not related may get jealous and wish for their death to inherit or steal their wealth. It is not only hard work and little money that make people move out of a village, but also the fear of witchcraft."[17] When we asked Tilele how to recognize a witch, she said only: "He who smiles at people, he who looks friendly, at night he may be a witch." In short, anyone may be a witch.

People are afraid of accusing somebody of practicing witchcraft. If indeed the accusation is right, how easy for the witch to destroy them utterly. Yet, when the Phiri family was expelled because of the murder of Dandaulani Mwale, some villagers said *mifiti zinayenda*—"the witch-people have left." They were so upset and sorry to have lost their relative that they forgot not to speak about the unspeakable.

Some people say, in the company of their closest friends, that Nkunku Sakala behaves in a strange manner and that he is a witch. But to confront him or anyone else with the accusation is best left to the diviner—*mwini wa mauola*—"the owner of the divining stick"—or the *ng'anga*—the traditional healer, witch-finder, and magician. Some *ng'anga* are witches who have turned their magic skills to good uses.[18] Theirs is the ambition to help rather than to harm. People who are possessed are by that very fact often able to identify witches and render their magic harmless. Square Banda is one such specialist and he explains: "Witches have come to my house to try their powers, but I am not harmed by them. I have some very strong amulets, and when a witch approaches he is captivated by the amulets and cannot run away before I see him. He becomes paralyzed and I can do whatever I want with him."

Not all *ng'anga* are equally competent, and the distinction between witch and witch doctor may sometimes be quite subtle. Headman Kefa tells this story:

"Konala Banda was my friend. One day he went to a *ng'anga* to ask for advice because his mind was set on getting rich quickly. But he did not notice that the witch doctor himself lived in a dirty straw house and wore rags only. My friend Mr. Banda failed to ask himself the question: 'Why, if this *ng'anga* had amulets to make people rich, was he not a wealthy man himself?' Well, Banda got some charms from the man, and after a while all his three children died, one after the other. Banda thought his relatives had bewitched the children, and he too wanted to make use of witchcraft to harm his brothers. He was better off than they and thought they were after his property. But I think it was the charms he got from the witch doctor that caused all his misfortune. Because the *ng'anga* himself was envious because Konala Banda had money and children, he lied about his powers, wanting Mr. Banda's money for himself. So please do not go to any *ng'anga* who says he knows how to control charms. In these matters, it is important to make inquiries so that you find the right magician."

Citanomoyo is another example of a person who serves as a warning to those who are tempted to get rich by the help of magic. Citano is mad and his madness is explained by his own greed and the ill advice he got from the witch doctor when he appealed for help to get rich quickly. Citanomoyo is a relative of Brighton Lungu, and Brighton made this report:

"Brighton has a brother [extended relative], Citanomoyo. Citano's mother is the sister of Lomanzi Tembo, who is Brighton's [proper] mother and the daughter of Ajesi Kamanga, who died last year. Citanomoyo is a grade seven man [i.e., quite educated as compared to most villagers] who sat for his final exam during the colonial government. Then he left Kefa village to earn. While working as a kitchen boy in Southern Rhodesia, Citano consulted a witch doctor to get rich quickly. The witch doctor told him to sleep at a graveyard and from the graveyard to go home and sleep with his own mother. Citanomoyo decided to follow the advice and went home to Zambia. Here he spent a night in a graveyard, and then he went to his own mother and begged for her permission to sleep with her. But the mother refused entirely to sleep with her own son in the same bed. Some say this is the reason why Citanomoyo went mad, while others say it is because he spent a night alone in a graveyard.

As Citanomoyo's madness grew, he was taken by the police to Chainama Hospital in Lusaka, where he stayed for three months before he ran away. "But Citanomoyo no longer wanted to be with other people. He stayed in the bush and, as people were fond of insulting him, he decided to chase away everybody he met on his way. The village residents appealed to the police to arrest him. But the police told them not to provoke the poor man. After that Citanomoyo improved, but to feed himself he had become a thief. People were aware that he took their chickens and green maize and they wanted to beat him but the headman refused to give his permission. So now we are getting used to him and do not trouble him when he steals things. After his grandmother Ajeso died, Citanomoyo has only his brother Brighton to depend on. His mother lives in Msukula village but does not look after him. When it was discovered that he had stolen three chickens and roasted them all, he was allowed to keep his relish. The headman said that because Citanomoyo was mad, it was up to us Kefa residents to look after our property."

It seems that in the case of Citano, as in other instances where village people are faced with the inevitable, the strategy is one of adaptation and cooperation.

Not everyone is ready to see witchcraft as the cause of every misfortune and every evil. When the young boy Ifenso Phiri died after only a short illness, the grandfather Kwerekani Phiri advised the boy's parents: "Please, do not cry too much for your son who died. Do not accuse people of the village that they have killed the boy. Death comes, even to the most undeserving, and need not mean that somebody has bewitched your son. *Cakanga cakanga*—what is gone, is gone. "But Rosemary, Ifenso's heartbroken mother, was convinced that the child had been killed by witchcraft and kept telling the husband, John Scout Phiri, to employ a witchfinder so that they could learn how their son had died.

John Scout did not heed her advice as he was not prepared to spend any more money; the boy was already dead and the funeral with all its expenses had been held. But Rosemary was not satisfied and a quarrel arose between Ifenso's parents. John Scout refused to give the wife money, and Rosemary no longer fed the husband or let him use her water to drink and to give to his pigeons. John Scout ate not from the wife, but from his mothers, and he bathed not at home but in Mtewe river.

When John Scout took this family problem to headman Kefa, the headman called a village meeting. Opening the meeting, the headman introduced the problem in this way: "I have not asked neighboring headmen, but you, my village elders and relatives of this woman [Rosemary], because the husband [John Scout] has asked that this must be considered a family matter, and not a case of witchcraft."

When John Scout and Rosemary had explained the problem as they saw it, Zuwaila Zulu said: "It seems that this is a case that is much older than what you are trying to make us believe. I remember at the *m'meto*— the hair-cutting ceremony that follows shortly after the funeral—Kwerekani [the grandfather] said, 'There are too many deaths in this village,' and 'We, the elders, must try to protect these our young relatives from the evil that seems to exist in this village.' I also remember that Rosemary's father said that 'Death and destruction have entered this house. Man's fruits are his children, and as the tree is proud when it bears so is man. But in this our children's house fruits do not mature. Every time this woman [Rosemary] bears a child, it dies. Something is very wrong. Now we see it happen again. But we must never allow it to happen a next time. Therefore I ask you to go and see a witch finder so that we can have an answer to this, our great worry, why children cannot grow in this house.' "

"I remember that we who were present then, agreed. But, since then, nothing has been done about the matter, as far as I know. It is my contention that what is now happening is that John's wife is trying to remind you, the parents, of the many deaths not only in her house, but also in the entire village, by quarreling with the husband. So the quarrel is not the problem. The real problem is the one you promised to look into, Mr. Kwerekani. Let us try to deal with that problem here and help each others to solve it to the satisfaction of these young people and to all of us who live together in this village."

After a few other people has spoken their minds, Kwerekani Phiri, John Scout's father, stood up and said:

"Ladies and gentlemen, one man is never right all the time. These children [John Scout and Rosemary] are mine because they stay with me here in Kefa village. But they need the advice also of the relatives of the wife [Rosemary]. Maybe my advice so far has not been good enough for their daughter. So now, to show your love, please sit down and discuss and help her so that all of us who love these young people can be together and correct our earlier mistakes and help them in every way possible." Zuwaila and others supported Kwerekani for his decision and went away so that the close family could review all the events that had led to their being together at the village meeting that evening.

Rosemary and John Scout were not the only Kefa residents troubled by the death of their children and the fear of witchcraft. Brighton Lungu was one of those eager to believe that a witch was determined to destroy the cooperation and trust that are the most vital foundation of any village. He made this report:

"Also in Shuzi Zulu's family there is no cooperation. Some family members are suspected of having killed Shuzi's son, Thomase, who died at only one-and-a-half years of age. The suspicion of witchcraft arose because Shuzi's grandmother had said it would be better for everybody in the village if Shuzi and Jenifa [the wife] went away to Shuzi's father's village. She said so because Shuzi had beaten her grandchildren, who had killed one of his hens. Shuzi wanted to teach the children a lesson. He said that unless they learn right from the beginning by the beating not to make trouble, they may kill a cow and then they would end up in court where they would be in real trouble. But Nyasakala Ngoma also told the parents of the children about the beating and they in turn started quarreling with Shuzi and Jenifa.

"When Shuzi saw that his family turned against him, he went to head-man Kefa to have the case resolved. Kefa Mwale admonished them that the fighting and quarreling should stop. But it did not. Nyakasa was not satisfied and told Shuzi to move out of her old house where he and Jenifa had been living ever since their own house fell down. It was while they were looking for a new house that Thomase, the small child, died. Shortly after the *m'meto*—the hair-cutting ceremony—Nyakasa said: 'Now, when you too have lost your child, perhaps you will grow up to become a man!' Shuzi and many others were utterly surprised to hear their grandmother say that it was on-ly after his children died that a man would grow up and be a man. James Phiri, Simon Sakala, Betina Tembo, and Isaac Phiri had already lost young children, and now also John Scout and Shuzi. And they counted the young men among them who had not yet lost a child and they were only Stephen Phiri and Jackson Phiri."[19]

A few days later Stephen and Jackson and some others came to Brighton to ask his advice. Brighton, speaking for all the young men, advised headman Kefa to call a magician witch-finder to search the village so that they, the residents, could know if their children and also others were dead from witchraft or from other causes. But Kefa refused to do anything.

Brighton reported: "After we had troubled the headman for five days, Kefa gave in and accepted our wishes."[20] Two days later Kefa and Brighton went to chief Chikuwe's court. They told the chief how the Kefa residents were crying for their deceased children and parents. Village residents were dying every week and there were some people in the village who said that children must die for their parents to grow up. They asked the honorable Chief to permit the best among the witch-finders in the area to come into the village and search for the witch if indeed there was one that had caused all this trouble.

The Chief agreed: A witch-finder could come and the two envoys should go back to Kefa village and tell the residents that the Chief knew of their problem. That very evening, headman Kefa struck his village bell and summoned his residents to a meeting. Having explained what had happened at the Chief's court, the headman posed the question:

"Do you want an African doctor magician to come and search this village so that we can know if witchcraft has killed our children and our parents?" he asked the crowd. And everybody shouted yes. But Chikwanda added: "I think our headman is cheating us. We asked him a long time ago to bring a witch-finder into the village, but he did nothing. Is it really so that now, after many years and so many deaths, a diviner of witch-people will be called?" But Kefa said only: "Brighton here will answer you."

And Brighton spoke: "Yes, you know what you have been told. Today the headman and I have talked to our Chief and we have his permission to call a witch-finder. Tomorrow we shall go back to his palace and get the letter of his approval that will permit the witch-diviner to come here. This year, I tell you, we shall surely see the magician here in our village. But it will happen only if all of us are willing to donate money, because such a magician will want big pay for such a big job."

"When Kefa, Brighton, and three other men went to get the letter of approval from the chief, the traditional Chewa leader asked: "If the witch-finder finds whoever is responsible for the evil deeds, what will you do with that person or those persons?" Kefa said nothing, but Brighton took the word and said that those who were found would surely be told to leave the village forever, so that all the others could live in peace and cooperate like before. And the Chief agreed and thanked Brighton for his answer.

When the delegates returned home, the villagers were called once again and informed about what had happened at the Chief's palace, and Brighton and Simon were chosen to go and look for the best witch-finder and diviner in the area. After three days the young men returned and again a village meeting was called. They had located the best witch-finder in Chief Mishoro's area. Here they had spent two days to see the man at work and they were truly convinced of his powers. He had agreed to come to Kefa village shortly; his only condition was that he wanted K. 2.50 from each Kefa resident. When the residents were asked if anyone present would not pay, they seemed to murmur their acceptance, yet under their breath some whispered that they had neither the money nor any idea of how to raise it, but nobody protested aloud. If they had others might think that they were the witch-people fearing to be identified.

A few days later Andrick Banda died. This time witchcraft was not suspected, as Andrick was old and ill, even if he rarely was too ill to drink beer. As he was mourned and buried there was a break in the witch talk. Then, after the funeral, Brighton and a few other young men set out to collect K. 2.50 from every adult resident. The job was not easy and was soon stalled. Because it was still several months until harvest time, most villagers simply had no money. And those who did hesitated to pay before their poorer neighbors did. Soon people started saying that K. 2.50 per resident would add up to K. 300 and even more and this was more than even the headman would earn from all his hybrid during a whole year. They found it a very stiff price even for the best witch-finder.

And while the villagers were discussing and deliberating, the green maize started to ripen. The green leaves and pumpkins followed suit, and all of a sudden there was plenty of relish everywhere and there were no more deaths.[21] Then Brighton was called away for some business prospects in Lundazi. As the headman remained just as passive as before, not wanting false accusations of witchcraft to destroy his village, the talk of bringing the witch-finder to Kefa grew fainter until it was nothing but an occasional whisper. However, that it will arise once more is only a question of time, because the causes remain: premature death, fear and anxiety, envy and even hatred.

Death

Once again, we should recall the words of Brighton: "I have counted the people who have died and who are still alive since the survey started, and we are missing sixteen persons." Within the short period of eighteen months sixteen family members from fifty-six households were dead—that is, almost one person from every third household. No wonder Kefa residents thought witchcraft was being wrought among them. Almost every third of the living huts in the village had had mourners cross their thresholds to give voice to the agony of meeting with the irrevocable, to express their love for the deceased, to comfort the bereaved, and to carry the earthly remains of yet another beloved family member to the resting place of the ancestors. Sixteen lives had ended: three infants, five small children, two older children, three adults, and three elders.

More than any other event, death commands the presence and participation of fellow villagers, that is, if the deceased has been given sufficient time to be recognized as a village resident proper. When a baby is still-born—*wakufa*—or a small infant dies, it is buried right away without ceremony. There is a special infant burial ground close to the village. Here women alone are the "conductors of ceremony." "Men are not allowed because the baby is so small that even the women do not cry," it is said. But no mother whose infant baby rests in a clay pot here just under the ground goes unmarked. One of the hardest hit is Evelinar, who within one-and-a-half years buried three children, including twins. When the first-born died, Mwada Simba organized the women and thirteen of them went to the burial ground early in the morning, dug the grave, and buried the clay pot, in only half an hour.

When older children and adults die, family members from near and far participate. This is a time when solidarity becomes tangible and even countable as the *antu a maliro*—the people of the funeral, or mourners— are counted to assess the popularity and status of the deceased. Tyford explained: "Each person puts a small stick in a hat or a container and the stick represents himself or herself. By counting the sticks the participants are counted and in this way it becomes known how famous the dead person was." In this way we know that 1,036 people mourned for Kakoche Mwale, Kefa's father; 580 person came to the funeral of Alesi Mwale; and 384 people to that of Grace Daka, the young girl made pregant by Jumapili Banda.

When death arrives in a village, every village resident is called upon to contribute to the funeral in one way or another and all ordinary work is laid aside. Those who do not join the preparations may be summoned before the headman. James Kamaswanda continued to weave a basket though Ifenso the young boy had just died. "Don't you know that we have a funeral in this village," the deputy headman admonished. "Everybody is so very sorry for the boy who died. On such a day nobody can work and those who do must be fined. That is why I will charge you K. 5 for not following the customs of this village."

According to the rules nobody is allowed to cry before the deceased has been washed and dressed and the headman has been notified. When Alesi Kamanga, Brighton's grandmother, died in the early morning, there was only a quiet flurry at first as the news was whispered to next door kin and neighbors. Soon silent shadows scurried through the dark, descending upon the small kitchen hut in which Alesi had collapsed and died. As the day started to break, women gathered, some to wash and dress Alesi, others to sit patiently outside the kitchen hut and await the arrival of the headman. But no one cried. By eight o'clock the men had come too. Now the headman had taken command and was busy organizing the *maliro*, the funeral. The women were told to cry aloud to give vent to their grief, and to relay to people in nearby villages and passing by on the road that death had descended upon Kefa village. To provide space for the mourners, Alesi's frail body was moved from her hut to a room in headman Kefa's brick house and the crowd was shifted from Brighton's compound to that of the headman, who was one of the several villagers who called Alesi *amai*—mother. Simultaneously, the headman and the village elders were busy organizing the *malodza*—the death messages. Every functioning bicycle was mobilized to take the youngmen of the village in all directions to deliver the sad message to neighboring headmen and to relatives. Time is short. Within forty-eight hours, preferably before if it is during the hot months of October and November, the body must be buried. By that time close relatives should have arrived to pay their last respect to the deceased and participate in the ceremony. Nobody wants to experience what Simon Sakala witnessed when he went to a funeral at Kaliyoyo village. Because the organizers of the funeral kept waiting for relatives to arrive from the Copper Belt, the corpse smelled so bad that people refused to carry it to the grave.

It is the village headmen who are informed about funerals and they in turn pass the message on to their village residents. Particularly in the cold season *malodza* sometimes seem to arrive almost continuously. When in August headman Kefa wanted to call the villagers to a meeting about the new housing scheme, Lemekani told his brother, "Please, let us wait to call people together until there is a death message. People are in the field and there is a lot of work to do, and they get tired having to go to meetings all the time." But Tilele, Lemekani's wife, who had just arrived from the big store at the crossroads said: "There is a funeral message. Mr. Kanjakuta has just died at Chiparamba rural clinic and he has relatives from this village." And so Kefa rang the bell.

Like many other village residents Mr. Kanjakuta was baptized at the end of the 1970s. Thus, on the news of his death, Mr. Ackim Zulu, who is a retired church leader, wrote letters to his fellow church leaders informing them that they had lost a church member. The letters were delivered by the youngmen, who could thus supplement the receivers with additional news through word of the mouth.

Since the middle of the 1970s there are two groups of Christians: the Catholics and the members of the Reformed Church. "This has brought some changes to our funeral practices," Simon Sakala told us. "Now, if the deceased is a Christian, church leaders conduct the funeral. But if he or she was a non-Christian, the number of attendants are often less, as some Christians have stopped crying at the death of non-Christians. Still, more people go to childrens' funerals, perhaps because Jesus loved children."[22]

The headman was not at all pleased with this new trend and he called together village elders like Lemekani Mbao, Robert Manda, Zuwaila Zulu, Sandikonda Daka, and a few other men to discuss the matter. Kefa said: "Why is it that you, my elders, do no longer attend funerals and give advice at the graveyard?" And Lemekani said: "I slept during the funeral because I was ill." And Sandikonda said: "I too was ill. You know that my leg prevents me from walking far." And Zuwaila said: "I am still sick with coughing, and that is why I sleep during funerals and do not attend."

But Kefa said: "This bad practice must stop. If the elders do not attend funerals, other people will also not attend. There are two churches in this village, the Reformed Church and the Catholic Church. But when there is a funeral everybody must come together. We cannot have funerals where people do not attend!"

Many people agree. What kind of village life is this where each man goes about his own business, not heeding the needs and wants of others? When two days later there was a funeral at Mpenyesani village, Mwanishupa said to her husband: "Please, do not work today, go to the funeral. Otherwise Mr. Kefa will say Mr. Daka does not love me, because if he did he would have come with me to the funeral. So you must go. Besides you are ill and you should not work. We will make bricks without you. Please accompany Mr. Kefa to Mpenyesani village."

Twice a day Radio Zambia Death Message Service spreads *malodza* all over the republic. That is how Sandikonda Daka came to learn that his child had died in Lusaka. Nason Phiri, who is a farmer living apart from the villagers, heard the message first: "Sandikonda Daka and Esitele Daka of Kefa and Mchenga villages! You are informed that David, the son of Justin, is dead in Lusaka." Hearing the very sad news, Sandikonda hurried to tell his sister Esitele in Mchenga village.

Because the honorable Chief is related to so many people in his chiefdom, he is one of the first to be informed about the death of a tribesman. And a person must approach an important person like the Chief with a token gift. When Alesi died, Micheck Phiri and Simon Sakala were given 20 ngwee by the headman and were told to inform the chief, who spent much of his time at funerals in one of the one hundred villages that fall within his realm.

A funeral is always expensive. To provide for whatever is needed the headman asks everybody to donate money or food. The money is spent on planks and cloth for the coffin, on flour-grinding at the hammer mill, on paraffin for light in the lamps at night, and on salt for the relish. Sonile Ngoma, who recently lost her husband, Andrick Banda, explained the funeral practices: "If the deceased is a woman, the husband is asked if he has money to buy planks to make the coffin and cloth to cover it. He is also expected to slaughter a goat or a cow if he has any, so that the funeral people will find good meat relish." If the deceased has no husband or brothers, relatives will help, as headman Kefa helped at Alesi's funeral by slaughtering one of his cows.

When Kefa's father, Kakoche Mwale, died some months later, Kefa refused to give up any of his cattle for relish, saying that he had fed his father well when he was still alive and that he had no more cattle for slaughtering. Mwazida Kefa's sister persuaded him to change his mind, and in the end both Kefa and Mwazida's husband Robert Manda slaughtered an animal to feed the one thousand mourners that came to Kakoche's funeral. Kefa also bought a ready-made coffin from Chipata for his father which cost K. 60. For Alesi it was Zindi Miti, Kefa's sister's son, who bore the costs of K. 29 for planks and cloth.

While the relatives of the deceased bear the main financial burden, every mourner is expected to give at least something. The total amount of money donated by the funeral people is another measure of the following of the deceased, and every ngwee is counted and accounted for. The individual donations vary from a few ngwee to fifty; occasionally a rich donor will give one kwacha. At Kakoche's funeral one thousand people coming from forty-two different villages, six separate farms, two shops, one beer hall, one agricultural extension camp, and one road maintenance camp donated a total of K. 18.72. At Alesi's funeral the donation amounted to K. 7.38, and at Grace's K. 11.38.

Sonile expained: "At funerals men are considered the conductors of the ceremony and the headman or his deputy is in charge. The women are under the supervision of the men, who organize them and tell them what to do. Although we all know what to do, the rule is that we women must obey the men. So we wait for their decision as to when to donate maize and to start pounding. That is why we go to the headman for our orders."

At Alesi's funeral the headman told Mwada Simba to organize the women and collect maize from every household in the village. By noon more that twenty pestles were in motion and the pounding rhythm flowed together with the loud crying to welcome every new mourner arriving in the funeral village. Timeke Daka was sent with three other women to cut grass to fence the funeral house. As the sun descended they returned from the grassland at the other side of Mtewe River. Once at the funeral house, the women quickly shed their burdens and the men took over. Their job was to construct the fence that would protect the hundreds of visitors who would sleep outside. As the sun set, the *malodza* had been carried throughout the chiefdom and mourners kept filtering into the lamenting village. By nightfall two hundred visitors had come to Kakoche's funeral and one hundred forty to Alesi's. Sweet beer was brewing, meat roasting, and *nsima* simmering on innumerable fires. The village women worked hard to feed them all and uphold their reputation of generosity and hospitality.

"The men have given themselves the task of preparing the coffin and digging the grave," Sonile continued. "Digging is the toughest job, so that is left to the youngmen, but elders stand by telling them what to do. To make a grave you need the measurements of the coffin, an axe to clear the small bush in the graveyard, a pick to break big stones, and a hoe with a short handle to use when the grave is getting deep. The depth of a grave is about the height of a man.

"To escape the stiffling midday heat, the grave is usually dug in the evening, when an old tire is burned to light up the site. When the job is done, most of the men return to the village, but some stay behind to guard the tools and the grave against the selfish witch-people."[23]

After all practicalities are completed, each group that has been doing a job reports back to the headman. When everything is ready, if the dead person was a Christian the church leaders read from the Bible. Then, the funeral attendants start moving toward the grave yard. The women lead the way. Songs accentuated by loud crying accompany the procession as a beloved family member is taken to his or her last abode. Along the lane, five hundred or even a thousand people, friends and relatives, move slowly toward the shady burial ground and the open grave. Somewhere in the middle of the procession is the coffin, covered in cloth. Men alternate to carry the burden so that as many as possible can say they have taken their relative home to the ancestors.

At the graveyard there is another short ceremony where church leaders read from the Bible. Then the coffin is lowered six feet into the ground. To cover up the grave every village present is called, one after the other, and at each calling five or six men spring forward, pick up hoes, and shovel earth onto the coffin. At the very end it is the children or grandchildren of the deceased who smooth the rough grave. Then, as the mourners return to the vilage, the local women carry the tools the men have been using and water so that the men who have worked with them can wash.

Back in the village the funeral people gather for the *zikhuzo*—the hearing. Time has come for the headman or his deputy to explain the cause of death: how coughing, bleeding, headaches, or purging killed the dead man or woman, elder, adult, or child. The *zikhuzo* is important to quench any rumors about witchcraft. After the hearing the funeral guests are urged to eat before they return to their separate villages and leave the funeral village so much emptier than before.

Mourning is not yet over. Close family members stay on for some days for the performance of the *m'meto*—the hair cutting ceremony. Kefa explains:

"The *m'meto* is performed to release the widow or widower and other close relatives so that they may forget their sorrow and continue their usual life, doing all the usual activities they stopped doing because of the death in the family. Until the close family members have had their heads shaven, relatives continue to sleep in the funeral house. This they do to help the bereaved person so that his or her heart will be a little bit settled. Otherwise the spouse who has been left alone may want to commit suicide for the sake of the beloved dead.

"Some families prefer to perform *kunyinda*, a special ceremony to protect them against the spirits of the deceased. After the haircutting is done and the hairs have been hidden in an ant hill, those who partake in the *m'meto* wash their heads. Then meat is boiled in a broken pot and mixed with medicine and each family member puts a hot piece of meat in his mouth and then spits it out on the ground. The second piece of meat they chew while they jump over the clay pot on the fire. The pot is broken and the remaining meat is burned on the fire. This they do so that their worries may leave them and the dead person will not trouble them in their sleep."

Other ways exist, too, to alleviate the pain of bereavement. Sonile explained how a woman who has just lost her husband sits with other women who rub her face with maize flour to prevent her dreams from being disturbed by her late husband. It will also protect her from *chidima*—being unable to find a new husband (or wife if it is a man).

"In the past the mourning used to last for one year," Sonile continued. "But now things are changing because funerals take place every week. The elders used to tell the bereaved spouse not to look for a husband or lover until one year had passed, but now people stay alone less than a month before they look for a new man or woman to sleep with. They hurry because someone else in the family may die, and how long can a person wait to get married again? If the spouse left behind is a women, she is not suppposed to cook *nsima*, touch the fire, and put salt in her relish during this time of mourning. That is why they want to do the hair-cutting ceremony as soon as possible to live like other village women. After the hair-cutting ceremony they [relatives] give *nsuzulo* [divorce money] to the widow[er] and she or he waits about two weeks before taking a man or woman to sleep with. If the person waits any longer the spouse that has lost the friend [partner] may run mad and have no chance of finding someone new to marry. But the Chief wants people to mourn for at least four weeks, not only two weeks as many people do now."

When a husband dies, any cattle, house, granary, tools, furniture, and money go to the man's relatives. Wife and children, as the thinking goes, will be provided for by the relatives, for the brother of the late husband will marry the widow. In a traditional subsistence society this may be a way of minimizing the disruptions that the loss of a head of household will cause. But in an expanding economy based on money, material possessions are becoming increasingly more important, as is inheritance. Newspapers are full of horror stories of how widows and orphans are robbed of their home and livelihood by greedy relatives who upon the death of the male head of household descend upon the family and carry away whatever goods they find, claiming the rights but shunning the responsibilities prescribed by the traditional society.

This is the background for a meeting to which the honorable Chief Chikuwe invited all his headmen. When the leaders of the many villages in the chiefdom gathered, the Chief spoke: "I have called you headmen here today to let you know that any relative who claims that he has the right to acquire any possessions from a deceased brother is by order of the government to produce a written paper to prove that this is so. And this written document he must show to you, the headmen and the elders. The reason is as you know. Very often the brothers and other relatives of a deceased husband have caused problems by taking all the possessions away from the children. So, unless the relatives can prove in writing that the things are theirs, all the inheritance shall from now on go to the children of the dead person, so that they will have something to live on."

Zindikani Miti is Kefa's sister's son. According to the rules of the matrilineal society he is Kefa's successor to the headmanship in the village. But Zindi is a modern man and he has endorsed the Chief's decision entirely: "The possessions belonging to Kefa Mwale should remain with the headman's proper children and mine are for my children. I am not stupid. I do not think that the headmanship will be mine. I represent my father. My mother is Kefa's sister; however I am linked not on that side, but on that of my father."

The Chewas are by tradition matrilineal—counting their ancestors through the *mother's* lineage. But with modern developments, this is about to change. Before, Zindi would be an obvious heir to the headmanship, being the son of Kefa's *sister* (a man was responsible for this sister's offspring, and his wife's brother would be responsible for his), but now even Zindi says he counts his roots to his father's kin, and not his mother's (i.e., to Kefa Mwale). What we see is a *revolution* of matrilineal to patrilineal thinking.

The new rules spoken by the Chief may improve the situation of orphans, but not necessarily that of widows. Most women live in their husband's village and cultivate what is considered "his" garden. When "the owner of a women" dies, she has two options: Either she marries a brother of her deceased husband, and continues cultivating her old field; or she goes home to her "own" village where her mother and/or brothers live.

If neither option is available—or acceptable—to the widow, she may find herself in a very difficult situation, particularly if she is old or ill and if she has no children willing to look after her.

> Tiku Banda, Kwezekani's widow, decided to go "home." She said: "I have no proper children in Kefa village and no relatives here; that is why I shall go to my mother's village." At a meeting among Kwezekani's brother, headman Kefa, other village elders, and Tiku shortly after the hair-cutting ceremony it was decided that Tiku would stay on in Kefa until March when her granaries would have been eaten and then she would go home to Chiduka village. Before she went, she would be given *nsuzulo* by Mr. M'kuduwavu, who "is brotherly related" to Kwezekani. The *nsuzulo* signifies that the mourning period is over and that the person is free to marry again outside the late husband's family (see page 143).

The loss of a close family member may mean the loss of a firm foothold, at least for a while. Even headman Kefa, so old and so wise, forgot his most elementary duties as a headman when confronted with the death of his own father. That is why, only four days after he had buried Kakoche Mwale, headman Kefa was summoned before the Chief. Traditions do not just happen, they are actively upheld.

The case against headman Kefa was held in Kefa's own courtyard. Because beer was ready in Kefa's compound and would be served after the judgment many people were present. The rule is that when a headman is to be judged the Chief himself, or the Chief's deputy as in this case, will preside. The Deputy Chief's advisor and the Chief's messenger were also present.

The Deputy Chief said: "We have come here today to learn how a funeral can be conducted so utterly wrongly. On Thursday Chief Mishoro and I were called for the funeral here. We kept waiting for the coffin to arrive. Then, all of a sudden, we heard the preacher start praying! But why not report to us, the Chief and the Chief Duputy? A headman is supposed to inform the Chief that the coffin has arrived! He is supposed to ask permission to put the body into the coffin! He is supposed to ask permission to start the prayer! This is our custom, but it seems that you, Mr. Kefa, you decided to play the Chief's drum with your own bare hands! It is about these matters that we have come here today. Where did you get the power to misbehave like this!"

Kefa Mwale answered: "I have attended many funerals. I know well that a headman is to report to the Chief about what is happening, step by step.

"On this occasion, and many people can be my witnesses, I was extremely busy. I moved here and there and got confused because there were so many requests from my friends who wanted to help. Because it was my own father's funeral, I expected people to know that it is our custom to inform you all the time as we proceed with the ceremony.

"When the coffin arrived, immediately James Daka told me to pass him the cloth to cover the body, and to pass him the screwdriver so that he could fasten the lid. Then he informed me that people should be prepared for prayers by the church leader of the Reform Church of Zambia, who is also James. What he did was to help me, and I accepted everything, thinking that my friends too know our customs. And this is where I was mistaken."

James Daka (Grace's father) said: "Yes, it is true. I was involved in violating our custom. But I was not aware of it. When I said what to do, Kefa always agreed." And Kefa said: "Yes, I agreed because I had so many things on my mind."

The Deputy Chief asked Mr. Daka if he had been in charge of the ceremony, and if so who had authorized him. And James said: "I am retired so I led the funeral procedure without any authorization from my church or from anyone else. I simply though it was suitable to assist in the funeral."

The Deputy Chief said: "Are you closely related, like some of Kakoche's grandchildren?" And James answered: "No. Anyway, I admit that I was wrong. But if I was wrong I made the mistake of assisting in the funeral at all."

The Deputy Chief than asked Kefa and James: "Do you think we can pass judgment in this case without calling anybody to defend you?" And both of them accepted.

The headmen from Mphazu, Mphindila, Mchenga, Kamanga, and Nyathani villages had been called for the hearing as a headman stood to be accused. Now, the Deputy Chief asked them to step aside and discuss between themselves what should be done with Kefa Mwale and James Daka. He encouraged them, saying: "The honorable Chief has given you this whip. Now use it and show what is left of it to the Chief, so that it can be seen that the guilty have been punished." What he meant was that the headmen had a case to solve, and their decision would be reported to the Chief for his final decision.

When they came back, headman Kamanga was their spokesman. Kefa Mwale was to pay K. 2 and James Daka K. 3 for their mistake in not reporting on the funeral proceedings to the Chief. Both culprits accepted the judgment, but James had to borrow K. 3 from Penelani Khosa to pay the fine.

The Deputy Chief then concluded by saying: "I have done this in order to set an example of what must be done when the Chief visits a funeral. I must go to ask Chief Misholo to excuse us. [Chief Misholo is a Ngoni chief whose customs may be different from those of the Chewa.] He will probably be talking badly about our Chewa customs and how we Chewa people treat our Chief. So let this be the end of the case. Now we can all go and drink beer! *Mfumu yaweluzidwa jmwini wace*—the headman who sits in judgment over others has been judged himself."

Notes

1. Asking a sample of people, we found that the average woman and man complained of 2 and 1.3 ailments respectively of which headaches and stomachaches were the most common. While some of the young men said they were healthy, hardly any women said so. Unfortunately we questioned adults only. Because many ailments are seasonally determined, our data are certainly not representative but may indicate general bad health among villagers. According to statistics from out-patient attendance at Chiparamba Rural Health Centre, the most common causes for hospital attendance were upper respiratory infection, malaria, fever, and diarrhea.

2. "The knowledge and use of herbs in Africa [are] extensive and impressive . . . Several concoctions tested and now in process of being analysed have proved to be effective in the treatment of parasitic and bacterial infection, malaria, tuberculosis, and even some forms of cancer. Oral contraceptives and drugs that induce abortion are known, and several local healers have demonstrated their use of a root infusion as an anesthetic when administered in the form of an enema." (Watson, 1982:152–53.)

3. "A ritual becomes a reality in its own right. It is not just something you do, or words you say, or the place you choose to perform. It may involve making a sacrifice to an ancestor or offering a prayer, swearing an oath or simply crossing the fingers. The details are unimportant, because they are not peculiar to the ritual. It is the whole of the procedure that matters." (Watson, 1982:119.)

4. ". . . divination works extraordinarily well. It functions first at a personal level, relieving doubt and anxiety. Divination is always associated with a situation that seems to call for a decision that cannot easily be taken. For each society there is a proper list of such occasions, which may include illness, death, marriage, calamity, loss, or merely unresolved conflict. Recourse to a diviner, whether the advice is good or bad, true or false, relieves these tensions and provides the psychological release which comes from conviction that a decision is in tune with the wishes of supernatural forces—in other words that it has the blessing of the spirits." (Watson, 1982:157.)

5. "Whether or not he or she is involved in healing, a diviner's prime function is to grasp consciously, and to bring out into the open, the secret and unconscious motives causing an individual to become ill, or creating a social disturbance.

   "Diviners are, in effect, the psychologists, psychiatrists, physicians, priests, confessors, counselors, and historians of their people. All these functions are wrapped up in a single and highly effective institution. A sympathetic study of the ways in which they work provides valuable insights into the origins not only of magical belief, but of all religion." (Watson, 1982:154.)

6. "The question of food taboos has bulked very largely in anthropological literature from the earliest days. Such ritual restrictions on diet seem to have struck the attention of European observers immediately. . . It may be said at once that the food taboo proper is not widely observed among these Central African people. The Bemba tribe is divided into clans named after various animals or plants, but in no case are totemic food taboos kept . . . Nor does there seem to be any food tabooed to one sex or the other, or considered appropriate to any particular time of life. Certain individuals regularly abstain from one or more types of relish. Such restrictions may be the result of an order given by a native doctor who may make a cure conditional on the regular observance a food taboo, or it may follow the individual's own conviction that a particular food eaten on some memorable occasion has brought him ill luck and is therefore likely to do so again." (Richards, 1939:62.)

7. "National figures for infant mortality officially quoted is between 140–160 per 1,000 live births but some estimates put it even higher. Measles (20%), pneumonia (16.1%), diarrhoea (11.4%), malnutrition and anaemia (11.3%), and malaria (10.2%) were reported as the five leading causes of death in children. According to local statistics from rural health centers in Kalichero and Luangwa Valley, a similar pattern of mortality is reported for the year 1978. These patterns of mortality suggested that malnutrition and disease associated with malnutrition, especially measles, diarrhoea and pneumonia, were responsible for about 55% of total childhood mortality." (K.M. Kwofie, 1980:8.)

8. "At any given day there were thousands of people all over Africa undergoing or watching someone else undergo what was believed to be possession by a spirit . . .

   "The social benefits of such belief are enormous. Information or advice given by a spirit, through a person possessed, acquires an unusual authority. . . The individual benefits are less direct, but no less profound. There is a remarkable sameness about the patterns of possessions. People in all parts of Africa tend to go into possession trance in much the same way, with the same sounds and movements. The behaviour seems to a very large extent to have become ritualized under traditional controls. This structure helps individuals to cope with what is essentially a terrifying experience. They know more or less what to expect.

"Possession is really the subjugation of self by something else, by an "otherness," but it does not produce schizophrenia. In most cases it seems to be a genuinely healing experience, leaving the possessed individual with a feeling of peace or euphoria when coming out of the trance. And it seems to have very similar effects on spectators." (Watson, 1982:124–125.)

9. Scott (1929:359): "*Mzimu*, a spirit, the spirit of the departed; supposed to come in dreams . . . also fortune and good luck. The spirit of the departed remain in life when a man is dead; they inhabit the spirit world and are with God and remain in something like the place where stays Mulungu [God], they know everything and they hear the plaints of man . . . but they have no intercourse with man, except in dreams and in the silent care which they can exercise over man, having power to lead men and watch over them with favours. . ."

10. "Throughout Africa, color plays an important role in symbolism, particularly related to medicine. The important shades are black, red, and white. Black is the color of night, death, excrement, and illness. White is daylight, life, food, and good health. Red is generally equivocal, indicating a transformation . . . Very often the medicines may be linked with a sacrificial animal, which is either pure black or pure white . . . 'The understanding of this matter of color,' said Rrasebe, 'comes with the knowledge of hot and cold. Illness causes the blood to be hot and is best treated with cool white medicines, or by pressing a smooth stone against all the joints of the body.' " (Watson, 1982:135-6)

" . . . spirit possession was most common in the most rigid and structured societies, and within these societies it is most often the culturally oppressed, notably women, who become possessed. In trance, they can give full expression to their personalities and act out their desires without fear of reproach. They can do so in a way that is positively beneficial to their society. It is not surprising, then, that the strongest personalities in a community frequently come to be its spirit-diviners. Furthermore, all these specialists are drawn to their calling as a result of an illness of some sort. They have thus been set apart from other people. The symptoms are clearly recognized as being different from those of ordinary illness, as being conditions of the mind rather than the body." (Watson, 1982:128.)

11. "The activities of diviner or spirit-medium are often taken up by people debarred from advancement in the secular field. In some societies they are professions for women . . . Spirit-mediums must have a special type of personality. They must be able readily to fall into a condition of dissociation and speak as though with a voice entering them from outside: they commonly find their vocation after a period of disturbance which a psychiatrist would probably call a mental illness. This disturbed state is usually taken as a sign that a spirit wishes to enlist the person in his service. But it is significant that we do not often hear of persons who hold positions of authority being 'possessed' in this way." (Mair, 1965:216).

12. "Zambian possessions, as described in the literature, display an enormous variety." Important dimensions of that variety include: "the nature of the associated beliefs (the participants' interpretation of the possession agents and of the latter's relationship with the possessed and with the community); the distinct institutional settings in which possessions and mediumship can occur; and the social organization of possession and mediumship in themselves." " . . . today possession cults (including those that receive no Christian reinterpretation whatsoever) are still very much alive not only in remote areas, but right in the centre of Zambia's big towns, waiting for adequate sociological research." (van Binsbergen, 1981:90.)

13. This is how Lyall Watson (1982:124–125) describes a possession by spirits. "All eyes now were on the woman, who had begun to shake and tremble. Her shoulders shuddered and her body leaned forward as though bowed down by a great weight. With a tremendous effort she shook it off and sat erect again, throwing her head to one side and blowing out her breath in a sharp cry like a sudden exclamation of pain. But the weight returned,

bending her over until she had to brace herself by flinging out her clenched fists to rest them on the ground. She screamed. For a moment she seemed to have regained control, but then the shaking started once more and she began to beat herself very hard on her shoulders and arms, making growling noises in her throat.

"The spasms increased until she was being jerked violently around, her teeth clenched and her face set in pain and resistance. The woman was clearly under attack and forced to defend herself, beating at her body and the air around her. The hut was filled with the sound of battle. At times the invisible assailant seemed to gain the upper hand as they rolled over and over on the ground. Then she would rise with an enormous effort, throw off her attacker, and breathe deeply two or three times, before falling back under a renewed onslaught.

"The agony continued until it became almost unbearable, even for those just sitting by watching helplessly. The air was charged with power and tension, punctuated by the woman's cries, which gradually grew more and more faint as she seemed to lose her strength and her ability to fight back. In the end, she gave up and the battle was over as suddenly as it had begun. She fell unconscious to the ground and lay there very still. . .

"When the old lady fell unconscious to the ground, nobody seemed particularly concerned . . . Several of the spectators began to sing softly, pleading with the spirits to return her, as there was still much for her to do. One of them produced a spirit broom and began to sweep and swish in the air about the fallen figure, running it gently along her arms and leg, stroking her back to consciousness.

"Soon she was sitting upright . . ."

14. "In most cases the spirit is given a personal name. It is clearly identified as an individual, usually a direct blood ancestor, but 'ancestor worship' is not an accurate description of the phenomenon. The *badimo* (spirits of ancestors) involved are still seen as distinctly human, with all the strengths and weaknesses of our kind. Many of them are petty and prone, if not treated in the proper manner, they cause hurt, harm, or even death. But they can also be instrumental in providing the positive benefits of health, prosperity, and fertility. All transactions with them are conducted in a formal manner, as befits their status as elders, but the people's attitude falls far short of reverence. . ." (Watson, 1982:124-5.)

15. Scott (1929:294): *Mfiti*—this is the centre of African darkness . . . The *mfiti* is the person who has acquired the knowledge of occult medicine by which he can kill his fellowmen. It is not by poison that he kills them, but by supposed power 'against' them through medicine. The knowledge is purchased from some doctor willing to sell such medicines and such power . . . What makes the power so dreaded is not that the *mfiti* exercises this power for reasons of spite, but (as it is dreaded) to eat the body . . . The association of the *mfiti* with demon or spirit clothes him with power of spiriting himself away, of dancing in the air, or being invisible to ordinary eyes . . . When a fox barks, there, says the listener in the night, is the messenger calling these midnight wretches to their awful orgies; when a fire is seen on a distant hill where no fire can be accounted for, there is the light of their dismal fire. The grave is supposed to be light, to shine with an uncaused light, where the *mfiti* gather! The dead man obeys the summons by his early name to come out of the grave, out even through a small hole he has to come. Then the trial by these torturers begins, the counts made: he is knocked down, divided limb from limb, and eaten." (Scott, 1929:294.)

16. "In most societies where people believe in witches there is a rich store of ideas about what they look like and how they behave. The essence of the belief is that there is no empirical way of detecting a witch's activities. Nevertheless there are many ideas about the nature of their invisible antics. What is important about these ideas is the symbolism of the anti-social. Night, when secret evil can be done, is the time for witchcraft, and night creatures are associated with witches, as are venomous creatures such as snakes." (Mair, 1965:220.)

17. "Other misfortunes are ascribed to witchcraft, but most attempts to identify a witch are made when somebody is sick . . . People ask who had a grievance against the sick man

. . . anthropologists have recently paid special attention to the direction that accusations take, and have found . . . they are typically made between persons who, according to the rules of the society, should be on friendly terms, but who are in fact at odds. Situations of strain are brought to a head by accusations of witchcraft, when nothing else would, to justify the termination of the relationship." (Mair, 165:220–221.)

18. "Most Cewa believe that certain persons are witches (*mfiti*, sing, and pl.) who impoverish, harm, or kill their fellow beings by using destructive magic and by performing supernatural feats of various kinds. That they are greatly preoccupied with this belief and its various implications is shown by the frequency with which they attribute death and misfortune to witchcraft, and by their related tendency to take precautions against possible attacks by 'witches,' e.g. by having their bodies and huts magically protected.

"Although Cewa distinguishes between the *phereanjiru*, who is a witch whose dominant motive is hatred, and 'real witch' (*mfiti yeniyeni*), who is motivated primarily by 'flesh-hunger' (*nkhuli*), they do not make the distinction between witch and sorcerer that the Azande make." (Marwick, 1952:215.)

19. In an in-depth study of nutrition in three chiefs' areas in Chipata District, Chief Chikuwe's area revealed the highest prevalence of undernutrition among children aged 1–5 years (38.8%). Chikuwe's area also had the highest child morbidity (39%). (Kwofie, 1980:16.)

20. "When threatened with disaster by some force apparently beyond your control, there are three things you can do. You can ignore it; you can pray for deliverance; or you can work magic through the performance of an established rite. . . . Prayer is certainly more soothing than doing nothing, but magic is the most comforting of all. . . . It deals at root with the unconscious forces governing individual and social behaviour. By bringing them into the open, suitably disguised in ritual or symbolized in tangible objects or actions, it makes them manageable. Far from being 'silly superstitions', they become essential tools for survival—and begin to be seen as such by most sensitive anthropologists." (Watson, 1982:120–121.)

21. "Data available from Chipata hospital and rural health centres, show a strong seasonality of occurrence of protein calorie malnutrition during the months of December to April due probably to exhaustion of food supplies in most subsistence families at the start of the planting season, high labour requirements and poor environmental conditions during the rainy season." (Kwofie, 1980:7.)

22. Most Kefa village residents are not churchgoers any more, though they may have been registered as church members. About three-quarters of the Christians are Roman Catholics. Some boys and girls sing in the church choir, and sometimes they also sing at home in the village practicing with drums as their main musical instrument. But it seems that many people are becoming disillusioned. They see that church members drink and smoke marijuana, just like non-Christians. And they do not agree with the church when it comes to having many wives and bearing children by damage. The following churches exist in the village: Roman Catholic, Reformed Church of Zambia, Mizimu Church, and the Watchtower Church.

23. "The belief that witches are necrophagous has important practical consequences. Whenever anyone dies, Cewa take elaborate steps to prevent witches from disinterring his corpse. They 'close' the graveyard with magical substances and, having set magical traps for the 'witches' keep a vigil at the grave-side for two or three evenings after the burial." (Marwick, 1952:215.)

CHAPTER 8   THE MODEL VILLAGE

Ndadziwa kale adamanga nyumba yopanda khomo
Who Said "I Know Everything" Built a House
Without a Door

*According to our way of thinking, a man with a brick
house is considered to be a rich man as such houses
are not common in the rural areas. Even people who
live well in good brick houses in towns consider
themselves bosses among others.*

A villager's view

"I have known both urban and rural life and have a clear understanding
of the advantages of village living," Gilbert Zulu, Kefa's grandson wrote to
us. "Since 1968 I have been working for Zambia Railways. I live in a permanent house here in Ndola, in a railway house. But the railway will not keep
me forever. One day I shall be useless to them and that is when I shall need
my own permanent home in Kefa village.

"We Zambians must have our villages. Towns were colonialist settlements
to which people flocked to exchange labor for gifts. That is how I see it.
It really bothers me how people suffer in towns. Squatters go about their
petty businesses and are rewarded with hunger. They have neither clothes
nor proper accommodations. Villagers are better off. They have free food
and free houses and land, while towndwellers only have a square meter
on which to build a shelter.

"It is better to be a peasant than a loafer in town. A peasant with a
permanent house can easily become a commercial farmer over the years.
That is better than to become a loafer or an armed robber overnight as we
see it happens in town.

"My ambition is to become a commercial farmer. The beginning is expensive, but—with this model village program that our humanist government
has started in my grandfather's village—I shall get a permanent home. Was
I happy when my grandfather wrote to me that his village has been singled
out to become a model village! As soon as I heard the news I decided to
take the three month leave I had accumulated and go home to Kefa village
and build myself a five-room house under the Kefa Model Village Scheme."

In was in 1975 that the honorable president Dr. D. K. Kaunda introduced the idea of village regroupings and model villages. He told the
public that, if people from several villages would come together and
cooperate with the government by making bricks, the government would
help them build permanent houses and provide their new and very much
larger villages with tap water and other modern facilities. Such villages,

he proposed, would serve as models for future rural life in which the standard of living between urban and rural dweller would not be as different as it was at that time. The president had stated the problems time and again: All the thousands of small villages scattered all over the country were an insurmountable problem for the government, as they could not all have nearby roads, bus service, depots, schools and health centers. Only larger rural settlements make it "worthwhile for the government to provide them with the amenities of life," the president had said.[1]

Because of its rather large size, because it was on the main district road, and because of the love of the Chief for headman Kefa, Kefa village was chosen as a future model village in Chipata District. This meant in practical terms, if the villagers would burn bricks and provide labor to build permanent brick houses, the government, through the Community Development Department and the Swedish-Zambian Intensive Zone Development Program (IDZ), would assist the villagers by contributing skilled builders, transport, and roofing materials.[2]

"No person should really fail to have a decent two- or three-roomed Kimberley brick house," the president had said. And the headman agreed wholeheartedly:

> "To make a brick house was always on my mind, since houses made of mud and poles fall down because of termites. Very early I decided to build myself a permanent house. After I had been employed for some years I invested my savings and built two brick houses with metal sheet [corrugated iron] roofs. Now my four wives live in brick houses, each with a room to herself. Other residents did not want to build permanent houses. They believed that my village would be shifted from one place to another, as we had already shifted once [a few years after the village was established]. They know that other headmen keep moving their villages around, but I have said that I never intend to shift the village again. Those who want to live in a village that keeps moving will have to go somewhere else, because my village will stay in one place. Now, my residents see the wisdom of my world. It is better to build permanent houses and to stay in one place."

Kefa is right. To stay in one place has many advantages. People are more inclined to invest time, effort, and even money if they have any, to improve their house and garden, and even the village. And increased investment is likely to result in better yield, better health, and better lives. From such a point of view, a brick house is an entry to the benevolent circle of increased prosperity for rural Zambia.

Unlike mud and wattle houses that have to be repaired every year and rebuilt every ten years or so, a brick house should stand forever. Obviously a brick home owner will never want his house or village to shift from place to place. But there are also advantages in the traditional system, where old gardens, old houses, and eventually old village sites are abandoned. Food is grown with less effort when it is left to nature to fertilize fields through the long-fallow system. Population pressure can be reduced and the exploitation of fields and forests, water, and fuel can be limited to an environment's optimal carrying capacity, as surplus population will move away to form a new village, having little or nothing of material value to lose in the process. This philosophy applies also to dissidents or troublemakers. They may accept being expelled or leave their old village voluntarily, to build new houses or cultivate new fields on virgin land. In this way village leaders are able to curb animosity and to prevent hostility and conflict among residents.

> "The past is gone, the future is tomorrow," Gilbert wrote. "Whether it will be good or bad depends upon oneself. I have been worried about my future, but with the coming of the Model Kefa village, I felt that my chance had come to take full advantage of this Government Programme. The Programme has enlightened me that, before you become a farmer or anything else, a permanent home is vital. I mean a really good house, a house made of burned bricks with a weatherproof roof.
>
> "The advantage of this Scheme is a healthy life all year round. Now, people do not concentrate hard enough on farming, because they have to think about repairing their houses each and every year. With the Model Village Scheme the idea that brick houses are only for the rich will be crushed once and for all in ordinary people's minds. Consequently they will try to earn more money and improve their standard of living."

The Model Village project involved a total reconstruction of the village. At the start of the project Kefa village had only six brick houses while fifty households lived in traditional mud and wattle houses. According to the Scheme each and every villager was to live in a brick house.

The headman was quite clear:

> "Those who are not willing to cooperate on the model house project must be prepared to leave this village. I shall not allow them to stay on even one inch of my land. I never asked the Government to make this Kefa village into a model village. It was the decision of the Chief and the District Governor. They promised to help us with builders, transport, and asbestos roofing sheets. But it is through the cooperation of its residents that Kefa village can become a model village. That is why we must all work together."

Making Brick

"To build even an ordinary three-room house you need a lot of bricks," Mwada Simba explained as she was resting from having made bricks all morning. "Brick-making is best done in the dry season, just after the rain when the earth is still soft. A good brick place is close to water and to an ant hill from where the best brick soil is taken, and close to trees because a lot of firewood is needed to burn the bricks." For these reasons most Kefa residents selected their brick-making places at the other side of Mtewe river, close to the *dambo*. To make the bricks most people cooperated in their traditional ways, with friends, neighbors, and or relatives. The average brick-making group had between four and six members, both men and women. For example, Simon Sakala worked together with his two mothers, Emelia Mbao and Mtole Mbao; Sandikonda Daka and the wife Mwani-shupa with Sandikonda's daughter and Laimen Phiri and his wife; and Micheck and Mwada with Sonile Ngoma and her sons' Kabanda and James and their wives.

In addition to water, soil, and woodfuel, also needed are *vikomboli* (brick pans), grass (to cover the bricks so that they do not crack while drying), and labor. There is a definite division of labor, at least as long as both sexes are present. The men dig the soil next to the anthill where it is just right to make the bricks hardy, mix water and soil and fill the brick pans. The women supply the water, carry the brick pans to the site and cover the newly formed bricks with straw. Gilbert Zulu, shrewdly observed that "the men who fill the brick pans are supposed to be the leaders of the entire brick-making operation. But having observed the work, I have reached the conclusion that it is tougher to run with the brick pans than to fill them up." Women filled brick pans, too, but only when the men were absent.

It was in August that the model village housing project started formally. Every villager, provided he or she was well enough to work at all, was expected to make bricks according to the plan drawn up by the Community Department and the IDZ. At a time when other villagers would be busy repairing their houses, visiting relatives, and drinking beer, Kefa residents were busy making bricks.

Tyford reported: "Men and women work in cooperation on the housing project. They contribute equally, some with food and some with other duties. While most of them work, some women bring plates and pots and baskets with whatever they need to cook food at the working place. They do it so that they do not have to go to the village for meals. Whenever necessary the men help the women draw water because a lot of water is needed to make bricks."

To make an ordinary two-room house takes 8,000 bricks. Gilbert Zulu, who is a well-organized man, kept a detailed account of the entire building process. His group, which varied in size according to how many people he could get to help him, made between 400 and 900 bricks each day, with an average of 600 bricks. Thus, to make enough bricks for a small-sized house would take them two full weeks. It would take them up to one month's work to produce only the bricks for a larger house, and many villagers wanted three and even four and five rooms.

No wonder those who could afford it looked for labor they could hire. Kwerekani Phiri, informed people that he would pay K. 40 to whoever would furnish him with 10,000 bricks. He had discussed the matter with his first wife Jessie and they had agreed that buying the bricks was the best way.

Gilbert Zulu talked the matter over with Kefa Mwale and, although the headman advised his grandson to buy bricks, Gilbert thought it would be less expensive if he made them himself and hired labor. His problem was that the working groups had already been formed. "As everybody in Kefa needs bricks for themselves, I have been careful not to tempt any of my own people to work for me. Instead I have gone to neighboring villages to search for assistance to make 12,000 bricks. What I found was two soil-diggers who each demanded K. 20, and two *vikomboli* [brick pan] boys who each wanted K. 12 for the job. Fortunately my mother had advised me to buy some *chitenge*—printed cloth—in Ndola for this purpose, and I found six women who volunteered to fill three drums of water for me every day for three weeks in return for two meters of *chitenge* [worth K. 7]. I myself ran with the *vikomboli* all day. It was really tough to lift all those kilograms of mud!" (We should remember that lifting the mud was the women's job.)

Like everybody else, Gilbert had a lot of problems getting the work done. His helpers fell ill, or were drunk and stayed at home, or went to funerals. After having worked for three weeks he had managed to make 8,000 bricks at a cost of K. 89.40 plus his own labor. Then he succeeded in buying 4,000 bricks from Iron Phiri for K. 40. "My brick-making got very costly," Gilbert explained, "because I did not plan properly in advance. Everything was done in a hurry. Because I am not a businessman, almost all those who helped me fixed their own payment. I am not looking for profits or advantages, I only want to build myself a permanent house in my grandfather's village.

Lubinda Mwale and Robert Manda participated in the housing scheme too, even though they already live in brick houses. Both were thinking of their children in the Copper Belt whom they hope will come home now that Kefa village is going to be a model village. Brighton reported:

"Lubinda has a worker who is Mefews Mwale and Robert has a worker who is Eliya Njobvu. Robert and Lubinda made an agreement; first they would build Lubinda's house and then Robert's house. But instead of Robert and Lubinda working, their workers did the job. Fatnes, Roberts' daughter, drew water for Mwazida, Robert's wife who has asthma, and Mwanizinga,

Lubinda's wife, did so for him. They cooperate very well. Whenever Lubinda rests, so does Robert and they see how the brick-making is progressing and discuss other matters. Robert and Lubinda seem to escape most of the hard work because both have cattle and are rich men."

Once the bricks had been made, time had come to construct the kilns where the bricks would be burned. Women and men, young and old stacked the sundried bricks one on top of the other into kilns that measured up to two-and-one-half meters in height and width and up to three meters in length. Meanwhile, the young and strong men of the village went into the forest to collect firewood, for a great deal was needed to burn the kilns. Gilbert described the operation:

"The size of the kiln will determine the number of doors and courses. One of the really big kilns had ten courses and seven doors, but it is advisable to keep the courses small because burning can be pretty difficult.

"To build a kiln took me two weeks because now I had only two helpers. I also had to go back to the Copper Belt [1,000 kilometers away] in search of extra cash to pay them. The size of the kiln and the number of doors determine the amount of firewood required. To cut the wood is no problem, but to carry the logs to the kiln may be a great problem. Big logs about one third of the size of the kiln are the best because they burn longer. If there isn't enough firewood the bricks will not be burned red. The best bricks are purple-burned. They are very strong but it is difficult to burn them purple because if the fire is too hot they will melt together and then they cannot be used. When the bricks are red, it is ready."

Before the kiln is burned, the whole structure is plastered with mud, except for the top and the doors. The doors are filled with firewood. The direction of the wind must be assessed and a fence erected to prevent the fire from concentrating on one side. The bricks are burned at night when it is cooler and less windy.

"To maintain the fire is the hardest of all the jobs," Gilbert continued. "It gets terribly hot, and the heat is just too much for my face and eyes. All my muscles pain because of lifting and throwing and pushing the logs into the kiln doors. When the fire reaches the unplastered top, it is a sign that this stage of the brick burning has been successfully completed. By then the heat is truly unbearable, yet now the firewood must be filled into the doors, to their full capacity. Then the doors are completely sealed off. In my group we started the fire at 5 p.m. After a complete shift of thirteen hours work, we sealed the doors at 6 in the morning. Now the kiln will burn by itself for as long as possible, but no less than two days and two nights. When the bricks cool down they are ready to be used."

The first government input in the model village housing scheme was to provide a lorry that would help the Kefa residents carry their bricks from the kilns into the village. It was headman Kefa's difficult job to see that his villagers were present and ready to load and unload bricks whenever the lorry came. But very often when the message had been passed that the lorry would come, people stood by waiting in vain. The rain was approaching and most people had not yet cleared their fields because making the bricks had kept them so busy. Their patience was wearing thin, yet many were very eager to have their new house built. Because they had been so busy on the housing project they had had no time to repair their old mud houses, and they worried that they would have to spend the rainy season in houses with leaking roofs and cracking walls. So they stood by, waiting and waiting for a lorry that sometimes came as promised, sometimes came late, and, more often than not, did not come at all. When the rain finally started, the situation worsened. Tracks hitherto barely passable were no longer accessible for the lorry. People had to carry their bricks to the nearest loading point, the fields had to be planted, and the old houses did indeed leak.

No wonder people got ill and died. No wonder the villagers were complaining. They said that this was the time to clear fields and to plant, and pointed out that other villagers had cleared their fields while "we in this village are pressed to work on the housing project. If we stick to this model village program we shall face great starvation, hunger, and poverty. If we are to build more houses this season it means that we shall be planting our crops too late. The headman said we would do this housing business in no time, but as we see it progress we expect that this job will take us more than four years!" They complained about not being able to do other jobs and earn money. And they complained about the lorry driver, who said he would come and move their bricks and did not, who transported the wealthy farmers' crops for money rather than Kefa bricks for free, and who was rude and uncooperative.

One day Sylvester reported the following incident:

"While I was seated at Square Banda's house together with the owner of the house [Square] and two other men, a woman came and knelt down [a usual way to pay respect] and said: 'I am sent by the driver to point out that you men are sitting idle when people have been asked to go and load bricks. We women have been working since early morning and we are now exhausted. We all feel the heat of the sun.' Mishael Mbewe replied: 'I am not concerned with that job. Not all people in this village work equally hard, and some of us have already done more than our share. Some people consider themselves bosses and even the driver is rude to us. He talks haughtily and with pride, and to me pride and rudeness are my enemies. If I had known that this was how we would work together, I would not have agreed to participate in the project. I shall do so this time, but if I see anybody boss-ing anybody around, I shall come back here and rest for the entire day. I can even stop making brick houses. I was not born in a brick house and I did not grow up in a brick house. So why must I die in one?"

A few weeks later, when the Department of Water Affairs came to Kefa village to bore for water, headman Kefa called all the men and told them to cut trees in the area where boring would be done. But Mishael Mbewe refused, saying it was none of his business and that he had work to do in his garden. Headman Kefa then summoned Mishael before the village meeting. The Chief's deputy, Mr. M'Kanduwavu, was present. Kefa presented the case: "Time and again I call you to work with us, but till now you never appear and you refuse to cooperate with us." Mishael replied: "I was busy in the field and the other time I was called I was delivering fertilizers for Mr. Manda." Sylvester was Kefa's witness and Zuwaila Zulu supported Mishael. During the hearing it was found that Mishael had been saying different things to different people concerning why he never contributed with labor when the headman called him. When judgment was passed, he was found guilty of uncooperative behavior, but Mishael still refused to admit his mistakes. To solve the deadlock Zuwaila Zulu and Penelani Khosa, Kefa's deputy, took Mishael aside and reminded him of the saying of the elders: *samva mnzako ndi tsiru*—"he who does not listen to his neighbor is a fool." And Mishael changed his at-titude and confessed his error.

It was the Deputy Chief who passed judgment. Kefa had asked him to do so because he considered himself part of the quarrel and wanted others to judge the case. The Deputy Chief charged Mishael a fine of K. 4 and said: "If this state of affairs continues, cooperation will come to naught in this village. The government was very pleased to see the prog-ress you were achieving. In Chief Chikuwe's area you, Kefa village residents, were chosen as an example for all of us. Why get tired now when you have come so far? People are admiring the fine houses you are mak-ing. Disagreement and quarrels must stop and all bad behavior end or others may copy your bad behavior rather than your fine achievements."

Building

To build the houses, the village residents were divided into two groups, the Northern and the Southern building sections. Sandikonda was asked to lead one, Penelani the other. The headman addressed the villagers: "These are your work groups and to go against the leaders is like going against me, your headman." Each building section worked with one of the two government of Zambia builders who had been stationed in the village as part of the Scheme. While the men built houses, women sup-plied water and provided the two builders with their daily food and water.

To draw water at the end of the dry season is no easy matter. At this time of the year the water hole is virtually empty and women dig for water in the parched river beds. To fill up the drums needed to make mud to build a house, some women would even get up in the middle of the night to collect water. At that hour the water level is higher than during the daytime, and the stifling heat of the day is greatly reduced. But to move at night is feared by most of the villagers.

When there is plenty of work to do, women-headed households are particularly pressed. Others may want to help them, but they too are busy, as there are so many households without able-bodied men to do what is considered a man's job. It is the headman's responsibility to see to it that his village functions as well as possible. When he saw that Romance and her daughter Lachel were digging out the foundation of their new house all alone, he called their working group and reprimanded the members for letting two women do a job that was clearly men's work. And the group went ahead and dug the foundation, with Lemekani in charge. When the group started building Romance's house Lemekani used the opportunity to teach David Mwale and Danga Banda how to build a good brick house. Romance in turn "helped the men with milk porridge and *nsima*," as Lemekani put it.

Still, Lemekani's group did not work well and Lemekani reported to his brother that "though we have been told to cooperate, some of the members assigned to us never show up. So from now on we who work will build only our own houses and not those of the inactive group members."

The other group had troubles too. Micheck had ordered the women in the group to carry his bricks from the kiln to the village, because the lorry had never come. But the women said that they would carry bricks when Micheck had cleared the path they should use. When he heard that he must make a path, Micheck got very annoyed and told Mwada (his wife) and Sonile (his wife's relative) not to bother, that he would carry himself and did not need to be helped by such uncooperative women. Micheck borrowed a wheelbarrow from Mr. Zulu, the builder, but the path was so poor that he could only carry a few bricks each time. Later James came with his bicycle, but he too was prevented from carrying many bricks because of the poor path. Then Kabanda joined them and the three men worked hard alone. When the women saw them, they too joined in, and the group worked well together for the whole day.

As it rained hard for almost a week all building activities stopped. When the group was to resume their work, only the builder turned up and again Micheck became annoyed. When he met with Kabanda who had spent the day planting maize, he told him not to help him ever again and that he, Micheck, would also not help Kabanda build *his* new brick house. Hearing this, Kabanda said: "Okay, if they are building and I refused to come, that is my business and I do not expect Micheck to help me back, but Micheck must remember that I helped him making bricks. If he refuses to help me make mine, I shall dismantle his house and fight him terribly." The headman called the men in Micheck's group to hear why they did not cooperate, and all of them gave excuses. Sandikonda had to plant groundnuts, Esidol had gone to see a sick relative, Kabanda had been at the grinding mill, James was busy hoeing, and John Scout had had a visitor. Headman Kefa resolved the case by saying that the working groups must cooperate better and finish all the houses. But Micheck was also to blame, because he had not planned to build his house according to the wishes of his working group, nor had he notified them when to start, "so how could your friends know that you were waiting for them?" asked the headman. And Micheck admitted that he too was to blame for the lack of cooperation.

By the end of November, people were really hard pressed. Tyford filed this report:

"Since Kefa people were depending on the brick houses, they never concerned themselves with repairing their old houses, or keeping their surroundings clean. As a consequence the village looks dirty and grassy. The village residents seem to say that if you clean your yard, you will be cleaning the yard of your neighbor whose brick house is going to be where your old house now stands. So they do not bother. Only when they move into their new brickhouses will they keep their yards free of grass.

"Some old mud houses are about to fall down. The owners have left them and moved into new brick houses. The headman decided to burn these old houses to make the village look cleaner. Some residents who lived in old and decrepit houses have moved into better, vacated mud houses. Others are eagerly waiting for their own brick houses to be build."

In December, when the rainy season was well under way, it was decided that the building groups would work from sunrise until noon, and noon until sunset every other day. In this way everyone could spend early morning or late afternoon in the fields, and the skills of the government builders could be fully utilized. At Christmas there was a short break before people resumed weeding their fields and guarding the growing maize against monkeys; no one had any time to spare on building houses. During January only one house was built in comparison to five and eight the months before. At that time only Robert Manda could afford to employ a laborer to help the government builder do the job.

In February five kilns were ready; two belonged to Zuwaila Zulu and one each to Jackson Phiri, Zindi Miti, and Gilbert Zulu. Lubinda Mwale, Zelenji Mwale, Robert Manda, and Gilbert Zulu had all completed their five-room houses; Jesina Kamanga, Micheck Phiri, Mtole Mbao, Lomanzi Tembo, Jessie Tonga, and a few others had completed their three-room houses, and Fatnes Manda had moved into her four-room house. Some 140,000 bricks had been made, burned, and transported to the village. At the same time gardens had been hoed and crops sown, weeded, and guarded. It was no wonder that people were tired and quarrelsome, that the entire village fabric of cooperation and concern seemed shaken, that villagers succumbed to illnesses and rumors of witchcraft were rampant.

To discuss, inform, admonish, and exhort, to solve problems and pass judgment, village meetings were called time and again.

Zuwaila Zulu was one of the troublemakers. Because he failed to work closely with his group, the group refused to help him, even though his two wives had carried water for the housing project, just like all the other village women. Andrick was the only group member ready to forgive Zuwaila. So at a meeting called to resolve the problem, headman Kefa concluded: "The only solution left is that Zuwaila finds another group to work with. It seems that the reason why Zuwaila has been refused by his group is not fully revealed. Maybe he is lazy, or else I do not know. As to Zuwaila's wives, they have definitely drawn water for the group and when Zuwaila builds his own house, the other women in the group must help back with water."

Suddenly the rumor arose that Zuwaila Zulu had sold the bricks that he and the wives had made and that he was about to move to Lusaka. When Lire Banda, Zuwaila's second wife learned that the husband had given away and sold the bricks they had made together, she asked Zuwaila: "Why give away bricks before we have built our own house?" He answered that he had only lent them to Mr. Tembo, but Lire saw that the husband had sold his goats, pots and pans, and even the door of their house, and that he had bought dried pumpkin leaves and peas leaves which he would sell in the Lusaka market. When he refused to tell her his plans, she went to headman Kefa.

Kefa discussed the problem with his deputy, Penelani Khosa: "What is happening in Zuwaila Zulu's house? It seems that Zuwaila wants to go to his house in Lusaka to stay there. [Rumors say that Zuwaila is a rich man with three houses in Lusaka! He is not a Kefa village man, but settled in the village because his second wife, Lire Banda, comes from here.] The wife cannot understand why he will not give her any bricks."

Kefa and his deputy decided to call a meeting. When people had gathered in Kefa's yard, Kefa asked Zuwaila Zulu if he had sold all his bricks, and if he had told his wife, Lire, about it.

Zuwaila answered: "I did not tell my wife; as to my bricks, I did not sell, I only lent them to my friend, Luciano Tembo, so that when I return from Lusaka, he must make bricks for me."

Tilele Zulu said: "If you were making bricks together with your wives, how can you lend them to Mr. Tembo before you make your own house?" Zuwaila answered: "I do not have the strength to make a house. I want to go to the hospital in Lusaka because I am ill." Penelani said: "If you are ill, why not leave one wife to look after your animals and the crops in the field? Zuwaila replied that the wives and the children will go with him. "I have no relatives in this village to look after them." Tilele said: "How can you look after them when you will be in the hospital? Also Lire has a child who is ill. What will happen to her if the mother goes to Lusaka?" Zuwaila said that Lire's daughter was grown up and could look after herself. But Lire reminded her husband that when she had married him, she had said: "I have children from my ex-husband. When you want to get me, does it include them, because they are in my care and I am looking after them?" Mr. Zulu had replied that he would look after her children when they were married. "So, now," Lire said, "I cannot go with Mr. Zulu when my daughter has no one to look after her. And I wonder why he will not take my daughter to Lusaka, when at the same time, he is not willing to provide us with a house here in Kefa village?"

Zuwaila only repeated that he was not concerned with the daughter of his second wife. He also said: "I cannot give my wife bricks because I cannot leave her behind in the village. Besides, a wife cannot build the husband a house! Did you ever hear about a wife making a house for the husband?"

Lire Banda said she would not go to Lusaka without having a home here in Kefa village. She had children whom she had produced from her first husband, and they too needed a home. And so did she, so that when she comes back from Lusaka, she would have a house like every other resident.

The case was deadlocked. People were utterly exhausted. But Zuwaila refused to budge and Lire Banda was advised to summon the husband before the Chief's court.

Ten days later, the matter was settled at Chief Chikuwe's court. Lire told the Chief how Zuwaila had sold goats, doors, and bricks, and that he refused to build a house for her and her children. "He also failed to inform me that he would go to Lusaka hospital. And if he divorces me, where will I live?" The Chief concluded: "Since you, Mr. Zulu have sold your possessions, this shows that you will not come back, because if you wanted, you could even have built two houses and your cattle could have provided adequately for this wife." The Chief judged that Lire Banda should get the bricks. She also got divorced as Zuwaila refused to take her with him to Lusaka. Soon thereafter the Northern section building group started building Lire's house and Brighton could report: "Now Lire Banda's house is completed and Zuwaila Zulu is put to shame. His wife made a house, though it was not for the husband."

Roofing material was part of the model housing package generously offered to the Kefa residents. The government had decided to used asbestos, which is a costly roofing material. To roof a three room house takes asbestos sheets worth K. 280, more than most people earned in a whole year. Asbestos is superior to the more commonly used corrugated iron sheets. Just like grass, it does not turn the house into a sauna in the hot season, and while the rain hammers on iron sheets, it taps only mildly on asbestos and grass roofs. But asbestos roofs are really superior to the grass roofs in that they are supposed to last forever, while grass roofs must be rethatched every year or every second year. So the Kefa residents considered themselves most fortunate when the government lorry came with the first loads of asbestos sheets.

Knowing the value of the asbestos, Kefa told the government builders to build the houses big according to the size of the sheets even if the owner wanted only a small house. Lemekani Mbao wanted a three-room house, but the builder asked him: "Do you think that three rooms will be enough for all your ten children?" Lemekani replied that also Mr. Kefa said he should build a five-room house because he had a big family. But Tilele said: "The problem is only this—that they cannot all come here at the same time. Five rooms will mean more credit for bricks from our neighbors, more cash for doors and window frames, and more hard work. We are far too busy as it is, even with a three-room house. If our children want bigger houses they can spend their own money and make them." And Brighton reported: "Hearing her views, Lemekani had no power to argue against the wife."

Danga Banda, too, protested loudly that the size of the asbestos roofing material should not determine the size of his new house. "I do not want a big house. I am not even married. What can I use so many rooms for? For me two rooms is enough. I am tired of always being ordered around in this village. Even my old house is just fine, but now the headman will pull it down. If he forces me to build more than two rooms, I will consider going somewhere else!" It was only when the villagers demanded that they call a government representative to confirm whether the housing scheme meant that they must all have large houses, that the headman gave in and permitted people to cut the sheets.

One day headman Kefa received a letter. It said that, though the villagers had got the asbestos roofing sheets for free, the government could no longer afford to assist the villagers with everything and that they would have to buy roofing nails, wire, and ridges out of their own pockets.

There was an outcry! How were people to raise the money? A heated debate arose. Some said it was their own fault, as they should never have accepted the scheme in the first place. Everybody knows that government never gives anything away for free. Some said they had known all along that the model village scheme would never work. Others said nothing because they had already lost courage. Headman Kefa, trying to think positively, suggested that they could roof their houses by just putting the sheets on the roofing poles without using nails to fasten them. But Lemekani opposed this idea, claiming that the sheets would surely break. Sandikonda Daka said: "If Kaunda [the President of the Republic of Zambia] fails to finish his development of this village, he had better keep his roofing sheets because it is a fact that we village residents cannot afford to fasten them." And Tilele added that they should let the government know that they had no money because everybody had been so busy with the model houses that there had been no time to grow cash crops for sale.

Finally it was decided to write a letter to the District Governor saying that Kefa village residents refuse to use the sheets unless they get wire and nails and that the government must come and take the sheets back.

Kefa asked people to choose the person to deliver the letter and said: "It must be a person who can explain the matter to the District Governor. The messenger must say that the letter is from the entire village and not only from Kefa Mwale." Simon Sakala volunteered and Kefa asked Micheck to accompany him.

Ten days later a Community Development Officer (CDO) arrived from Chipata to discuss the problem. When the CDO opened the meeting, which thirty-two men and twenty-three women attended, she said, "You Kefa village residents cannot expect the government to help you with everything. Now the turn has come for you to help the government by helping yourself. The government has reached the time when it will not continue aiding this particular village."

But Kefa Mwale answered: "The District Governor promised that the government will assist us with everything and not only transport, and already it has failed to provide us with cement. We are building houses with mud and some have fallen down before they were up." Sandikonda Daka continued: "If we had been told right away that we would have to buy things for money we would certainly not have agreed to participate in this development project. Look at us. Where is the money. Where can it come from?"

When the CDO asked if somebody could afford to buy nails and wire, Isaac Phiri answered that he would buy nails if the government would provide the wire and roofing ridges for free. On hearing the price for the nails, which was K. 2.50, Enelesi Mawarera said: "*Chabwino,* if that is the price, we can all buy, and those who do not have the money can do piecework or brew beer and earn their nails." In the end the CDO was told to carry the message that Kefa residents would buy the nails if ridges and wires were given them for free. If not, the government should come and get their asbestos sheets and forget about the whole model village.

The view of the villagers was accepted and nails as well as wire and ridges for the asbestos roofing were included in the model village package. But the problems were not over. When the government nails finally did arrive, Kefa stored the boxes in his house. Soon people started grumbling: "What is this? It seems the headman has got nails after all . . . We village residents have been looking for nails ever since the government told us to buy nails ourselves and alone, but nails seem to have come to this village and the headman advertises nothing! What he wants is first to roof his grandson's house and the houses of others whom he favors, and only then will he give nails to us. He is a very bad headman. Even roofing poles are not shared equally. Some people receive none and some get bent ones, but those in the Southern section get the good poles, while we here in the Northern get very thin ones . . . Those nails came here for all of us to use, but the headman hides them in his house . . . How can we cooperate when things are like this?"

Settling In

In December the first houses were ready. From then on, almost every week, one family after the other left their old, familiar mud house to move with pots and baskets, blankets, clothes, and utensils into their new brick house. It was a time of transition and great ambivalence, a time when village elders and the young affirmed their identify with the past and the future, respectively. The young saw their dream of living in a permanent house come true, while the elders, like Mwanishupa Phiri, considered it the final proof that an epoch was indeed at its end:

> "To live in a brick house is a different thing altogether. I tell you, even dreams are different when you live in a brick house. I must confide in you that my sleep was much better in my old house. In this new house there are strange noises. We all hear them. It is as if stones are thrown on the roof, invisible birds whiz through the air, and knocks are heard at the door, but when we look there is nobody outside. We are not used to living in brick houses and we have no charms and amulets to protect our lives. How can we prevent the witches from approaching our houses at night? I feel that some of us will die shortly. And as you know already there are so many who have died. Because of all that has happened in the village, witchcraft is growing strong here. There is jealousy and envy and anger among the people."

Sandikonda, Mwanishupa's husband, was also worried, but for other reasons. His problem was all the help that Kefa residents had received from the government. "We never thought the government would do all the things they said they would do. Many other villagers have made bricks, but they were never helped like us. When the government said they would provide us with transport and builders and roofing materials we strongly doubted it, but they did. We here in Kefa village have got so many things for free that we worry. It is well known that when the government does something for people, later on they are forced to work hard or pay for what they got in some other way. Now we worry because any day the government officials may come and ask us to pay to live in the new houses.

Black Banda fully agreed with Sandikonda: "Everybody says so, that the government cannot lose its money for nothing. If it gives us help, it will surely claim something in return. Whoever fails to give the government what it wants will probably be chased away and his houses given to those who can afford to pay whatever the government charges them."

A rumor circulated that in the future, when all the mud houses had been replaced by brick houses, the village would no longer bear the name of the headman. "It is plain for all to see," some people said, "that all the new brick houses are built in a line just like the locations in Chipata and Lusaka. When the government finishes with this village, it will be renamed 'The Location,' and the headman will regret that he ever got involved in changing his village so utterly." A further proof was that the houses were constructed in a line at the outskirts of the present village, and that in the middle there was nothing. Here the government would surely build a school, or a hospital, or perhaps government offices. "How can this remain Kefa village with a government building right in the middle?" they asked.

The logic seemed irrefutable. It was accentuated by the fact that those who were born in mud houses and who had spent their entire life in mud houses strongly felt that their new houses were less comfortable than the old. "These new brick houses are no good. They are cold at night when it is cold, and too hot during daytime. They are not like our mud houses that warmed us at night and provided a cool shelter for us during the heat of the day. We cry to go back to our old houses, but the headman has burned them!"

But the headman was adamant:

> "People outside this village are envious when they see how we progress and cooperate. Do not let us put our ears to rumors. Let us stop this futile talking and listen to the government. *Mugwilizano* and *utaogoleli*—cooperation and leadership—those are the words that the Community Development Assistance has used to encourage us. And now we see the result. Last year I had six residents here with modern brick houses. This year I have twenty-eight and next year I will have even sixty. This is my plan and those who live with me will see that from now on our problems will diminish. Our roofs will need no thatching and our walls will not crumble during the rain. With these permanent houses, youngmen like my grandson Gilbert and

many others will want to come and stay close to us, their elders. And we can make full use of my village land. It is better to be a permanent farmer than a jobless school-leaver in town. We have committed ourselves to the government and for a long time now we have agreed to cooperate. Therefore we accept to do whatever the government decides and shall continue to do so with excitement. People in Kefa village will never become disappointed but continue to cooperate strongly and that is how we can progress. And those who refuse to cooperate, it is my firm decision, can go somewhere else."

Kefa village residents cooperated and the village scene was indeed transformed, even if those who had said it would take four years turned out to be right. By then, the success of the housing scheme and model village was clear for all to see. People in Kefa no longer died in mud houses, and their children were no longer born there. Where earlier mud houses were scattered all over the landscape, there are now neat rows of brick houses. But the effort that lay behind this transformation is invisible and will soon be forgotten except by those who built the village with their own hands, and the many who lost a parent, a relative, or a child during those years of intensive mobilization. It is more than likely that some of the sixteen persons who died were victims not of witchcraft but of too much work and too little food and care.

Modernization is a tough process, particularly when it is intitiated from outside and the people affected are given the option: adapt or leave! This was the predicament of the Kefa villagers once their headman decided to join forces with the change agents of the government. Yet headman Kefa too was caught in the same predicament. Being a wise elder with much love and concern for his villagers he knew that the African village had to adapt to the new demands of the national and international centers, to survive at all. The headman also knew that in the process of change many cherished cultural traditions and values would die.

But culture, unlike people, can be replaced. It was the survival of his villagers that was Kefa's main concern. And that, he judged, depended on revitalizing the village to make it attractive for the young people. The Kefa model village was built for the young—for people like Gilbert Zulu who would come with his tractor and for Stephen Phiri and the others who knew town life and had a specialized skill with which they could further develop their home area. But the elders felt estranged. They saw their own subsistence agriculture disappear well realizing that a future of tractors and clean shirts was not likely ever to be theirs. And they also knew that they had lost forever to the Kefa model village much more than their mud huts and grass roofs.

Notes

1. The Zambian political philosophy behind the rural policy of regrouping is specified, i.e., in Kaunda: *Humanism in Zambia and a Guide to Its Implementation.* (Zambia Information Service, 1975.)

2. The model village scheme, or Domestic Housing Improvement Scheme, as it was called by the Intensive Development Zone Programme (IDZ) through which it was financed, was described thus in the IDZ Co-ordinator's Annual Report and Progress Report for 1975:

   "The supplementary budget of 25.9-1975 provided for . . . a start of a pilot project on domestic housing. . . . An experimental scheme of support to the Department of Community Development in its efforts to promote group housing schemes. . . "

   "The aim of the Group Housing Project is to improve the standard of housing and sanitary facilities in the rural areas, in accordance with the guidelines in the SNDP [Second National Development Plan] by promoting establishment and efficient supervising of group housing projects on self-help basis through grants and technical assistance."

   Target
   "To provide building materials for 40 houses. The distribution of the material will be done by the Department of Community Development, and the construction work by the participants . . .

   Physical Progress
   " . . . The material will be distributed to the applicants early 1976. IDZ has requested funds for 1976 to support the project, and to enable the Department of Community Development to employ building organizers, i.e. qualified craftsmen, to guide and supervise the construction work.

   Financial Progress
   "Allocated K. 4,500. Spent K. 4,496."

3. "It may seem surprising, in view of the primitive tools used in shifting agriculture, that families can produce their food and some cash crops with so small an input of labour as that of the African cultivator families. . . The explanation is that in regions with a favorable land/man ratio, the system of shifting cultivation requires less input of labor per unit of output than primitive systems of permanent cultivation. As long as population densities remain relatively low, labor-intensive systems of land improvement and fertilization need not be applied and it is possible to avoid cultivating land with a low yield due to soil exhaustion after frequent or permanent cultivation without the use of fertilizers." (Boserup, 1970:32.)

APPENDIX A   THE KEFA TIME ALLOCATION STUDY

Ukayenda m'chire wayendera zonse
When You Go into the Bush You Go for Everything

*It is difficult, of course, to calculate exactly the time
and energy expended on any kind of work which is
not subject to industrial conditions . . . It would
require a specialist study by someone familiar with the
economic calendar and methods of work . . . who was
able to concentrate on this particular problem by
means of records of individual activities and daily
diaries.*

Richards, 1939:381

The Kefa time allocation study records how a random sample of Kefa villagers spent their time between June 1977 and July 1978. The sample was observed by a team of local assistants from before sunrise to after sunset and all their activities were recorded for a total of 500 mandays. In addition, the sample was asked if and on what they had spent money and if and where they had been travelling. Of course, the time observation study was also a prerequisite for the qualitative data that have been presented so far in this book.

Time observations provide unique insights. They offer a most objective account of what people do which is often quite different from what they say they do. Time observations are comparatively easy to carry out—one needs only motivation to do the job properly and a certain amount of literacy. And time budgets offer an inroad to consciousness raising and social mobilization as they make everyday affairs accountable and provide a frame of reference within which priorities and preferences can be identified and discussed.

Sample

At the outset of the sociological study Kefa village had 56 households. On the basis of a census, 10 households were selected at random for the time allocation study. The selected households included a single male-headed and a single female-headed household, one polygamous household (two wives of whom one was observed), two households where husband, wife, and children were living in close cooperation with other family members (extended family households), and five households with husband, wife, and children of different ages. The sample households were representative of the village households in terms of marital status of heads and number and age of children.

Only the heads of household were observed, that is, seven married couples and two single people. Observations were discontinued in one household when the male head went to prison. One household was replaced by another of similar marital and economic characteristics when the male head refused to be observed.

Observation days were chosen at random. Days when total observation time was less than 9 were hours eliminated from the study. The final analysis included an average of 36 observation days per observed person, and an average of 12.9 hours of observations per observation day. Thus, the data below are based on a total of 498 days or 6,424 hours of observation.

Data Gathering

We focused our observations on what people did, the duration of their activities, and a few other things. To collect the information our sociology team of three men and two women worked 5 days per week and in shifts.

I, an expatriate sociologist, was the leader of the team. I had found the team members in Kefa village and its surroundings, and their most basic qualification was that they all spoke some English. On each day one male and one female villager, usually a married couple, were observed, the man by our male recorders and the woman by woman recorders. The first shift of recorders worked from before the sun was up until noon, when the second shift took over.

All observed activities were recorded into a logbook that had the following headings:

Observed person		Simon		Data	5/12		Recorder	BKKL	
Activity	Time	Things worked on or with	Price if any	How acquired	For whom	With whom	Who decided	Remarks
getting up washing eating	6.09 6.12 6.18	previous day nsima		brought by wife made by wife		son, 5	self	will go to Chipata

The recording proper was preceded with a four-week trial period during which the method we had chosen was adapted to the reality we wanted to record. The recorders were not all used to writing in English. When they did not know the English word, they used Nyanja. For most activities auxilliary information about price, raw material involved, for and with whom the activity was done, and so forth, was irrelevant. When it was relevant, it occasionally provided us with useful information, but not often enough to be included in the final electronic data processing.

As time passed, the recorders got very used to routine recordings. At this stage they started to write down fragments of discussions or events that took place in their immediate surroundings. For this purpose they had a special notebook that was regularly picked up by myself, and the information it included was typed, handed back, and discussed. It was a method of learning by almost instant feedback and it worked well. No scrap of information was considered too insignificant for such treatment, and this encouraged my co-workers to continue to observe and record.

Processing

Most of the tables that follow are the result of ALGOL and FORTRAN programs executed on edited files, and some—the recall study—are the result of the DDPP statistical program developed at the University of Oslo. Two files were made, one for the DDPP-processing for the more ordinary sociological analysis, and one suitable for standard computer programs. Some editing was done. Data about a couple who had been observed for less than 25 days were excluded, as were those about days when observation time amounted to less than 9 hours. Classification of activities was simplified from more than 100 activities to 57, and a simpler version of the files was created where activities were reduced to 16 categories. Information regarding season, and sex and age was coded into the file. Not much editing was needed for the recall study on money use and travels.

Punched data from the observation formula were used as input for the computer analysis. Processing was done during 1979–1980 on a DEC-10 computer system used by the University of Oslo. Information was organized into two parts: (1) observation of daily activities, and (2) interviews about nonobserved activities (the recall study). Some error processing and restructuring of data proved necessary for the observation study. Initially, information was organized as a sequence of activities including all relevant information and duration, grouped on a day-to-day basis. Each day included a few other variables such as day and week of the year, weather, and health of the observed person. For the electronic processing single activities were made primary units of analysis; however, all other useful data for each activity, including day of occurrence, were kept.

Only a rudimentary analysis of the vast amount of data is presented below. As was agreed between Zambian authorities and IDZ, all data files stored on tape and ready for further analysis were handed over to the Rural Development Studies Bureau, University of Zambia, in 1982.

Kefa Time Uses

Observations were carried out only on days when the observed person spent most of his or her time in the village. Thus, time recorded on activities like travelling, going to funerals, and seeking medical care was much too low. As such activities usually took people outside the village for the whole day or several days, observations were discontinued. *Our data are representative only of what villagers do on days when at least half their time is spent inside the village.*

A major finding, not the least surprising, is that women are far busier than men. Not only do they work an average of 8 hours and 33 minutes per day as compared to 5 hours and 10 minutes for the men (Table 1), but they are also involved in many more activities in terms of specific tasks that can be delineated. Contrary to findings elsewhere in Africa, Kefa village women spent less time cultivating than did the men. It was the male villagers under forty who contributed to the male agriculture dominance. Above the age of forty, the average woman in our sample spent almost one hour more than the men on agricultural work (Table 2).

Table 1. Average Percent of Time per Day (Hours) Spent by Men and Women on Different Groups of Activities

Activity by Main Group	Men %	Men (hours)		Women %	Women (hours)	
Food preparation and related activities	3.7	(0.46)		37.0	(4.62)	
Housekeeping	0.3	(0.04)		5.8	(0.73)	
Child care	0.2	(0.03)		1.5	(0.19)	
Agricultural activities	19.8	(2.48)		16.1	(2.02)	
Animal husbandry	1.5	(0.19)		0.2	(0.03)	
Model house construction	7.2	(0.90)		3.2	(0.41)	
Maintenance and repair work	4.6	(0.58)		0.6	(0.08)	
Meetings and discussions	1.7	(0.21)		0.6	(0.08)	
Funeral attendance	2.0	(0.25)		1.6	(0.21)	
Medical care	0.2	(0.03)		1.5	(0.19)	
Work and Other Duties			41.2 (5.17)			68.5 (8.56)
Eating	6.0	(0.75)		5.8	(0.73)	
Drinking beer	7.4	(0.93)		1.4	(0.18)	
Personal hygiene	2.1	(0.26)		2.6	(0.32)	
Going outside the village	3.5	(0.44)		2.6	(0.31)	
Other Activities			19.0 (2.38)			12.3 (1.54)
Recorded Leisure			39.1 (4.89)			19.5 (2.44)
Total time observed per day			100.0 (12.50)			100.0 (12.50)
Number of days observed		245			253	
Number of hours total		3062			3162	
Number of months		12			12	
Total number of persons observed		8			8	

The data clearly tell about a gender-based division of labor, even if it is not absolute. Although men cook and carry water if there are no women around to do it for them, they do it mostly to satisfy their personal needs and not those of their families. Women sell crops at the market if they have some to sell and no husbands to do it for them. In agriculture there is both cooperation and specialization, as only men cultivate vegetables in the dry season. And men spend time on animal care, while child care is the concern of women. More than any other cluster of responsibilities, food preparation dominates the lives of village women. According to the time allocation findings, the average woman spends 4 hours and 30 minutes every day on preparing the daily meals for her family of 4.1 persons (Table 1). This amount is more than twice the time she spends growing food and cash crops. While men and women spend about the same amount of time eating, drinking was mostly a male activity, as men spend 7 hours per week drinking beer and the women 1 hour.

Table 2. Average Percent of Time per Day (Hours) Spent by Men and Women over and under 40 Years of Age on Different Groups of Activities

	Men		Women	
Activity by Main Group	Under 40 % (hour)	Above 40 % (hour)	Under 40 % (hour)	Above 40 % (hour)
Food preparation and related activities	5 (0.56)	3 (0.38)	38 (4.71)	36 (4.54)
Housekeeping	0 (0.02)	0 (0.05)	6 (0.69)	6 (0.76)
Child care	0 (0.05)	0 (0.01)	3 (0.33)	1 (0.06)
Agricultural activities	24 (3.03)	16 (1.94)	10 (1.26)	20 (2.70)
Animal husbandry	1 (0.14)	2 (0.20)	0 (0.01)	0 (0.05)
Model house construction	7 (0.87)	8 (0.94)	2 (0.32)	4 (0.49)
Maintenance and repair work	4 (0.55)	5 (0.62)	1 (0.10)	1 (0.07)
Meetings and discussions	1 (0.18)	1 (0.12)	1 (0.10)	0 (0.05)
Funeral attendance	1 (0.14)	3 (0.36)	1 (0.12)	2 (0.28)
Medical care	0 (0.15)	0 (0.05)	1 (0.17)	1 (0.10)
Work and Other Duties	43 (5.69)	38 (4.67)	63 (7.81)	71 (9.10)
Eating	7 (0.85)	5 (0.67)	5 (0.80)	5 (0.68)
Drinking beer	5 (0.62)	10 (1.22)	0 (0.05)	2 (0.28)
Personal hygiene	2 (0.29)	2 (0.24)	3 (0.34)	2 (0.30)
Going outside the village	4 (0.54)	3 (0.33)	3 (0.35)	2 (0.28)
Other Activities	18 (2.20)	20 (2.46)	11 (1.54)	11 (1.54)
Recorded Leisure	36 (4.51)	43 (5.37)	25 (3.15)	15 (1.86)
Total time observed per day	100 (12.50)	100 (12.50)	100 (12.50)	100 (12.50)

Keeping the home clean and tidy is another women's job; repairing tools and granary bins is that of men. Men spend three times as much time on meetings and discussions than do women or altogether 1 hour and 30 minutes per week compared to 30 minutes by women. Men also travel more than women, but not very much more, at least not when they spend most of their day in the village.

Individual variations are considerable in every main group of activities.

Even the amount of time people spend eating varied—because of the habit of Kwerekani Phiri to nourish himself on beer rather than food. The range is most marked in agriculture. Maximum time input (daily average) is 4 hours, minimum 0.1. Time spent by women on food preparation varies between 5.6 hours and 3.4 hours (Table 3).

Agriculture

We recorded everything that people did. Under the heading "agriculture" we included planting, sowing, hoeing, weeding, harvesting, collecting and spreading manure and fertilizer, preparing cash crops for sale, selling cash crops, walking to and from the field, and "other fieldwork."

On average men spent 2 hours and 30 minutes and women 2 hours on "agricultural work" daily throughout the year.

Only in the midst of the weeding season (December) did we decide to record the crop on which the observed person worked (Table 4). Thus, only for 33 of 107 entries concerning weeding do we know the crop. Of the 1100 hours the sample listed as "agricultural work," 300 hours were spent walking to and from the field, looking for tools, and otherwise preparing for fieldwork. Of the remaining 800 hours, crop worked on is known for 57 percent of the observed time, that is, for jobs done between December and July.

In Kefa village tomatoes, rape, bananas, and tobacco are "men's crops," while men as well as women cultivate groundnuts, maize, pumpkins, sweet potatoes, and other small crops. Unfortunately, we could not distinguish between time spent on cashcrops and that spent on subsistence crops. For local and hybrid maize we could have, but for groundnuts the amount sold depends on family needs and not primarily on the amount grown. Nevertheless, men spend more time on hybrid maize than women. In our sample two of eight women cultivated cotton. As a result, one fourth of the women/hours in agriculture was spent on cotton. This is not representative of the time village women spend on crops for sale. Our data are biased because Tilele Zulu, the female cotton entrepreneur, happened to be in our sample. She used little paid labor and got little help from her family. Hers was the highest agricultural time input among women: 3:3 hours as a daily average. Evelinar Njobvu had the lowest number of hours: 0.9. Among the men Simon Sakala was the most hard-working cultivator with an average of 4 hours daily. Kwerekani was the lowest, but Kwerekani worked at the Public Works Department and came to Kefa village only on weekends to see his wives and have a good time. Lemekani Mbao, who spent an average of 1.2 hours on agricultural work, also earned money doing odd jobs outside the village.

Table 3. Time Allocation: Hours Spent on Various Groups of Activities: Individual Daily Averages

Respondent		Food Related Activity	Eating	Drinking	Agriculture	Animal Husbandry	Housing Project	Repair Maintenance	House-keeping	Travels	Funeral
Men											
Square	0*	0.9	0.9	0.9	1.7	—	—	1.0	0.1	0.2	0.2
Lemekani	01	0.1	0.7	—	2.2	0.5	1.8	0.4	—	0.5	0.2
Michek	02	0.4	0.8	2.1	1.2	0.2	0.8	0.4	—	0.7	0.1
Sandikonda	03	0.2	0.7	1.6	2.4	0.2	1.4	0.7	0.1	0.2	0.5
Kabanda	04	1.1	0.8	—	3.4	0.3	0.7	0.4	0.1	0.3	—
Simon	05	0.3	0.9	0.2	4.0	—	1.4	0.2	—	0.5	0.3
Kwerekani	06	0.1	0.2	3.5	0.1	—	—	0.1	—	0.6	0.8
James	07	0.3	0.9	0.1	3.9	—	0.6	1.2	—	0.7	0.2
Women											
Faides	1*	4.7	0.8	0.2	1.1	—	0.5	—	0.5	0.5	—
Tilele	11	4.8	0.6	—	3.3	—	0.5	—	1.0	0.2	0.1
Mwada	12	3.4	0.6	0.9	1.9	—	0.6	0.2	0.8	0.2	0.2
Mwanishupa	13	5.6	0.7	—	3.0	0.1	0.6	—	0.5	0.1	0.2
Evelinar	14	4.0	0.7	—	0.9	—	0.2	0.1	0.7	0.1	—
Tisalire	15	5.3	0.8	—	1.6	—	0.4	0.1	0.7	0.6	0.2
Tisauke	16	4.0	0.9	0.4	2.4	—	0.2	0.1	0.7	0.8	0.8
Dorothy	17	5.1	1.0	—	1.7	—	0.2	0.1	1.0	0.2	0.4
Men		0.5	0.8	0.9	2.4	0.3	0.9	0.6	—	0.4	0.2
Women		4.6	0.7	0.2	2.0	—	0.4	0.1	0.7	0.3	0.2

*Notes: 0 and 1 are single. 0 is also a cripple. 0, 01, 03, 11, 12, 13, and 16 are all over 40 years of age. 06 is permanently employed and lives outside the village except for weekends. 01 is married to 11, 02 to 12, 03 to 13, etc.

A mild specialization, but first and foremost cooperation dominates the gender division of labor in agriculture. Watering is the single activity that only men do, because only men cultivate cash crops in the dry season. Weeding too is done more meticulously by the men in their cash crop vegetable fields, than by women and this is reflected in the time study (Table 5). Only men make use of fertilizers and manure. Both men and women prepare cash crops for sale: Groundnuts and maize are shelled and cotton packed in bales, all very time consuming activities mostly done by women. The actual marketing is mostly done by men for two obvious reasons: men grow more cash crops than women, and men have fewer duties at home and consequently more time to spend at the market place.

Table 4. Agricultural Work on Different Crops Performed by Men and Women Between December and July

Crop	Men %	Women %	All %
Groundnuts	16	13	14
Maize (hybrid and local)	36	31	33
Tomatoes	14	0	8
Rape	9	0	5
Pumpkins	4	4	4
Beans	0	13	6
Sweet Potatoes	3	2	3
Bananas	2	0	1
Cotton	0	27	13
Tobacco	4	0	2
Other crops (minor)	12	10	11
Hours of observations	244	414	458

The small size of our sample prevents us from making any detailed analysis of how age influences agricultural work input. Still, we divided the sample into those over and those under forty years of age and found that older men worked less and older women more than younger men and women. As Kwerekani did not do any agricultural work, being employed outside, we excluded him from the account and the male–female difference among those over forty disappeared.

The difference among older and younger men and women, however, remained. Among women the difference was as much as one hour and 30 minutes per day. One obvious reason is that, while younger women have small children to look after, older women are relieved of some of their duties at home by *their* children. Older women seem more set on earning money, too, because of necessity or because their children provide them with the opportunity and the motivation. Cultivating cash crops to pay school expenses is quite common among women. Whether younger women too will become more economically self-reliant when they grow older, or whether a new division of labor is being established where women are becoming more dependent on men, our data do not reveal. It is worth noting that the agricultural work input by the household, or married couple, remains virtually constant whether the couple is over or under forty years of age: about 4 hours and 30 minutes daily.

Because people try not to work on Sundays, the average working day is really longer than the 2.24 hours in Table 4. Besides, agriculture is markedly seasonal. In the busy months of December and January, the average working time is 5.1 hours for men and 4.3 hours for women. When we recorded *working time*, people truly worked. Talking to passers-by, eating in the field shelter, and resting were *not* included. The average figures include performances by people like Square the cripple and Evelinar, notorious for her refusal "to work hard." Thus the average times imply some very long working days for those villagers who were healthy and dedicated and who made agriculture their main concern.

Table 5. Time Spent by Men and Women on Different Agricultural Activities (Percent of total agricultural work input)

Activity	Men %	Women %	All %
Planting, sowing	6	5	5
Hoeing	10	18	14
Watering	4	0	2
Weeding	25	16	21
Making ridges	3	7	5
Harvesting	10	24	17
Using fertilizers/manure	2	0	1
Walking to/from field	20	20	20
Preparing cash crop for sale	2	6	4
Transporting/selling cash crop	8	1	5
Other fieldwork	10	3	7
	100	100	100
Total hours observed in agriculture	607	511	1127
Average hours observed in agriculture per day	2.48	2.02	2.24

The observations were supplemented by questioning and one of the subject matters we discussed with our sample of villagers was which spouse decides what to do in a given field of work (Table 6). Only decisions about when and where to clear new land are commonly assigned to the men; otherwise men *and* women seem to think that most agricultural decisions are taken by themselves or by both spouses. Lemekani Mbao and Kwerekani Phiri are exceptions to this general rule. Both of them said they left decisions as to what and when to cultivate to their wives. Considering that both the men spend a large part of their time outside the village, that seems a sensible thing to do. Irrespective of their husbands' views almost all the women say they themselves decide what crops they would grow, when and how they would plant and harvest, or that they would do so in cooperation with their husbands. Among the men the picture is more varied.

Table 6. Decision Making in Agriculture by a Representative Sample of 16 Villagers According to Marital Status and Marital Relationships

Couple		To Clear New Land	What Crops to Grow	When to Plant	When to Harvest	How to Cultivate	What to Sell
				Who Decides			
1	husband	h*	w	w	w	w	w
	wife	h	w	w	w	w	w
2	husband	h	b	b	b	b	h
	wife	h	w	w	w	w	b
3	husband	h	h	h	h	h	h
	wife	h	w	w	w	h	w
4	husband	h	h	h	h	h	h
	wife	h	b	b	b	b	b
5	husband	h	b	h	h	h	h
	wife	w	w	w	w	w	w
6	husband	w	w	w	w	w	w
	wife	h	w	h	h	b	h
7	husband	o	b	h	h	b	h
	wife	o	w	w	w	w	w
Single	man	h	b	b	h	b	b
	woman	o	w	w	w	w	w

*Abbreviations: h = husband, w = wife, b = both, o = other.

Food Preparation and Related Activities

Under the heading "food preparation and related activities" we included shelling and pounding maize and groundnuts; drying and storing food; gathering, borrowing, and buying food; making beer; cooking, roasting, and frying food; bringing food to others; and carrying water and collecting firewood (Table 7).

Of all groups of activities none are more time consuming than these. On average Kefa village women spend 4.6 hours and men 30 minutes on food preparation every day during the 500 days they were observed. The daily averages among women vary between 5.6 hours (Mwanishupa, 55 years old) and 5.3 hours (Tisalire, 25 years old), each with a husband and two children to cook for, and 3.4 hours (Mwada, 45, also with husband and children, but who often eats with relatives or friends). The other women in the sample spend between 4.0 and 5.1 hours on daily food preparations.

Table 7. Average Time per Day (Hours) Spent by Men and Women on Food Preparation and Related Activities

Activities	Women (hour)	Men (hour)
Shelling, pounding, sieving	1.24	0.03
Soaking and drying food (including tabacco)	0.25	0.02
Carrying maize to and from the mill	0.35	0.06
Collecting or borrowing relish	0.14	0.05
Storing food and collecting stored food	0.05	0.01
Frying or roasting food	0.05	0.07
Cooking food	1.20	0.05
Bringing cooked food to others	0.11	0.00
Buying food and other household items	0.03	0.05
Carrying water	0.70	0.00
Collecting firewood, making fire	0.23	0.10
Other food preparation activities	0.27	0.03
Total hours per day	4.62	0.47

Only to process the maize into flour takes a woman an average of 1 hour and 45 minutes per day, and we may have underestimated the time spent carrying the maize to the mill. As pointed to in Chapter 3, the *nsima* production process includes shelling, pounding, sieving, soaking, drying, carrying to and from the mill, and drying the flour once more.

The actual cooking of nsima and relish takes another 1 hour and 15 minutes. This is not the time when the pots simmer over the fire, but the time women's attention is on cooking to the exclusion of other activities. In the rainy season women gather leaves, tubers, and mushrooms in the forest. During an average week, food gathering takes the women about 1 hour, but as food gathering—like so many other activities—is seasonal, the actual time spent on picking wild growing eatables varies considerably from one month to the next. (Harvesting cultivated crops was registered under "agriculture".) Usually men and women eat separately and women bring the cooked food to the men. Occasionally a mother may wrap *nsima* and relish in a banana leaf and take it to a child in school, to a friend who is ill, or to a male relative whose wife is away. On average, "serving food to others" takes the women 7 minutes daily.

Kefa villagers are largely self-reliant, but those who can afford it buy sugar, salt, matches, and a few other items from local shops or itinerant pedlars. They buy fish and meat from individual pedlars or fellow villagers. The time spent buying household and other goods was recorded as 1 hour 45 minutes per *month*. As purchases are often made away from the village, this time input does not adequately reflect how often people spend money, but indicates that men spend more time on buying things than women. More will be said about this below.

Women carry water to the home for their menfolk and children to wash and to prepare food. To economize on energy, women generally wash utensils and clothes at the water hole or in the river. The amount of water brought to the home depends upon season and availability, on the size of the household, and on the number of women and girls who share in the duty of bringing water to the home. On average, water carrying takes the women 42 minutes every day.

Kefa village is surrounded by forest and firewood is easy to find. On the way home from the field, women and occasionally men make a detour into the bush to collect branches from fallen down trees. Collecting firewood and lighting fires takes the women 15 minutes a day, the men 6 minutes.

Though beer plays an important role in village life also from the point of view of labor inputs, brewing is not included as a separate food-related activity in Table 7. To make beer means to draw water, collect firewood, and pound maize and millet, activities that were recorded under their specific headings and not as separate beer-brewing activity. As should be clear from Chapter 3, beer-making takes a lot of time during the five days of its most visible preparation.

Though food preparation is the job of women, men do prepare food. They may want to help their wives, like Micheck, live alone without wife or close female relative who can cook for them, like Square, or have a lazy wife like Kabanda. A considerable part of Kabanda's daily input of 1 hour and 6 minutes was spent on taking maize to the mill for grinding. Square spent 55 minutes a day preparing food for himself; the other men spent less than 25 minutes on food preparation. Collecting firewood and making fire is the most time consuming male activity under the general heading "food preparation." Men also cook and particularly roast food, mostly to eat it themselves (Table 3).

The impact of the local processing and conservation methods is considerable in terms of the time it takes to feed a family. In addition to the daily 4.6 hours invested by women and the 0.5 hours by the men, children also and particularly girls spend time helping their mothers preparing food. We did not study the time uses among children and adolescents, but it seems likely that about 7 hours of work daily may be needed to feed an average family of 4.1 members adequately.

There is surprisingly little seasonal variation in the amount of time spent preparing food.

When and what to cook and when to brew is clearly within the women's sphere of authority. Decisions concerning when to buy household goods or food items, and to slaughter goats and pigs are less gender bound. Here, the tendency found in the agriculture sector seems to prevail; each gender assumes more decision-making power for itself than what the spouse accords it. Still, on the whole, women's authority seems to dominate (Table 8).

Table 8. Decision Making in Household-Related Matters According to Marital Status and Marital Relationships

Couple		What to Cook	When to Cook	When to Brew Beer	When to Buy Food/Soap/Things			When to Slaughter Goat/Pig/Hen	
1	husband	w*	w	w	h	b	b	h	w
	wife	w	w	w	w	w	b	h	w
2	husband	w	w	w	w	w	b	b	b
	wife	w	w	w	w	w	b	w	w
3	husband	w	w	w	w	w	b	b	w
	wife	w	w	w	w	w	w	w	w
4	husband	w	w	w	b	h	h	h	w
	wife	w	w	w	h	h	b	b	w
5	husband	w	w	w	w	w	b	b	w
	wife	w	w	b	b	b	w	b	b
6	husband	w	w	w	w	b	b	w	w
	wife	w	w	w	h	w	b	h	h
7	husband	w	w	b	b	w	b	h	b
	wife	w	w	w	w	w	w	w	w
Single	man	w	w	w	h	h	w	b	w
	woman	w	w	w	w	w	w	w	w

*Abbreviations: w = wife, h = husband, b = both.

Eating and Drinking

Among the men time spent eating varies between 56 and 14 minutes per day, the 14 minutes being spent by a regular beer drinker. Among women time eating varies between 60 and 36 minutes. Half the meals are *nsima* meals, i.e., *nsima and* relish. Maize in some other form than *nsima* comprises 19 percent of the meals (porridge, maize on the cob, etc.) Pumpkins are registered in 7 percent and fruits and other snacks in 7 percent of the recorded meals.

Availability of food and beer, and the amount of work waiting in the field determine how much time people spend eating and drinking (Table 9). February–March–April is the time of plenty and this is reflected in our findings. At this time people spent almost 1 hour eating per day, while the average for the rest of the year is 40 minutes.

Beer drinking is no male prerogative, but compared to men's 0.92 hour per day, women spend little time on beer, 0.18 hour. In fact, the average man spends more time drinking than eating. It is particularly some men's habit to spend most of the weekend in a "house of beer" that contributes to the high figures. Individual differences are greater when it comes to drinking habits than any other activity. Some people do not drink at all, while the heaviest drinker in our sample, Kwerekani, spends an average of 3 hours and 30 minutes per day on drinking beer.

Table 9. Time Spent Eating and Drinking According to Season and Sex (Hours)

	February–March	May–July	August–October	November–January	Men	Women
Eating	0.92	0.67	0.67	0.69	0.76	0.74
Drinking	0.32	0.58	0.96	0.46	0.93	0.18
Food preparation	2.57	2.45	2.63	2.69	0.46	4.62

Washing pots and pans and clothes, keeping the home clean and tidy, airing blankets, and preparing the paraffin lamp at night were recorded under "housekeping." On average women spend 40 minutes each day on such activities while men spend 2 minutes. Sweeping the house and the compound is the most time consuming single activity under the general heading. And as a result Kefa always looked nice and tidy.

Child Care

The average time a women spent on "child care" was registered at only 11 minutes a day. Young women with one or more children under five spend a daily average of 20 minutes on child care, while their husbands spend 3 minutes.

More than anything else the figures underline how little *specialized time* children receive from adults and the high degree to which children are integrated into the community. This practice makes it difficult to record adequately time spent on "child care" (Table 10). Firstly, the recorders repeatedly failed to register the presence of small children when a women was doing her daily duties. Secondly, activities involving children, including breast-feeding a baby, were usually considered a secondary activity by the recorder, who would concentrate on the fact that a nursing mother was also chatting, smoking, or eating. Thirdly, activities like cuddling a child or chatting with him or her were often registered as "leisure" time. Fourthly, child care often means to be available and to keep an eye on a child in case he or she will need adult attention. Needless to say, such alertness cannot be reflected in time studies based on observations of what people do. What may have been recorded as "being idle" may in fact have been this particular type of child care.

Table 10. Decision Making Concerning Children

| | Male Respondents | | | Female Respondents | | | |
	Husband	Wife	Both	Husband	Wife	Both	Total
Schooling	4	0	4	2	5	1	16
Marriage	7	0	1	4	4	0	16
Medical treatment	1	3	4	0	7	1	16

The activities that have been recorded under "child care" are those that concentrate on children exclusively, like dressing them, washing them, and putting them to bed.

Though women are responsible for a child's daily up-keep, on important issues fathers take decisions, though perhaps not quite as often as they would like to think (Table 11). Decisions concerning schooling were considered by four fathers but only two mothers to be that of the man. Concerning who and when to marry, seven fathers and four mothers said it was the man who decided. Regarding when to seek medical assistance or treatment, men as well as women said the mother or both parents decide.

Animal Husbandry

The nine households that we observed looked after a total of 24 goats, 10 pigs, 3 cattle, and 80 hens at the time we carried out our census. All animals are closed in at night. Dogs and pigs are fed regularly. Cows are milked once a day and cattle are herded during the rainy season and watered during the last months of the dry season. On average, men spent 10 minutes a day and women 2 minutes on such activities and on building and repairing pens, sheds, and kraals. The inability of the observation method adequately to reflect time spent on children applies also to animals. In addition, adolescents perform much of the herding and consequently it is not included in our recordings.

Table 11. Hours Spent on "Leisure" Activities by Men and Women (Average per Day)

	Men	Women
Observed leisure time	4.99	3.07
Drinking beer	0.93	0.18
Not observed leisure time	0.49	0.00*
Total leisure	6.41	3.15
Percent of total working day (13.15 hours)	47%	23%

*On average women were observed 30 minutes longer than men every day. The reason is that observations were stopped at night when the observed person retired to rest or chat. As men usually did so earlier than women, the 30-minute differential has been listed here as leisure for the men.

Other Economic Activities

A housing scheme represents an anomaly in a village time budget. Men spent an average of 1 hour per day, and women 25 minutes, on the housing scheme. How would the time have been spent had there been no Model Village project? We can only guess. The villagers complained that because of the scheme they did not have sufficient time to hoe and weed their fields. It is also likely that activities like brewing beer and cultivating cash crops suffered. Individual differences were considerable, even if we exclude Square the cripple and Kwerekani who worked outside. With 1 hour 50 minutes per day Lemekani represented the maximum input. He was a skilled builder set on making a house for his handicapped son as well as for himself. Among women time investment varied from 12 to 36 minutes a day. Labor inputs were highly seasonal. In the slack season average daily input was 1 hour and thirty minutes, in busy November–December 15 minutes.

Time spent on "repair and maintenance" is also seasonal. In May–June every man must set family granary bins in order to receive the year's harvest. During these months repair and maintenance take an average of slightly more than 30 minutes per person. In the peak agricultural season between November and January only 5 minutes per day is spent on repairs. Seven-eighths of the time spent on repair-maintenance is that of men.

Leisure

When people did not do anything in particular, when they chatted with friends and relatives, waited for something, took a nap during daytime, went to church or to a dance, it was registered as "leisure" (Table 11). According to our findings men have twice as much "leisure" as women, or 6 hours and 30 minutes per day to women's 3 hour and 10 minutes. However arbitrary our definition of "leisure," the findings highlight a basic inequality in the rights and opportunities vested in traditional and also present-day sex roles. In a world of increasing opportunities men have a very much better starting point for trying out new crops or agricultural methods and to avail themselves of advice and credit. For these and other reasons they are also considered more attractive participants in the modernization process by change agents commissioned to promote new types of economic exchange. Not only spare time but also access to information and personal networks are important prerequisites for successful participation, and men have more of it than women. However, "leisure" as defined in the study is not necessarily a commodity that can be converted into any other activity without limitations.

A more refined analysis could have distinguished between "voluntary" and "involuntary" leisure. Particularly during the rainy season villagers spend a lot of time waiting for the rain to pass, in order to get on with their work. As a consequence, 30 percent of the observed time during the busy rainy season was recorded as "leisure" time.

Women under forty were recorded as having more "leisure" than older women. Some of it undoubtedly could have been recorded as "child care" or "cooking."

In a subsistence society where virtually all production is for personal and household consumption, and accumulation is limited to a few durable crops, time is a scarce resource only at certain critical moments, like during sowing and planting, weeding and harvesting. Outside these peaks, people are not in a hurry. But at the critical times the availability of sufficient labor is vital to the well being of the family. It is this vulnerability that makes secondary productive activities—in Kefa village, for example, vegetable growing in the dry season—of much importance.

Time alone is not sufficient to increase labor inputs. In the time budget, elderly men come out with a lot of spare time. One type of "involuntry leisure" is the time people spend resting simply because they are not fit to work. It should be clear from Chapter 7 that illnesses and ailments are prevalent in a village like Kefa and will necessarily deeply affect production and productivity.

As we shall discuss below, time studies have many shortcomings when one tries to understand adequately the functioning of a subsistence society. Our findings clearly underline the large work burden of women, the tremendous labor input needed to process a family's daily food, and the clear, but not absolute gender-based division of labor.

Methodological Problems: The Problem of Interpretation

To study what people do over time is to study behavior. As a data-gathering method, time observations share with operationalism, pragmatism, and stimulus-response research the basic structural principal of "reductio ad actionem." As a method of data-gathering, behaviorism had its breakthrough in the 1920s. It was a mechanistic and materialistic reaction to the long and largely inconclusive study of mental or introspective processes. Since then, it has been pushed back to a very much less absolute and more specialized field in the study of people. The reason why is obvious—particularly so in sociology. The social scientist is generally less interested in behavior than in the sociopolitical and economic structures and processes that determine and/or restrict what people do, and structures and processes do not easily lend themselves to observations. The fact is that time observations say little about the social, economic, political, cultural, and/or ecological conditions that determine and in turn are determined by what people do.

There are other problems as well. In time allocation studies, the behavior "bit" or activity is the most ready unit of analysis, whether everything a person does is included as in our study, or only selected activities. Whatever approach is used, the flow of life is cut up and parts are isolated; activities are separated from their context and alienated from the whole onto which they must shed light. Thus, time allocation studies need to be supplemented by other methods, at least if the objective is not only to describe but also to explain social behavior.

African time allocation studies are few, and they are often quoted because of the precision of their data. For descriptive purposes they may be unique, but their analysis poses definite problems. In the Kefa study we found that "women spend 4.62 hours preparing food every day," or "men over 40 spend 1.22 hours daily drinking beer, as an average." "Men spend an average of 2.48 hours per day on agricultural work, and women 2.02 hours." What do such figures say about necessity, preference, quality, variations, or optimal time use? If women have better tools will they spend less time on preparing food or invent more time-consuming cooking practices as women have done in other parts of the world? If women spend less time preparing food, will they spend more on growing it? Or on drinking beer? Is it at all necessary to improve tools to reduce time spent on food preparation, or can women speed up their ways of doing things if there are other activities they would rather do? There certainly seems to be scope for doing things differently from the way our findings on time allocations indicate. Whenever there is a funeral or whenever a relative living far away is ill, a women who spends a daily average of 9 hours on "work" arranges with family and friends and goes away for days and even weeks.

Older women work longer hours in the field than younger women. But do they accomplish more? Some women sweep their home and compound several times every day. Is this work, or restlessness, or "leisure?"

From a Western point of view the dichotomy "work/leisure" is quite meaningful, but can it be used at all to analyze behavior in a subsistence society? By dividing our data into "work" and "leisure" we may fail to grasp the social and material implications of the traditional division of labor within its original setting. Who says that "cooking" has less potential to it than "chatting to a friend," or that "sitting idle" is more rewarding than "thatching a roof anew"?

When we use concepts like "work" and "leisure," it is with the acknowledgment that subsistence considerations are no longer the sole determinant for behavior in Kefa village. In rural areas all over the world new ways of thinking and new priorities are becoming increasingly forceful. Capital, labor, and land are acquiring new significance as entrepreneurs use them as means of exchange in the market. And as labor is becoming a commodity with a specific market value, so is leisure. As a result, concepts once devoid of meaning may become important analytical tools, necessary to analyze the effect of technical and economic innovations on men and women.

What frame of reference ought we to select when analyzing a culture different from our own? Theirs or ours? Or both? Is it at all possible to internalize a different culture to a degree that enables us to use it as a frame of analytical reference? And if we seek refuge in our own culture to make what is different intelligible, is not our purpose immediately thwarted? There is no simple answer to this dilemma. But its solution is clear. We must encourage Third World scholars to develop further the indigenous rationality embedded in their own culture. But they should hurry, because rationalities, just like culture, wither and die without ceremony.

Methodological Problems: The Problem of the Odd Case

The study of only one or a few cases is always vulnerable when the aim is to shed light on more general issues, and most studies are ambitious enough to have such aspirations. So also the Kefa time allocation study. It was done only in one village, it included 18 persons, and it was carried out throughout an entire year. We might have included one hundred people and observed them for one month for about the same cost, but the problem of the odd case would still be with us as no month is typical of any other month in a subsistence society. Because participants were picked at random, the Kefa sample was representative.

No doubt the study pictures life in this particular village, but how typical is Kefa village? To find out we compared Kefa village—in terms of basic characteristics like demographic structure, housing conditions, water supply, cash crop involvement, and access to social services—with other villages in the District and with national data. The findings indicate that Kefa does resemble thousands of other villages. But more about that below.

However, like every other village Kefa is also unique. Furthermore, at the time when the sociological study was carried out, the externally initiated model house scheme contributed to making the village rather special. From the point of view of understanding social change, this status may be an advantage. Because of the model house program the study sheds light on how a society meets the challenge of social transformation.

The Kefa Recall Study

While problems regarding validity and analysis are common to most sociological methods, those concerned with how to render rare events adequately may be particular to time observation studies. They stem from the fact that the importance of certain events in no way corresponds to their duration. Yet such events may determine behavior and may play a decisive part in people's lives.

In Kefa village earning and spending money are rare events. Money is a major concern to many villagers, but when in the village, and even when outside, they spend and earn so little money that its importance cannot be rendered through a time study. The importance of travelling is also invisible when a study focuses on what people do *while in the village.*

To catch odd events, on each observation day we asked the observed persons about travels, incomes, and expenditures on the two days prior to the observation day. The result was one thousand recall days. The recall study makes it possible to assess the validity of data regarding events and activities that did not happen very frequently. It also provides us with information on travelling.

Expenditures and Incomes

Like most people, Kefa village residents did not like to talk about their income, so instead we talked about their outlays. During the one thousand days that our respondents were asked to recall, total outlays amounting to K. 420 (U.S. $500) were reported. This equals K. 155 (U.S. $186) per adult per year. Individual differences were considerable and estimated yearly incomes varied from K. 611 to K. 20 among men and K. 430 to K. 20 among women.

Because they are so busy catering for family needs, women have less time to earn money than do men. They also spend differently the little money that they have. More of what they have goes to satisfy family needs, and less is spent on themselves (Table 12). On 42 percent of the occasions when men spent money they bought something for themselves, while women did so on 18 percent of the occasions. On 7 percent of the occasions both men and women bought something for the spouse.

Most money was spent on clothing (30 percent). Food accounted for 7.5 percent; household goods for 7 percent; seeds, fertilizers and domestic animals for 14 percent. Entertainment in the form of beer, liquor, card games, and tobacco comprised 10 percent.

Table 13 reflects differences in spending patterns between men and women. While the men spend 14 percent on entertainment and 5 percent on food, women's priorities are the other way around (4 percent on entertainment and 13 percent on food). Women also spent 65 percent on clothes, soap, paraffin, and grinding mill compared with the men's 23 percent.

If we assume that the median is our most accurate measurement, a household consisting of husband, wife, and children has an average of

Table 12. The Spending of Money (Percent of Occasions on Which Money Was Spent by Men and Women)

For Whom or What	Men %	Women %
Self	42	18
Spouse	7	7
Child(ren)	4	2
Household	34	61
Other	8	6
No information	6	6
	101	100
Number of days on which money was spent	187	136

K. 230 to spend during a year (1977–1978). Of this K. 13 would be spent on food of which the man pays K. 8 and women K. 5, K. 62. on clothes of which husband and wife each contribute K. 31. Entertainment would cost K. 31 of which the man would spend K. 25 and the women K. 6.

As men earn more than twice as much as women, it is not surprising than women occasionally spend their husband's money (on one of five occasions)—however, men also spend money which they consider belongs to their wives (Table 14).

While people spent money on one of three days, they received money on one of ten days. The amounts were mostly very small. Large sums of money, i.e., in the range of K. 20–100 are received, if at all, once or twice a year when crops or domestic animals are sold. As they happen so rarely, such transactions are not adequately reflected either in the observation study or in the recall study.

Sale of vegetables and fruits was the reported source of about half of the men's incomes. If we exclude the sale of a cow worth K. 120, which would otherwise loom large in the statistics, 36 percent of women's incomes came from brewing beer. Fifty-seven percent came from gifts from husbands and relatives (cow excluded). In fact, on two of three occasions when women got money, it was as a gift, and men got money gifts on one of four occasions when they received any money. The amount varied from 2 ngwee to 10 Kwacha, the mode as well as median being 20 ngwee. The eight men in the sample reported having received gifts to the total amount of K. 17, while the figure for the eight women was K. 7. It seemed that those more likely to repay a gift were more likely to receive one.

Travelling

The recall study confirms that most journeys are of short duration and distance (Table 15). Men are more mobile than women. On average men go outside the village on 1 of 3 days, women on 1 of 5. Seventy-five per-

Table 13. Items on Which Money is Spent by Both Men and Women
(Percent of Recalled Expenditures during 988 Days)

Items	Men %	Women %
Maize	0.5	3.3
Vegetables	0.2	0.9
Fruits	0.4	0.6
Bread, biscuits	0.7	0.6
Sugar, salt	1.3	2.7
Meat, fish, milk	1.3	1.8
Other food	0.5	2.7
Food total	4.9	12.6
Grinding mill	1.6	8.2
Paraffin, matches	1.0	2.0
Soap	1.5	2.3
Clothes	18.4	52.5
Household items total	22.5	65.0
Seeds	4.9	—
Fertilizers	2.4	0.3
Animals, hens	12.6	1.8
Investments total	19.9	2.1
Liquor	1.0	1.0
Beer	4.5	2.2
Cards	7.3	—
Tobacco	1.1	0.3
Entertainment total	13.9	3.5
Transport	5.9	0.7
Funeral	12.5	—
Other things and more than one item	20.3	16.1
Total expenditures	99.9	100.0
Kwacha spent	279.44	140.55

cent of men's trips and 59 percent of women's take them no further than to neighboring villages. Women go to the grinding mill almost every 3 weeks (19 times a year), men once every 2 months (7 times). The health center, 10 kilometers away, is visited by women four times per year, by men three times. And both men and women went to the market once during the 12-month period. Men go to Chipata or thereabout once per month, women once every 4 months. Travels beyond Chipata (30 kilometers away) are undertaken by men 6 times per year, by women once.

Table 14. Whose Money Men and Women Spend (As Percent of Occasions on Which Money is Spent)

	Men %	Women %
Own money	84	63
Spouse's money	5	19
Other people's money	4	4
No information	7	13
	100	99

Visiting and funerals are the most common single purposes that take women away from home, while men go to buy things and to drink beer. Meetings outside the village are mostly attended by men. Men said they have more than one reason for going away on one of five occasions. Women, whose work burden probably encourages them to plan ahead, have more than one purpose for being away every second time they go outside the village.

Table 15. Purpose of Journey According to Sex (Days per Year)

Purpose	Men		Women	
	Days/year	%	Days/year	%
Funeral	16	13	9	13
Meetings	10	9	1	1
To buy things	21	18	7	10
To sell things	13	11	0	0
To visit people	10	9	15	21
To drink beer	17	15	7	10
More than one purpose	25	22	30	44
No information	4	3	0	0
Total	116	100	69	100

Women mostly walk, whereas men walk or go by bicycle. Men go to Chipata by bicycle, in a private car or on the bus, women by bus only. It seems that men have better access than women to private transport, since they have more time to wait and also can leave for a journey the moment they have the chance of a free lift.

Thus, travelling is also less expensive for men than for women, who have to plan ahead, which mostly means to plan for the bus.

While men usually travel alone (57 percent of occasions), women journeyed in the company of others on three of four occasions. On one of five trips men travelled in the company of children.

Kefa Village—Unique Yet Representative

Just like any other village, Kefa is unique. In some villages, past and future seem further apart than elsewhere. But in Kefa village in 1978, social order and economic priorities were very much those of its colonial and neo-colonial past. The market played a modest role in everyday village dispositions, yet young people and surplus agricultural production continued to be sucked away as men and foodstuffs were and still are devoured by market forces all over Africa. Thus, in this and a number of basic characteristics, Kefa represents not only itself, but villages elsewhere.

Size

Village sizes in Chipata District and elsewhere in Zambia vary. According to Marwick (1952:131) a Chewa village had between 40 and 400 huts around 1950. A sample survey carried out by the Intensive Development Zone Programme in 1973 found that the average village in Chief Chikuwe's area had 14 households, the median being 12 and the mode only 6 households. In Kefa village in 1977 we found 56 households although the IDZ had counted 35. Kefa village is quite large. Yet small villages are often clustered or regrouped so that what appears as one fair-size village is considered as two or three villages by those living there.

Access to Social Amenities

Most rural Zambians live in mud-and-wattle houses, just as Kefa village residents did prior to 1978. In Chipata District, 45 percent of the villages surveyed by IDZ in 1973 had only mud houses; 6 percent had more than six brick houses. Prior to the housing project Kefa village belonged to the category of 51 percent villages with a few brick houses.

In half of the villages the water supply was unsatisfactory and in 37 percent it dried up during the dry season; so also in Kefa. Furthermore, 77 percent of the people interviewed walked less than three-quarters of a kilometer to the water source, as did Kefa village women.

In regard to access to a health center, 10 kilometers away, the primary school 3 kilometers, shopping facilities 3 kilometers, and the bus 3 kilometers, Kefa compares with other villages in Chipata District.

Like nine of ten villages in the area, in Kefa village, too, land is still abundant.

Market Involvement

According to the 1973 IDZ survey, only 3–5 percent of the rural population in the district cultivated crops or reared domestic animals for the market (Table 16). Like virtually all other villagers, Kefa residents too were firmly rooted in a subsistence economy, but on average it was perhaps slightly more "commercialized" than that for the rest of the IDZ survey population.

Table 16. Market Involvement among 1,800 Heads of Household (Intensive Development Zone Programme Survey 1973*)

1% sold more than 5 bags of maize (hybrid)
1% grew more than 1 acre of cotton
2% grew more than 1½ acres of tobacco
2% used tractor to plough and to transport corps
8% used oxen
3% had more than 10 cows
5% had more than 5 pigs
1% had more than 12 pigs
1% had more than 18 cows
1% had more than 6 goats or 25 layers or 10 broilers
4% were in the habit of using paid labor
6% owned an iron plough
3% owned an ox cart
4% owned a ridger
4% used more than 7 bags of fertilizers
3% grew hybrid maize on one hectar or more

* Data Sources: In 1973 Intensive Development Zone Programme (IDZ) made two surveys in Chipata District. One comprised a study of village amenities and other characteristics collected from 199 village headmen. The second collected information regarding agricultural performance from 1,870 male and female heads of household. It is the findings from these two surveys and from the 1969 national census on population and housing that are used here to shed light on the basic characteristics of Kefa villllage.

Though agriculture is the source of livelihood for virtually everybody, a few villagers have ventured to make a craft or art their full-time specialty. In a study of artisans, Hans Hedlund (1975) found that 11 percent of 114 villages in Chief Chikuwe's area had a blacksmith, carpenter, bricklayer, or pitsawyer. In Kefa no resident relied only on cash income, at least not when living inside the village. Thus in terms of lack of occupational differentiation Kefa is similar to other villages in the area.

Demographic Characteristics

According to the 1969 national census, 24 percent of all Zambian households were headed by women. The figure for Kefa in 1977 was 27 percent. The average Zambian household had 4.7 members; that of Eastern Province had 4.1, as did the average Kefa village household. The average female-headed household in Kefa, with only 3.3 members, also compares well with the Zambian average. In Zambia as a whole, 5 percent of households were polygamous. In Kefa the figure was 15 percent, but, both in the nation as a whole and in Kefa, four of ten households were either single-person households or were headed by women.

In terms of male-female ratio, Kefa differs from national averages. But with its large proportion of women it is similar to rural areas all over Zambia; 64 percent of the adult population were women, which is about what Tuthill et al. (1968) found in the two Chewa villages they studied in 1967 (64 percent and 61 percent). Most unmarried women in Kefa were divorced or widowed, while most unmarried men were young and not yet married. In Zambia as a whole the large majority of widows and divorcees are also women (86 percent in 1969).

A simple comparison of basic village characteristics does not answer the question of representation. But it does indicate that in terms of population structure, family size, marital status, occupational differentiation, market involvement, housing, and access to water, land, and public services Kefa is similar to many, many other villages.

This has been the story of how Kefa village residents organize their lives and make use of their resources. That they do so is another characteristic that they share with villagers everywhere.

APPENDIX B   THE KEFA VILLAGE DIARY

Chakudza siciyimba ng'oma
What Comes Does Not Beat a Drum

In the main text of the book, the data about Kefa village have been presented within a framework suggested by the headings of its various chapters. By doing so, I have attempted to present an orderly picture of village living. However, what is missing are the dynamics of everyday life, the incessant movement of time and being as day follows day and event supercedes event. It is for that reason that I present the Kefa Village Diary as an appendix, perhaps meant less for reading than for browsing. The advantage of a diary is that it presents life as it reveals itself, bit by bit, day by day. And just like life itself, it makes no attempt to explain or to interpret events. The diary is based on the notes that Sylvester took while participating in everyday affairs in Kefa village.

Sylvester's Diary

July

The weather is mostly quite cold. The cattle are free to graze without a herdsman. Wild fruits mature. Grass fires are frequent. The ECU market is now open to receive the cash crops from those who have crops to sell.

15. Women and girls dance *Chimtali* at night in the full moon. The dance is to honor the IDZ sociologist who moved into headman Kefa's house yesterday.
18. *Mlandu* (village meeting): Mwada Simba consulted her segment clan members to solve the dispute between herself and the husband Micheck Phiri who, she complains, gets drunk and does not respond to her as a spouse should. 10–15 people present. As only 2 supported Micheck, the husband was told to improve his ways.
20. Alesi Kamanga, Brighton's aunt, died early in the morning. The headman organized the funeral. 140 visitors came to sleep overnight.
21. Alesi was buried. The Zambia Reformed Church members sang funeral songs. Donations, K. 2.84. Chief Chikuwe was present.
26. Lomanzi Tembo and her daughter and Tilolele and her daughter did piecework shelling maize for Mwanizinga Mbewe. They were paid 5 ngwee for each basin of shelled maize.
29. Timeke Daka and others went to Kamanga Village to shell maize with the Roman Catholic Church group. There were 17 women and 3 men and they all worked to earn for their church group. 4 bags were shelled.

31. Dandaulani Mwale, the son of headman Kefa, was found dead, hanging from a tree in the forest. Dandaulani was a man with two children and lived in Kaliyoyo village.

August

August is usually chilly. The lowest morning temperature measured was +10 C. During the first 3 weeks morning temperature was around +15 C.; by the end of the month, +22 C. During the whole month people were busy making bricks. Some kilns are already burned and Lubinda's house is almost up. The Community Development Assistant came several times to supervise brickburning and building. Because people are so busy making bricks, they have little time for house repairs and beer. August, like September, is a time for visiting relatives who live in other parts of the district and of Zambia.

1. *Mlandu* is held concerning the circumstances leading to the death of Dandaulani Mwali.
2. The village is virtually empty. Everybody has gone to the funeral of Dandaulani at Kaliyoyo.
3. A message has come that Jessie Tonga's mother died in Chiwayo village. Kefa women come to cry at Jessie's house. The death message came so late that the funeral had already taken place.
4. Kathontho Mwale has hired a tractor to carry his 4 bags of maize to the ECU (Eastern Cooperative Union) Market at Kalichero.
6. Titar Nkhoma has been admitted at the Maternity Ward at Chiparamba Health Center.
8. *Mlandu:* Matrida Sakala (Kefa's divorced wife, mother of Dandaulani) and Kefa Mwale accuse Laimen Phiri of having murdered their son. Laimen admits the crime. The meeting resolves the case by expelling Laimen and his family from Kefa village.

   Eliah Phiri's second wife asked permission to continue to live in Kefa village and this is accepted. (In other words, she is divorcing Eliah.)
9. Villagers buy household items from the Phiris, who have booked a car to take their maize and groundnuts to Malambo in Luangwa Valley. Some villagers who are related to the Phiris help them pack.
10. *Mlandu* is held at Chief Chikuwe's *bwalo* with Kefa village elders and Laimen Phiri. Laimen is publically accused of murder in front of the Chief but denies being guilty. The Chief expels him and the rest of the Phiri family from his chiefdom.

    Mr. Njamini came to hire Lemekani Mbao to make a platform for the cotton market, which is to open shortly at Gia's store in Kalichero.

12. The Phiris hired a tractor to carry their things from Kefa village.
14. Now that the Phiris have gone, many fields, gardens and houses have been vacated. Residents who want to use these assets ask the headman for permission.

   Beer is ready in two Kefa households. All the beer is sold as it has been brewed to raise money. Many people from inside and outside the village come to drink.
18. At Jessie Tonga's house 8 women are pounding millet. They do not help her out of love, but because they want her to help them when they are preparing beer.
21. Jenifa Banda bore a baby today. Shuzi Zulu's family members cooked and drew water for the family. Evelinar Phiri—Jenifa's mother—has been expelled, so Jenifa had no family to help her.
22. Shuzi goes to Mnukwa to inform his wife's relatives about the baby.
25. Evelinar Phiri, Jenifa's mother, came from Mnukwa to see her daughter. She asks the headman for permission to enter the village.

   Eliah Phiri decides to spend a night in the village (at his second wife's house) without asking anybody about it. When people learn of his whereabouts, he runs away. Kefa organizes the youngmen to find him. Kefa informs his residents not to accept the Phiris unless they have received permission for a visit.
26. Micheck is employed to clear Mr. Sakala's field.
27. Kamawanda Njobvu has slaughtered a pig and sold meat for K. 22.70.

   Kefa organizes the youngmen to look for Laimen Phiri, who is said to be around the village and to have threatened women on the way to the grinding mill. Laimen Phiri is now wanted by the police.
28. The 7-days beer of Tilele Zulu is ready. It will be taken by Lemekani Mbao as *vipheko*—a token gift—to his son-in-law in Chimimba village. People from Kefa village will go to Chimimba village to try the beer.
31. Timeke Daka has started preparing her beer today. Some women help her draw water.

September

September is a busy month for all village residents. People are making bricks with their working groups and kilns are made and burned. Like August, September is also a month of bush fires, mice digging, and all kinds of repairs.

September is much warmer than August, but temperatures are still pleasant. The most ardent farmers have started clearing their fields.

1. An Agricultural Assistant (AA) came to see headman Kefa about training a pair of oxen for him. Since there was nobody in the village who could help them catch the animals, the AA had to leave.

Sandikonda Daka, Mwanishupa Phiri (wife), and Timeke Daka (daughter) left for Kapatamoyo to visit Mwanishupa's sick mother. Sandikonda dropped into the beer hall on the way and got drunk.

3. Mwanizinga Mbewe has gone to Chipata to stay with relatives for a few days.

4. Lubinda is selling groundnuts at the Cooperative Market, now open. Lubinda goes on his bike, leaving the transport by ox cart to his worker, Eliah Nkhoma.

5. Some people like Jackson Phiri have already started to clear their land for planting.

6. Titar Nkhoma is moving to her parents' village near Chiparamba. Because her husband is hardly ever in Kefa village, she wants to be closer to her family.

7. Laimen Phiri is still around. Kefa Mwale, Micheck Phiri, and Penelani Khosa went to Chief Chikuwe to seek the assistance of other headmen in the area, so that Laimen can be caught and handed over to the police.

    Evelinar Njobvu gave birth today after 5 months of pregnancy.

8. Evelinar's baby died. The women bury the infant.

12. Kefa organizes the youngmen to catch Laimen, who is observed in a neighboring village. 7 men and 1 woman are involved.

    Mlandu: Mr. Njobvu was paid 1 pig to make bricks for Agrippina Sakala. Now the pig is slaughtered and sold by Mr. Njobvu, but he has not yet finished making the bricks. Agrippina has appealed to the headman to find out why.

13. Eliah Phiri is in the village. He says the chief has given him the permission to bring a gift of relish to his granddaughter. The headman tells him to leave, but to report to the chief on his way. He is escorted by some youngmen to see that he goes.

14. Kefa, his son David, and Jackson Phiri go to the chief to see if Eliah reported there the previous day. (He did not.)

    Lubinda sold 1 bag of maize and 1 bag of groundnuts at the cooperative market.

15. Laimen was caught by 4 men from Kefa village. The police were notified by telephone and took him to Chipata Prison. The headman told people not to beat him.

    Gilbert Zulu has come from Ndola to make bricks.

16. Kefa invites Chief Misholo to taste beer brewed by his fifth wife. The chief brought 7 men and they were all drinking in Kefa's yard.

18. Problems in Robert Manda's house: A tractor driver who is in love with Robert's daughter ploughed Robert's fields for free. Then the foreman of the tractor came and charged Robert K. 6 for the job. Today the owner of the tractor arrived. He was very angry and demanded K. 18 from Robert saying the job must have taken several days.

19. The police returned with Laimen Phiri to collect evidence for the murder case.
20. *M'meto* at Evelinar's house for the baby that died.
22. *Mlandu:* Accused: James Njobvu: plaintiff: Angrippina Sakala. About 10 people were present to solve the case. Mr. Njobvu had promised to make 8000 bricks, but now he refuses to make more than 3000 for the meat he has received worth K. 22.70. The case was solved by Kefa who asked Mr. Njobvu to pity the woman and help her make all the bricks, even if the payment was not enough.
23. Lubinda Mwale beat Kwezekani Mbewe on the head at night when Kwezekani came to Lubinda's house to complain about a dog that had killed 3 of his hens.
24. Kwezekani is taken by car to Chiparamba Clinic. In the evening he dies at Chipata General Hospital.
25. Lubinda is taken to Chipata Prison by a policeman (who happens to be his son-in-law who came to visit him in Kefa village).

   There is mourning in the village because of the death of Kwezekani. All arrangements for the funeral are done, but there is no crying because the body still has not come back from Chipata.
26. The body arrives at 2:30 P.M. and the funeral takes place, though Kwezekani's wife, Tiku Banda, has not yet come from Chipata.
27. Shuzi, Elisabeth Phiri, Esidol Mwale, Thomase Banda, Brandin Nkhoma, and Lomanzi Tembo, all Catholics from the Caritas group, went to a church meeting at Kalichero.
29. Today is the day of *cizimalupya*, the first rain that puts out the bush fires.
30. A lorry has come from Chipata to transport bricks. The bricks belong to Gilbert Zulu, Fatnes Manda, Isaac Phiri, and John Ngoma. Many people were involved in loading and unloading the bricks.

October

In the whole month of October water is very scarce. This is a time when dug-out wells less than 4 meters deep go dry. Women sometimes draw water in the middle of the night, thinking that there is more water at this hour.

During the month people spend increasingly more time in their fields. Those who have vegetable gardens really have a problem watering their plants.

2. Dorothy Banda gave birth to a daughter today, and many people have come to see her and the father, James Phiri.
3. Rachel Ngweni had a nightly visitor in her room. The visitor was a

teacher from Kamanga village. When he was caught and taken before the headman, he insulted the headman. Rachel is a member of our sociological team.

Mlandu: The teacher and Rachel are accused of bad behavior. The teacher's wife was also present and said her husband had a bad character.

5. IDZ coordinator and marketing officer came from Chipata. They wanted to see with their own eyes the progress of the building scheme. They were taken around by headman Kefa and Zindi Miti. They promised to send a lorry to transport bricks very soon.

6. Funeral in Kamanga village. Many Kefa village residents attended. Some stayed overnight.

   Police came to gather more evidence for the Laimen Phiri case.

   Kefa village residents were informed that a lorry would come tomorrow to carry bricks, and that they must be ready to assist in loading and unloading it.

7. People waited in vain for the lorry.

   Evelinar Njobvu and Faides Banda have gone to a maturity ceremony in Masupe village.

8. The lorry came this morning. Many women and also some men helped carry bricks.

   Beer at Esidon Mwale's house. 10–15 visitors are enjoying it.

   Mlandu: The case concerns problems between Gilbert Zulu and his wife. The wife is found guilty of bad behavior and warned not to repeat it.

9. People continue to drink beer at Esidon's house.

   The IDZ lorry came again and people are shifting bricks.

   Headman Kefa has employed two laborers to repair the door and to plaster a wall in Janet Lungu's house.

10. Men and women cooperate with the lorry and 8 loads of bricks have been carried to their owners.

    The District Governor and his staff came to Kefa village to discuss the work to be carried out during Humanism Week to celebrate the 24th of October (Independence Day).

    Shuzi has gone with his uncle to the Valley to hunt elephants.

    Tisauke Mwale, Zindi Miti's second wife, had a premature stillbirth today.

11. Women of the village went to bury the baby. Some men, like Simon Sakala, went to see Zindi to mourn with him.

12. The lorry carried bricks for Esidol and James Phiri. People are busy collecting firewood to burn in the kilns.

    James is selling tomatoes almost daily.

    Mwada Simba is brewing beer, which will be ready by Saturday.

Eliza Phiri is also brewing beer. Jessie Tonga is making *kavinde,* special secret beer that is not for sale, but only for her husband Kwerekani and his friends.

13. Shuzi is back from the hunt with meat.
14. The headman informs his villagers that the lorry will come tomorrow to take the youngmen to Mphomwa hills where they will cut poles for the new houses. Some men are told to stay in the village to help the women shift bricks, as the lorry will come back once the youngmen have been dropped in the forest.
15. Dynamo, the Kefa village football team, is playing against Kampheta village team. Dynamo won 2–1.

   Beer is sold at Micheck's house (Mwada's beer) and Zuwaila Zulu's.

   Lemekani Mbao has got a job as a bricklayer outside Kefa village.
16. The lorry came and took 8 youngmen to cut poles at Mphomwa hills. Then it returned and women and men were shifting bricks. Kefa informs the residents about Humanism Week. Government servants will assist in building model houses here in Kefa village and the women are told to contribute mealiemeal and relish. The men must also contribute relish to feed the visitors. Particularly those with vegetable gardens are asked to provide for the visitors.
17. Lemekani has returned from his new working place to say hello to friends and relatives.

   The District Governor and 8 officials have come to assist in building houses because of Humanism Week.
18. Meeting at 8:20 A.M. People are told to work hard and to accept the help of 4 visitors from outside who have come because of Humanism.

   Government lorry came to transport people who would go to the airport to greet President Kaunda. Micheck and some others went.
19. Mtole Mbao's house is being completed under the supervision of GRZ builder Mr. Tembo.

   Mr. Ezidon Zulu from Kamanga village is making 4 door frames for Kefa village brick houseowners. Each costs K. 1.50.

   Mlandu: The problem is a dog that Micheck has been looking after. The dog seems to belong to Matias, but he lost it 4 months ago. Now he wants it back, but Micheck charges K. 4 for having fed and kept the dog for so long. People who came to resolve the case agreed with Micheck. Matias must pay if he wants the dog. So Matias pays K. 4.
20. 4 government officers have come to do Humanism Work. They are roofing Zenaida Mwale's house.

   8 men worked on Sandikonda's house and 5 women drew water. Sandikonda shouted at them that they must draw more water.
21. *Milandu:* Residents are told to contribute mealiemeal and 10 ngwee for the Independence Feast at Chief Chikuwe's Palace. Farmers and

businessmen have been consulted and have agreed to paying K. 1. Some businessmen like Staff Mwanza have agreed to pay K. 2, K. 1 for the person and 50 ngwee for each wife.

22. The Reform Church of Zambia members with 9 participants from Kefa village and from other villages, have been gathering bricks from the fallen down church building outside Kefa village. They want to put up a new building.

   As they did last week, James and Simon went to Kamanga village to look for girls and to see *vibanda* dancing.

23. Everybody is washing clothes and preparing for the Independence celebrations tomorrow. People have already contributed mealiemeal and money.

   Kwerekani Phiri has called the father of his daughter's husband to pay the remaining marriage payments.

   Mlandu: Kwezekani Mbewe's widow is Tiku Banda. It was decided that Tiku stays in Kefa village for another year, to eat her maize. Then she will go home to her own village.

24. Independence Day: The festival ceremony was held at Kalichero Agricultural Station. The arrangement includes dances, football, and food. Some people brought their businesses—selling buns, sugar-canes, and medicines. Food was provided and water was supplied from a tap. Many people celebrated in the beer houses and beer halls in the area. About 6 P.M., Mwada Simba started beating Micheck, the husband, saying: "Why did you leave me behind? You have been with girls."

   In the evening it rained, a sign that the rainy season will start soon.

25. People seem to be resting after the celebrations yesterday. Some people have gone to the field to prepare their gardens.

26. Simon Sakala came to report to Kefa that from now on the village building groups work morning and afternoons every second day.

27. A man from outside came today to ask the headman if he can settle for some time in Kefa village to carry out his business, which is to carve mortars and pestles.

   There was a football match at the Kefa sportsground. Dynamo lost 3-1.

30. It is raining very hard, and people stay inside or visit neighbors in their houses, waiting for the rain to stop.

31. Now, with the first rains, everybody is clearing their fields.

   Some people like Jessie Tonga and Zenaida Mwale were heard pounding their maize in the middle of the night to avoid doing this hard work in the heat of the day.

   There is a funeral in Kamanga village and most Kefa village residents have gone to mourn at the funeral. Just a few stay because they have some urgent work to do, like Titamenji Nkhoma, who is pounding.

November

November is a very busy month. By the end of the month the maize is sprouting and people start to weed. At the same time Kefa village residents are in a hurry to complete their houses, as the rain threatens to wear them down.

The presence of Water Affairs workers is disturbing the daily doings in the village. Some of the workers have brought their women and children, and others seem to want to marry Kefa girls.

Cattle and goats have to be herded as they cannot roam around without supervision.

Many people get up early and work all day before they eat at night.

1. Rose Nyirenda from Kamanga village is possessed by *vibanda* spirits who claim to have caused her miscarriage. Titambenji Mwale and Square Banda from Kefa village have gone to help her.
2. Shuzi Zulu went to Lusaka to learn how to drive a car and be employed as a driver.
3. Andrick Banda's house is under construction. 7 men work on it, supervised by Mr. Tembo.

   Kefa village is visited by Elfasi Phiri, a handlemaker and blacksmith who will do various jobs for money.

   People are busy preparing for the agricultural season. The men are preparing their tools. Micheck is carving an axe handle, James Njobvu is making ox-yokes and others set their hoes and maize and groundnut bins in order.

   The women are busy in the field hoeing and preparing to plant. The Water Affairs people came today to start boring for water, as part of the model village project. The headman organizes the youngmen to cut the trees and clear the place for the boring. The Water Affairs people have put up their tents and will live here at the outskirts of the village.
4. Caritas Church Group brought fertilizers with a tractor to Mr. Manda's house. The fertilizers are for the Caritas members in the village. Robert Manda is their leader. Members are Rosemary Lungu, Misauel Phiri, Enelesi Mawarela, and some others.
5. The marriage between Jones Mwale and Bernadette Tembo was celebrated today. Marriage payments amounted to K. 190. There was chicken as relish and plenty of beer.
6. Lemekani Mbao has now stopped working as a builder outside the

village. Today he reminded the headman that cattle owners who keep their animals in Kefa's herd must now take over responsibility for their animals. As crops have started growing, people must herd their own animals.

7. There is beer at Kefa Mwale's house. Close friends like Micheck Phiri and many others are invited to drink.

   11 houses have been roofed.

8. Kefa calls people together to find out why the Southern section group does not help Lomanzi to build her house. The group promises to improve their performance.

   The headman also informs about the registration of grade 1 schoolchildren at Mtewe School. Parents with children must go to the school to present themselves. He notifies people that the following day he will go to Chief Chikuwe's court with headman Nyanthani who has grabbed his land.

   Robert Manda had his field ploughed by tractor.

9. Milicka Mwanza has packed her things and gone to Lusaka. (People say that she usually does so at this time, when fieldwork is getting fierce.)

   The headman and some other men from Kefa village have gone to Chief Chikuwe's Court. According to Mr. Kefa, Chindola and Nyanthani villages were given permission to build their villages next to Kefa's but they should clear land outside the Kefa village land. Now it has been found that some villagers are using Kefa village land.

   Robert Manda is selling goat meat. One of his goats died after being trapped in the cattle kraal.

   Two carpenters from Chipata Rural Council have been sent by the District Governor to roof model houses. They brought 162 asbestos sheets for the roofs.

   Mlandu: Zindi Miti accuses Faidani Daka and John Banda of ambushing him. The two passed him in his plantation, without saying *"zikomo."* The group present and Mr. Kefa warned people to say *zikomo* when approaching anybody's place. They also warned Mr. Daka and Mr. Banda not to repeat their mistake.

10. A poultry farmer has come to negotiate some land from Mr. Kefa.

    Mlandu: A letter has come from the Community Development saying that the villagers must buy their own nails, ridges and wire.

    Two new *indunas* (deputy headmen) are chosen by the meeting. They are Jackson Phiri and Penelani Khosa.

11. Some women have decided to buy their own nails (in spite of the meeting yesterday).

    A message is received that a lorry will come on Saturday.

Lemekani has decided to train Kefa villagers to become house builders. He and three apprentices are now building his house without the help of a GRZ builder.

Rain fell yesterday and everybody is busy preparing seeds for planting.

12. The lorry came and carried only three loads. Simon Sakala and some others refused to shift bricks. They have gone to their fields.

13. An Asian came to buy an ox from Mr. Manda, but he left without buying.

14. Evelinar Njobvu was beating on Margret Banda's drum. After a short time, she stopped.

There is a lot of rain these days.

15. Dynamo football team did piecework in Zenaida Mwale's maize field. She paid them K. 5.

3 Asians came to buy goats. One goat belonged to Zindi Miti's wife, but Zindi pocketed the money. Micheck, Thomase, and Penelani helped the Asians load the goats onto their lorry and were thanked with 20 ngwee each.

16. The Asian who wanted to buy Mr. Manda's oxen returned today. He brought roofing, nails, and cash so it seemed they had reached an agreement.

The Water Affairs people did not work today because they had no fuel and no water to use when boring.

17. Zalenji Mwale's and Robert Manda's houses were roofed.

Nasom Phiri came with oxen and transported a drum of water to Gilbert's house construction.

At night a vehicle got a flat tire just outside the village. There were 5 male and 5 female passengers plus children. They were accommodated in Staff Mwanza's house.

18. Medical Assistant from Chiparamba Health Centre came to talk about preventive health. He warned people not to throw things around, but to make a pit for wastage and to make pit latrines.

For the past days 3 women residents were making beer to raise money for their houses.

19. *Mlandu:* Rahaby Sakala accuses the husband James Njobvu of being a poor provider. Micheck has been appointed negotiator.

21. Kaondwa Kangachepa slaughtered a pig to pay people who will work for him.

22. Kefa has employed people from outside to work on Gilbert's house. He has also asked his brother Lemekani to book the Mechanization Unit Tractor to plough his fields after the 29th.

A child at the Water Affairs Camp in Kefa village died.

Mlandu: Kefa accuses Mishael Mpasi of being uncooperative. Mishael is fined K. 4 by the Deputy Chief.

23. People from other villages and Kefa village residents mourn the Water Affairs child.

    The water in the dug-out well is now so dirty that people have stopped using it. Instead the women go to a well 2 km away.

24. Kefa calls people to warn them that goats and cows must be herded, because the maize has started to germinate.

    Mlandu: Faides Daka took her children and left her husband, who lived in Lusaka. Now the husband wants to divorce her.

25. Mr. Poison Daka, the owner of Soft Grocery, has been summoned to the local court, because of a land dispute. Many Kefa villagers have gone to follow the case.

26. Mishael Mpasi's house is being roofed.

27. Fatnes Mbewe and James Phiri went to church to pray.

    Beer is sold at Nabien Banda's. About 40 people are drinking there. Many come from the Water Affairs camp. As it is Sunday, people want to enjoy themselves.

    A football match should have been played, but Mkule football team did not turn up, so the Dynamo members just played between themselves.

28. The Water Affairs people have struck water, at 40 m.

    People are waiting for the IDZ lorry, which did not come.

29. The men gathered awaiting transport to take them to Mphomwa Hill to cut poles. Afterward, bricks were transported. 12 women and 5 men loaded and unloaded the bricks.

    Kefa Mwale went on Lemekani's bicycle together with Micheck Phiri and his fifth wife Nyamanda to Mgubudu in Chief Chanje's area to settle a dispute in court with the former husband of Nyamanda.

30. Abel Ngoma does piecework for Lelia Mbewe, making a new roof for her maize bin.

    The Water Affairs people are testing the water pump in the new bore hole.

    For the whole week nobody has made beer. It seems that people have started to economize their maize. But today Mwanishupa Phiri's beer is ready for sale.

December

December is the month of intensive fieldwork. The rain keeps falling and everything grows. It is also the time when crops must be watched against monkeys.

1. *Kacasu* is on sale in the village. 1 bottle costs 60 ngwee.
2. Kabanda Nyuni refused to be observed any more by the sociological

survey team. Many people heard his loud complaint. *Mlandu* was held and after some time Kabanda accepted that we continue to observe him.

4. The village men are working to clean the roofing poles that were brought last week.

Mwada Simba wants to run away from the husband who has been beating her all night.

6. People have started ridging their groundnut fields.

8. Village residents are spending their days in the field because monkeys have come to spoil their crops.

10. Some people work in Sonile's and Andrick's fields with beer as payment.

11. Beer is sold at Zuwaila's house.

12. Heavy rain in the morning kept people from fieldwork.

13. Though it is Sunday, most people have gone to their fields.

Dynamo played against Kapara and lost.

14. People from Chipata market have come to buy bananas from Zindi Miti.

16. Most people are away all day in their fields. Some have gone to drink *kacasu*—liquor—in Kamanga village.

19. Most villagers have weeded for the first time, and some are busy weeding for the second time.

People have stopped buying relish because their fields provide them with enough fresh ochra leaves, green leaves, etc.

There is less work now. The men stop work before the women, who remain behind to pick relish.

20. Jessie Tonga employed about 10 people, mostly relatives, to clear away grass and weed. They were paid with sweet beer.

23. People are preparing for Christmas, washing their clothes and looking for cash.

25. Christmas: Some village residents have gone to Kachenga to the funeral of the beer hall owner in Chiparamba, some to the church to celebrate Christmas, some to their field. In the evening people entertained themselves with beer and dancing. Those who had money to spare drink tea and eat bread.

26. Tisabenji Daka is making beer at Jesinao's house. Her own house is too small.

27. Faides Phiri gave premature birth and the baby was stillborn. The women buried the baby.

28. Most village residents are busy weeding, and nobody is seen in the village.

29. *Milochi*—the rain that pours continuously. Housebuilding has stopped for two weeks so that people can do fieldwork.

30. *Mlandu:* The problem is the disappearance of 14 hens and 10 eggs from villages around Kefa village. 20 people are present, all men.

Dorothy Banda arrived back today. She has been in her home village since December 23.

January

In January and February people are busy in their fields, weeding and guarding crops. Some men have established vegetable gardens growing tomatoes, rape, and cabbage. Some also have time to repair their possessions. Women brew beer even now in the wet season.

1. There is a dance at Kawaza village to the music of saxophones. At Chikuwe village there are traditional *chimtali* dances.

    Kefa Mwale and Robert Manda (or rather their wives) have beer, which is given out for free.
3. Beer at Kefa's house.
4. Sandikonda Daka killed a snake just outside his house.
7. People are working in their plots also on Sundays. Monkeys are creating a problem.

    Some residents have gone to the church this afternoon.
9. Dynamo boys are doing piecework at Msekera. Lefati Phiri is selling hoe handles that he made himself.

    Rain filled Mtewe River this afternoon and those cultivating on the other side could not cross before midnight, when the water was down a bit.
10. The IDZ coordinator and some other Europeans come to look at the model houses.

    Headman Kefa slaughtered a sheep for his granddaughter, who is marrying in Chimumba village.
14. Micheck, Mwada, Evelinor, and Faides went to Kapita hills looking for mushrooms.
15. A football match was played. Many people were present. They have left their fields, fearing that the river will swell again so that they would not get home.
16. Because of rains, the builders did not make any houses.
17. A Medical Assistant has come to the village to talk about tsetse flies and dirty water.
18. *Milochi:* Only women are out. They are looking for relish.
20. Kefa and Yanzulani exchange a cow for a bull.
21. Headman Kefa informed his residents of a funeral at Mcacha village, and that surveyors will come to Kefa village and the village residents must feed them.

Beer was sold at Sandikonda's house, brewed by Jackson's wife.

22. Mwanishupa's beer is brewing, and customers insisted on drinking her beer, even if it was not ready. As is the custom, Mwanishupa gave the headman a gourd for free.

25. Mr. Mumba, the new Community Development Assistant from Kapara, has come to introduce himself. From now on, he is responsible for the housing project.

26. A few people who have finished the difficult part of farming are now planting sweet potatoes.

   Yanzulani's son has been killed in a car accident in Lusaka.

27. People come to mourn at Yanzulani's house.

28. Headman Kefa informs his residents about two funerals. Donations collected amounted to 48 ngwee.

29. Kwerekani is selling pig meat to buy mealiemeal from Chipata.

30. Rumors say that the death message received by Yanzulani was false.

31. It was raining all night and Square Banda's house is full of water so he did not sleep.

February

1. People go to attend to the Mobile Mail Van, which comes every Wednesday to Dalala stores. Zuwaila Zulu, Zalenji Mwale, Tilele Zulu, and Simon Sakala are some of the people who save money at the Mobile Post Office.

2. Zuwaila Zulu and Lucien Tembo have gone to attend the Parent Teacher Association meeting at Mtewe School.

   Agnes Banda's husband's mother in Malawi has died. People come to their house to give their condolences.

5. After a break, house building has started again.

8. *Mlandu:* Micheck's working group does not function well. Only the women in the group seem to cooperate. The men were told to improve their ways and work with Micheck and the women on Micheck's house.

10. Cattle were taken to Chief Chikuwe's court where a cattle dip has been installed.

13. All the headmen in the area have been called to a UNIP (United National Independence Party) meeting at Chiparamba. They are informed about the election that will take place this year. They are also told to improve the performance of the Productivity Committees. (In Kefa village the Village Productivity Committee is nonfunctioning.) About 100 people were present at the meeting, almost all of them men.

   In Kefa village the residents are worrying about Ifenso Phiri, the deadly ill son of John Scout, who has been taken to Kapara Health Centre.

14. *Mlandu:* Penelani Khosa complains that the elders do not attend funerals.
15. Mourning at John Scout's house because of the death of Ifenso.

    Europeans have come to see the model village.

    Ifenso is buried. Many people from neighboring villages came and left again as they had two funerals to participate in. After the funeral people went to guard their crops.

    A message was received from Chipata that the Minister of Agriculture will come to see Kefa Model village.
16. The Minister, the District Governor, and the IDZ coordinator with many staff visited Kefa village and saw one model house.
17. People are attending to their fieldwork, but because it is very hot they only guard for monkeys. Green maize and pumpkins are now ripening.

    The Dynamo boys cut grass in the football yard.
18. *M'meto* (hair-cutting ceremony) held at Kwerekani's house for the boy Ifenso.
19. Timeke Daka is brewing secret beer for a youngman who intends to marry her daughter.
22. Some villagers have gone to Mtewe school to elect a new representative for the Mtewe UNIP branch.

    Others have gone to funerals as there are three funerals in neighboring villages.

March

By the end of March, the maize is getting dry and monkeys are no longer a problem. There is not much work in the fields. Women are busy drying relish, which they store to eat in the dry season.

1. Headman Mphindila died and was buried today.

    Housebuilding has stopped because of excessive rains.
2. The sun is shining again and women are busy drying relish to store for the dry season.

    Many people complain about malaria fevers and headaches.
3. *Mlandu:* James Njobvu is requested to pay K. 30 as damage money for Rahaby Sakala.
4. Beer sale at Daresia Banda's. 34 beer drinkers have come. Most of them are men.

    Kacasu is also sold in the village. 1 bottle is now 70 ngwee.
5. The Reform Church of Zambia held a meeting in Katelina Daka's house in order to ask the headman to give them land where they can have their own churchyard.

Dynamo played against Msukwala village team and won!

7. Some Europeans from IDZ have come again to see a model house. They are taken around by Mr. Kefa.

8. *Milochi:* People take advantage of their new houses and collect rain water from the asbestos sheets.

13. It has been raining hard for 3 days and not much work has been done.

14. Kakoche Mwale died. The village is mourning. The villagers, mostly men and relatives, stay in the funeral house at night.

15. Funeral preparations. 200 visitors come.

16. Kakoche is buried. 1000 mourners follow him to the grave.

17. With the assistance of Ticoke, Regina Shawa, Kefa's third wife, is brewing beer.

18. Beer is sold at Regina's house. About 50 people have come to drink.
    Women are busy drying relish.

19. Dynamo boys have gone to play against Mulire village team.
    M'meto at Kefa Mwale's house.
    Mlandu: Kefa Mwale is accused of not conducting his father's funeral properly.
    As it is Sunday, some people have gone to church.

20. Bernadette Tembo gives birth to her firstborn.

24. Kamanga village residents complain that Kefa cattle have grazed in their fields. They report the case to Headman Kefa, asking for compensation.

25. *Mlandu:* Cattle trespassing. Eliza accuses cattle owners. A big tree has fallen down in the village, and the headman asks the men to take their axes and chop it up.

26. Chief Deputy, Headman Kefa, and Kefa village residents have come together to release Tiku Banda (Kwezekani's widow) with *nzuzulo* so that she can go home to her own village.

27. *Mlandu:* Marriage troubles between Rahabe Sakala and the husband James Njobvu are discussed.

29. Mr. Mumba, Community Development Assistant, has come to make a speech about the housing scheme to Kefa village residents. 20 men and 2 builders attended.

30. Beer sale at Lelia Mbewe's house. Customers were more numerous than usual as some men had come from Kalichero Agricultural Station.

31. Some men have started making *nkhokwe* for the coming harvest. *Chimtali* was danced at Margret Banda's house in the evening. Most women in Kefa village attended, and some men came to watch.
    People from the Rural Information Department came to tape information about Kefa model village. Everybody gathered to give information to be broadcast all over Zambia.

April

In April the rain is subsiding and the maize is drying. People start harvesting, storing their maize in granary bins. Now the *dambo* gardens are drying and are ready for use. Some youngmen grow vegetables for sale. When the maize is dry enough to be transported to the village, grass is also dry enough to be used to thatch roofs. April is almost the dry season and some men hunt for bush animals and mice.

1. Kefa, Sandikonda, Tikoce, and others are drinking beer at Lelia's house. Angrippina and others have gone for *m'meto* at Taswela village. Others are busy making houses. Women are cooking, pounding, and washing.
2. James Phiri, Stephen Phiri, and Thomase Banda have found three roasted chickens that were stolen by Chitani Moyo. The chickens are taken to the headman, who will decide later what to do about the theft.
3. Kefa and Lelia Mbewe have gone to Chipata. Micheck and Mwada have gone to Lundazi.

   A vehicle brought mealiemeal for sale. Whoever had cash bought some.
5. Headman Kefa rang his bell and informed his residents that a meeting would be held at the Chief's Palace.

   As there was a funeral in Chiwayo, some villagers spent the night there.
6. Beer is ready at Nyokasa's house.

   A few Kefa residents have gone to attend the Chief's meeting.

   Ms. Jere, a Community Development Assistant, visited Kefa village to register the progress of the housing scheme. She brought some Europeans.
7. A meeting was called to inform the residents that two women must go to Kalichero Training Center and learn domestic science, which they can later teach their fellow women in the village.

   About 40 people are drinking beer at Nyokasa's house. Most of the beer drinkers are women. The men have gone to some other house to drink.
10. The Water Affairs people have left the village to go elsewhere to look for water. Vast Manda has been left by her Water Affairs husband.

    Mwanishupa started harvesting groundnuts today. Cotton also is being harvested. All growers are busy in the fields.

    Lemekani Mbao has been booked by Mtunduwatu to repair her pigeon house.
12. Gilbert Zulu has come from Ndola to mourn his great-grandfather Kakoche, who died.

At a village meeting the headman informs his residents that the IDZ lorry will come to transport bricks, and that the Chief does not accept that any of his residents distill *kacasu.*

13. People are repairing their granary bins. Some have started to harvest maize.

    Villagers with a registration card have to register at Mtewe School to be able to vote in the presidential election.

14. Kefa sends Penelani Khosa, Margret Mbao, Lemekani Mwale, Mtole Mbao, and some other very close relatives to take Gilbert to see his great-grandfather's grave.

17. Schoolchildren are back in the village on holiday.

    Eliza Phiri has started making beer. Regina Shawa, Tilemekeze Daka and Nyamanda help her draw water.

    Lemekani Mbao, Zuwaila Zulu, Isaac Phiri, and Esidol Mwale have gone to Chiparamba with a Member of the Central Committee to attend a meeting in Lusaka.

18. *Mphasi*—small biting ants—have forced Margret Mwale and Aida Mbewe to quit their old huts.

    John Poison, Georg Zulu, and Joseph Mwale are three youngmen who make maize bins to sell for money.

19. Kefa calls a meeting: Only residents with a valid registration card are allowed to stay in the village. He also informs village residents that Health Department Staff will visit the village tomorrow and everybody must be present.

20. The bell is rung early in the morning. The villagers are told to produce their registration cards. They will be listed by the headman, who will give the list to the Chief, as requested by the UNIP people at Chiparamba.

24. Meeting: Fatnes Manda and Betina Tembo, who have been trained in how to run a woman's club, are back from their course and exhibit dresses and things they have made. Women were informed that a Kefa Women's Club would be started. Entrance fee is 50 ngwee.

25. Kefa's fifth wife is brewing beer. This week beer has been on sale every day somewhere inside the village.

    A tractor came to shift bricks and people helped as the headman ordered.

May

In May vegetables are grown and cash crops are harvested and packed. People cut grass, hunt mice, and finish their various jobs in the field.

1. Villagers are asked to harvest faster so that they can proceed with the house building.

Milk-selling business in the village seems to grow. Robert, Kefa, and Kwerekani sell milk regularly.

2. People are very busy in the field, but today many have returned home early to attend the funeral of Grace Daka.

3. People were waiting for the tractor to shift bricks, but it never came.

4. Kefa Women's Club met for the first time. During the meeting the headman asked the women to harvest Betina's and Fatnes' field because they had been away on a course for two weeks. 16 women participated.

Mlandu: Zuwaila Zulu wants to leave Kefa village and has sold his bricks.

6. Some people have formed working groups to transport each others' maize from the field to the village. They are all women.

7. The problems of John Scout Phiri and Rosemary Banda and of Zuwaila and Lire have been solved by headman Kefa and the village residents.

8. Today, yesterday, and the day before yesterday, the tractor was here to shift bricks. 10–15 Kefa villagers helped, most of them women.

10. Robert Manda sold a cow to Chipata butchery.

Zuwaila and wife and some other village residents have gone to Chief Chikuwe's court to settle the problem of Zuwaila's bricks.

Kefa Women's Club held its first proper meeting at Tikambenji Mwale's house. The first lesson was skirtmaking. The teachers were two female extension workers from Kalichero. 26 women attended.

17. Two Asians came to buy a goat, but nobody in Kefa village wanted to sell, so they left.

18. People are busy getting the maize in the *nkhokwe*. Lubinda's and Nason Phiri's oxen are hired for transport. Some women use headloads.

Some men are busy in their vegetable gardens.

20. Lire Banda (Zuwaila's wife) has been granted bricks and today she shifts them to her house site.

Men wait for the tractor to go and cut more poles.

21. Though it is Sunday people are as busy as on work days.

In the afternoon there was to be a football match, but the other team did not show up.

22. The Women's Club was visited by Chiparamba Community Development Assistant.

23. People from Mtolo, Chimdola, Kamanga, and Kamphera villages have come to Kefa village to play cards for money.

25. James Njobvu used Robert Manda's oxen and his own self-made cart to transport people's bricks for money.

26. A cotton demonstrator from the Agricultural Camp came to visit Kefa village cotton growers.

27. Lemekani woke up late because he played cards all night from around 6 P.M. until morning.

28. 10 men cut poles at Mphomwa Hill. Later men and women took the bark off and cleaned the poles.

Fatnes Manda, Esidole Mwale, and Regina Shawa hired a tractor to transport their maize and paid K. 6 for a load.

30. Kamaswanda Njobvu the basketmaker went to the Valley to collect plants for his basket making. The plants are picked for free in the bush.

June

In June the late workers are in a hurry to bring their crops home. Any day now the bush fires will be started by youngsters or others. They are eager to go hunting for mice or other small animals to supplement their vegetable diet. The successful farmers will soon have filled their granary bins and women are preparing beer from their surplus maize. The men relax in the village or visit friends in other villages.

1. Yesterday the grandson of Kefa's fifth wife died, and people have gone to Kamanga village for the funeral.
2. Catholic church members have gone to a two-day meeting at Kalichero to meet with the Bishop of Chipata and Eastern Province.
4. It is Sunday. The boys are playing football, and the Women's Club members are playing netball at Kefa sports grounds.
5. A lorry came to transport men to cut poles, but most Kefa village residents have gone to a funeral at Mcache village.
6. Most Kefa residents have finished harvesting and are busy making bricks.
7. Women's Club met for sewing lesson given by the leader Fatnes Manda, aided by Ms. Mbewe, the government teacher from Kalichero Training Centre.

   Police came to notify Kefa Mwale and other witnesses that the case of Lubinda Mwale and Laimen Phiri will be judged on June 12.
8. Some villagers were sent to attend a meeting with the Chief. They are told that the Chief refuses people to drink *kacasu*—liquor.
9. Bushfires have started. Young people went to hunt mice. Most people are not happy because they have not yet had time to collect grass for their roofs, and some have not even finished harvesting their maize.
10. Tilele Zulu has gone to Lusaka and Kitwe to see her grandchildren, who are ill.

    The police came with a Landrover to pick up witnesses for the murder cases. 9 men and women were brought from Kefa village.

    An army officer came to buy a goat.
13. Numero, Faides Phiri's son, has been admitted to Chiparamba clinic with measles.

16. Rothia Sakala, the daughter of Simon Sakala and Tisalire Banda, died of measles. Village residents mourn.
17. Funeral in Kefa village.
19. The Dynamo boys have made a vegetable garden to earn money for their team.

    Cattle owners have now released their cattle to graze wherever they want. Today 28 cattle were observed in Zindi Miti's field.
20. Villagers visit Headman Kefa to learn about the judgments in Chipata Magistrate Court concerning the murder cases.
21. Water Affairs people have come back to lay pipelines from the bore hole to the center of the village.

    A European from IDZ came to inspect the Women's Club.
22. Kefa Mwale, Simon Tonga, Fatnes Manda (for Robert), Bernhard Mwale (for Kathontho), and Lemekani Mbao went with people from Kamanga village to settle a case of cattle trespassing at Chief Chikuwe's Court.
23. Kabanda Nyuni was selling pork.

    Beer at Aledi Phiri's house.
26. News is received that Lubinda Mwale has been released from prison and admitted at Mwami Hospital.
28. Water Affairs lorry has brought cement and bricks to construct a pump house and water tank.
29. Catholic Church members have gone to do piece work at Gia's Store. The money will be kept by the church.

    Most people are washing their clothes and preparing to go to the annual Chiparamba Agricultural Show.
30. Agricultural Show: The Women's Club members have taken their best sewing and clay pots to exhibit at the show. Most young Kefa people have gone to Chiparamba to participate in the show, which will last until late at night.

Postscript

Brighton reports about Lubinda Mwale:

"Lubinda was released from prison. After one week in the hospital the old man came back home to Kefa village where he slaughtered a very fine cow to celebrate his release. Some of the meat he gave to the headman and to Kefa's wives. Some of the meat he sold to people passing by on the road. Some village residents wanted to buy meat from Lubinda, but as they did not know how to approach the slayer of their kinsman Kwezekani Mbewe, they never came forward.

"The close family members of Kwezekani Mbewe were very uneasy about seeing Lubinda back in the village. They went to headman Kefa and stated that if Lubinda were to stay in the village, every day they would face the killer of a beloved family member. Because Kefa did not know what to say, he went to ask advice from the Chief. The Chief told him to go home and discuss the matter with the families involved, and Kefa then called the Lubinda family and the family of Kwezekani Mbewe as well as village elders.

"At the meeting, the Mbewe family members repeated that they would not stay in the same village as the slayer of their kinsman. And headman Kefa spoke to Lubinda and said: 'Please, Mr. Lubinda, Kefa village residents used to love you very much. But as you happened to kill one of them, our villagers now fear you, thinking that you may kill some of them again, as you already killed one of them. That is why we ask you now to leave us, to go to some other place.' And Lubinda agreed without arguing to leave Kefa village. He was old and had no strength to discuss. Kefa also asked him to go alone, not to take any family members with him. They had not killed anyone, and they were friends and relatives of other village residents. Again Lubinda accepted what headman Kefa said, but he also said that if any of his family would come with him, he would not mind.

"As Lubinda prepared his departure, it turned out that his relatives also prepared to go. They stopped making bricks and building houses.

"At this point the Deputy Chief, Mr. M'Kunduwavu, heard what was about to happen in Kefa village. He called Headman Kefa and asked him why this case of expulsion had been conducted without his presence and why the headman had not informed him?

"Kefa answered: 'I did not inform you, but I informed the Chief, and he gave me permission to discuss the matter at home with the families of Kwezekani and Lubinda. The Chief also said that I should come and inform him of the decisions taken at the meeting.'

"But the Deputy Chief said: 'You have no right in resolving such a case without my presence, or that of the Chief. Now it is necessary that we reopen the case and discuss the matter over again.'

"When Lubinda came back from looking for a village where he and his family could move, the Deputy Chief was called and a new *mlandu* was held. The Deputy Chief said that they had come together again because the decision of the previous meeting was taken without the permission of the Chief, though it was a matter of expelling a village resident. Then he pointed out that Lubinda had already got his punishment. He had been in the prison for more than one year, away from family and friends. As everybody present could see, Lubinda had suffered in the prison. He was an old man. He was certainly no threat to anyone. At the same time he recognized the pain of the family members of Kwezekani. Now, Kwezekani's children were orphaned, had no parents and no one to help them.

"To settle this case once and for all,' said the Deputy Chief, 'let Lubinda and his family stay as part of the village. They had lived here for so many years, they were even related to the Mbewe family, and to that of the head-man. But let them repent and help the relatives of the man who died by paying three cattle to them.'

"And that is what happened."

GLOSSARY

amai	mother; includes the biological mother, her sisters, and the father's brother's wives
amai ang'ongo	"little mother": niece; or any young female relative
ambuye	grandparents; or any elderly relative
antu a maliro	"the people of the funeral": mourners
aphungu	the wise elderly women; specifically, a woman's advisors during childbirth
aphwa	nephew
atate	father; includes the biological father, his brothers and the mother's husbands if she has remarried
atsibweni	the mother's brothers
bwlao	the meeting place where *mlandu* are conducted
chabwino	okay
chamlomo	a small cash gift from a boy's family to a person negotiating a marriage
chibwabwa	pounded and roasted maize eaten by people with poor or no teeth
chidima	being unable to find a new mate after the death of a spouse
chidulu	ash water—an alkaline solution—used to soften and give flavor to leafy vegetables; made from burned groundnut leaves
chidumu	damage money (from *dumula*, to do something unexpectedly for someone)
chikomboli	pans used in brick-making (pl. *vikomboli*)
chikwati	a big basket (pl. *vikwati*)
chimalo	bride wealth
chimbala	"maize that has slept": leftover *nsima* eaten the next day
chimtali	a women's dance
chinya	beer on the fifth day of its brewing; enjoyed very much by women and children who do not drink the regular beer with its full alcohol content

chitenge	a piece of printed cloth
chitundu	a type of deep basket used for food storage
chiwanda	one of two types of spirits; dance spirit (pl. *viwanda*)
cimanga	maize; the staple crop
cizimalupya	the first rain that puts out the brush fire
dambo	wetland by a river
delele	ochra leaves, used as relish for *nsima*
dengo	a type of deep basket used for food storage
dimba	a small vegetable garden
dowi	"English-style" cooking involving the addition of tomatoes and onions
dyonkho	a free taste of beer
dzinja	the growing season, roughly November to April
fisi	hyena; associated with *mifiti*
foula	a type of gourd thought necessary to be avoided during pregnancy
fushala	boiled dried maize
induna	deputy headman
kacamba	sweet potatoes
kacasu	liquor made from maize husks and sugar
kamaswanda	basket; also the name of the village basketmaker
kapenta	a small, tasty, and inexpensive dried fish brought to the village by itinerant fishmongers
kavinde	the secret beer made in small quantities to attract and please husbands and best friends
khola	cattle enclosure
kudya	to eat; used also to call pigs: "*kudya, kudya, kudya*"
kuikijya	the "putting out system"; a system of keeping and looking after other people's animals, or having friends or relatives look after yours, with many social and economic benefits
kunyinda	a special ceremony sometimes following a funeral and the *m'meto* to protect remaining relatives against the spirit of the deceased
Kwacha	the primary unit of currency; in 1979 the value of the *Kwacha* was about U.S. $1—in 1989 it was less than 10 cents
licelo	a type of shallow basket used for sieving maize and carrying small amounts of flour and groundnut powder

lobola	a payment in addition to *chimalo*—bride price—paid to transfer the right to children from the mother's lineage to the father's
madimbi	a children's game in which little boys and girls act as a married couple
malimwe	the gardener's off-season, from May to October
maliro	funeral
malodza	message of a death in a neighboring village
manda	grave; also a clan name
mankhwala	medicine
masese	"the seven-day's beer": named because it takes five days to make it and two days to drink it
mashanga	picking up leftovers from the fields
mawele	fingermillet; used in beer brewing
mbatacice	Irish potatoes
mbwelela	the second weeding of the season
mfiti	a person who has acquired the knowledge of what in the West would be called black magic (as opposed to a more benevolent white magic)
mfumu	chief
milochi	the all-day rains of the rainy season
mlandu	a meeting for discussion of some claim or right, lawsuit or quarrel
m'meto	the haircutting ceremony that follows shortly after a funeral
mowa	beer made from germinated maize
mowa wapya	new beer, after five-and-a-half days of brewing
mphanje	a newly opened field
mphala	a special meeting place
mphindule	fields that have produced for several years
mpongozi	mother-in-law
msele	a food made from the very small grains that are left when the maize has been pounded twice; cooked with salt, sugar, and mashed groundnuts
mtawa	beer on the first day of its brewing; it is sweet and can be drunk
mteteka	the water in which maize has been allowed to soak and germinate (germination increases the vitamin B content of the maize); used to make porridge or soup, to brew beer, or to feed animals

mudzi	village
mugwilizamu	cooperation
mvula	rain; also a clan name
mzimu	one of two types of spirits; "the spirit of the departed" (pl. *mizimu*); see also *chiwanda*
ndinda	field shelter
ng'anga	a traditional healer and diviner
ngwee	there are 100 *ngwee* in a *Kwacha*
njala	hunger
njobvu	elephant; also a clan name
nkhokwe	granary bins made of bamboo woven into a cylinder
nkhoswe	wise older friend or relative who serves as marriage counselor
nkhunyu	"the falling sickness": epilepsy
nongo	a clay pot used to drink beer
nshawa	groundnuts; also a clan name
nsima	boiled mealiemeal (ground maize); the staple food
nsuzulo	divorce token, these days usually a small coin
nthayo	a "cold" human being
ntwilo	pounded groundnuts
otentha	a "warm" human being
palila	the first weeding of the growing season
pepani	"I am sorry"
phala	porridge made from water in which maize has been soaked for a couple of days
phiri	hill; also a clan name
shawa	groundnuts; also a clan name
tate wamkazi	the father's sisters
thobwa	beer on the second day of its brewing; can be drunk
tuyobela	the "somber art" of the *mifiti*
unjise	an illness that can strike the last-born if the mother becomes pregnant again too soon; *kwashiorkor*
utaogoleli	leadership
vikomboli	pans used in brick-making

vikwati	dried bundles of vegetables and green leaves to be used as relish during the dry season
wakufu	a still-born infant
zikhuzo	"the hearing": after a funeral, the village meeting for the official explanation of the cause of death
zikomo	a common greeting; also "please" and "thank you"

BIBLIOGRAPHY

Boserup, E. 1970. *Woman's Role in Economic Development.* New York: St. Martin's Press.

Bruwer, J.P. 1948. "Kinship Terminology Among the Cewa of the Eastern Province of Northern Zambia." *African Studies,* December 1948:185–187.

Bruwer, J.P. 1955. "Unkhoswe: The System of Guardianship in Cewa Matrilineal Society." *African Studies,* Vol. 12, No. 3 (1955):113–122.

Dahlschen, E. 1970. *Women in Zambia.* Lusaka: NECZAM.

Ehlers, J., and J. Child, ed. 1975. *Songs of Zambia.* Lusaka: Longman.

Elliot, C.M., et al. 1970. *Some Determinants of Agricultural Labour Productivity in Zambia.* Universities of Nottingham and Zambia, Agricultural Labour Productivity Investigation.

Government of Zambia. 1969. *Census of Population and Housing.* Lusaka: Government Printer.

Government of Zambia. 1973. *Intensive Development Zone Progressive Survey.* Lusaka: Government Printer.

Government of Zambia. 1973. *Third National Development Plan 1973–83.* Lusaka: Office of the President.

Government of Zambia. 1975. *Crop Memo.* Lusaka: Department of Agriculture, Research Branch.

Hall, R. 1976. *Zambia 1890–1964.* London: Longman.

Harvey, R.H. 1973. *Some Determinants of the Agricultural Productivity of Rural Households—A Report of a Survey in Kalichero District, Eastern Province.* Ministry of Rural Development, Mesekera Regional Research Station, Chipata, Zambia.

Hedlund, H. 1973. *A Survey of 199 Village Headmen in Chipata District.* Chipata: Intensive Development Zone Programme.

Hedlund, H. 1975. *A Study of Artisans in Chipata District.* Chipata: Intensive Development Zone Programme.

Hedlund, H. 1980. *Small Farm Development in the Periphery.* Lusaka: University of Zambia.

Hedlund, H., and Lundahl, M. 1983. *Migration and Change in Rural Zambia.* Research Report No. 70. Uppsala: Scandanavian Institute of African Studies.

Hellen, J.A. 1968. *Rural Economic Development in Zambia 1890–1964.* Munich: Weltforum Verlag.

Heney, J.A. 1973. *Farm Management Handbook.* Mimeo, Mesekera Regional Station, Chipata, Zambia.

Kaunda, K.D. 1975. *Humanism in Zambia and a Guide to its Implementation.* Lusaka: The Zambian Information Service.

Keesing, R. 1981. *Cultural Anthropology.* New York: Holt, Rinehart & Winston.

Kwofie, K.M. 1980. *Introducing Nutrition Considerations into Agriculture and Rural Development Projects—A Case Study of Zambia.* Paper 3.14. Rome: Food and Agriculture Organization.

Lombard, C.S., and A.H.C. Tweedie. 1972. *Agriculture in Zambia Since Independence.* Lusaka: National Education Company of Zambia, Ltd.

Mair, L. 1965. *An Introduction to Social Anthropology.* Oxford: Clarendon Press.

Marter, A., and D. Honeybone. 1976. *The Economic Resources of Rural Households and the Distribution of Agricultural Development.* Lusaka: University of Zambia, Rural Development Studies Bureau.

Marwick, M.G. 1952. "The Social Context of Cewa Witch Beliefs." *Africa,* Vol. 22:120–135, 215–233.

Milimo, J.T. 1972. *Bantu Wisdom.* Lusaka: National Education Company of Zambia, Ltd.

Price, T. 1966. *The Elements of Nyanja for English Speaking Students.* Blantyre, Malawi: Church of Central African Presbyterian, The Synod Bookshop.

Richards, A. 1939. *Land, Labour and Diet in Northern Rhodesia.* Oxford: Oxford University Press.

Roberts, A. 1976. *A History of Zambia.* Nairobi, Ibadan, Lusaka: Heinemann.

Skjønsberg, E. 1978. *A Preliminary Sociological Report from Kalichero and Kalunga IDZ Areas.* Mimeo, Chipata, Zambia.

Skjønsberg, E. 1981. *The Kefa Records: Everyday Life Among Women and Men in a Zambian Village.* Oslo: University of Oslo, U-landseminaret.

Tuthill, D.F., et al. 1968. *Shifting Agriculture in Two Chewa Villages.* College Park, Maryland: University of Maryland.

Tuthill, D.F., et al. 1978. *Agricultural Sector Assessment: Zambia.* Mimeo, for Southern African Development Assistance Project.

Scott, Rev. D.C. 1929. *Dictionary of the Nyanja Language.* Edited and enlarged by the Rev. A. Hetherwick. London: The Religious Tract Society.

van Binsbergen, W.M.J. 1981. *Religious Change in Zambia: Exploratory Studies.* London and Boston: Kegan Paul International.

Watson, L. 1982. *Lightening Bird.* Sevenoaks, Kent: Hodder and Stoughton Ltd.

Whitby, P. 1972. *Zambian Foods and Cooking.* Mimeo, Lusaka.

INDEX

at funerals, 174, 178
brick making, 192, 193
carrying, 51, 62
cultivation, 33–35, 38, 108
feeding livestock, 98
firewood and water, 38, 87
food preparation, 51, 69
gathering vegetables, 77
grass cutting, 64, 89
hoeing, 50–52
housing construction, 196
making pots, 71

men doing, 50
milking, 95
rationale for, 50, 62, 87, 140
winnowing, 74
World War, I, 23–24

Y
Youngmen, 20, 29, 31, 131
   at funerals, 178
   cash investment in food crops, 35–36
   and model village project, 204–205